LOVE TROUBLES

NEW DIRECTIONS IN CRITICAL THEORY

NEW DIRECTIONS IN CRITICAL THEORY

Amy Allen, General Editor

New Directions in Critical Theory presents outstanding classic and contemporary texts in the tradition of critical social theory, broadly construed. The series aims to renew and advance the program of critical social theory, with a particular focus on theorizing contemporary struggles around gender, race, sexuality, class, and globalization and their complex interconnections.

Critical Theories of Anti-Semitism, Jonathan Judaken

Subaltern Silence: A Postcolonial Genealogy, Kevin Olson

Contesting the Far Right: A Psychoanalytic Critical Theory Approach, Claudia Leeb

Another Universalism: Seyla Benhabib and the Future of Critical Theory, edited by Stefan Eich, Anna Jurkevics, Nishin Nathwani, and Nica Siegel

Fascist Mythologies: The History and Politics of Unreason in Borges, Freud, and Schmitt, Federico Finchelstein

Selected Writings on Media, Propaganda, and Political Communication, Siegfried Kracauer, edited by Jaeho Kang, Graeme Gilloch, and John Abromeit

Crisis Under Critique: How People Assess, Transform, and Respond to Critical Situations, edited by Didier Fassin and Axel Honneth

Praxis and Revolution: A Theory of Social Transformation, Eva von Redecker

Recognition and Ambivalence, edited by Heikki Ikäheimo, Kristina Lepold, and Titus Stahl

Hermeneutics as Critique: Science, Politics, Race and Culture, Lorenzo C. Simpson

Critique on the Couch: Why Critical Theory Needs Psychoanalysis, Amy Allen

Capitalism on Edge: How Fighting Precarity Can Achieve Radical Change Without Crisis or Utopia, Albena Azmanova

A Time for Critique, edited by Didier Fassin and Berbard E. Harcourt

Transitional Subjects: Critical Theory and Object Relations, edited by Amy Allen and Brian O'Connor

For a complete list of books in the series, please see the Columbia University Press website.

Love Troubles

A PHILOSOPHY OF EROS

Federica Gregoratto

Columbia University Press
New York

Columbia University Press
Publishers Since 1893
New York   Chichester, West Sussex

Library of Congress Cataloging-in-Publication Data

Names: Gregoratto, Federica, author.
Title: Love troubles : a philosophy of eros / Federica Gregoratto.
Description: New York : Columbia University Press, [2024] |
Series: New directions in critical theory | Includes bibliographical references and index.
Identifiers: LCCN 2024024919 (print) | LCCN 2024024920 (ebook) |
ISBN 9780231217620 (hardback) | ISBN 9780231217637 (trade paperback) |
ISBN 9780231561822 (ebook)
Subjects: LCSH: Love—Philosophy. | Sex—Philosophy. |
Sex—Social aspects. | Critical theory.
Classification: LCC BD436 .G72 2024 (print) | LCC BD436 (ebook) |
DDC 128/.46—dc23/eng/20240913

Cover design: Milenda Nan Ok Lee
Cover art: Yves Klein, *Untitled Anthropometry (ANT 154)*, 1961. Dry pigment and synthetic
resin on paper. © Artists Rights Society (ARS), New York / ADAGP, Paris.
Photograph by Ben Blackwell © The Estate of Yves Klein c/o ADAGP, Paris.

Love Troubles

A PHILOSOPHY OF EROS

Federica Gregoratto

Columbia University Press
New York

Columbia University Press
Publishers Since 1893
New York   Chichester, West Sussex

Library of Congress Cataloging-in-Publication Data

Names: Gregoratto, Federica, author.
Title: Love troubles : a philosophy of eros / Federica Gregoratto.
Description: New York : Columbia University Press, [2024] |
Series: New directions in critical theory | Includes bibliographical references and index.
Identifiers: LCCN 2024024919 (print) | LCCN 2024024920 (ebook) |
ISBN 9780231217620 (hardback) | ISBN 9780231217637 (trade paperback) |
ISBN 9780231561822 (ebook)
Subjects: LCSH: Love—Philosophy. | Sex—Philosophy. |
Sex—Social aspects. | Critical theory.
Classification: LCC BD436 .G72 2024 (print) | LCC BD436 (ebook) |
DDC 128/.46—dc23/eng/20240913

Cover design: Milenda Nan Ok Lee
Cover art: Yves Klein, *Untitled Anthropometry (ANT 154)*, 1961. Dry pigment and synthetic
resin on paper. © Artists Rights Society (ARS), New York / ADAGP, Paris.
Photograph by Ben Blackwell © The Estate of Yves Klein c/o ADAGP, Paris.

To Marisa Nibale (1932–2024)

CONTENTS

viii

CONTENTS

Chapter Five
Joy as an Act of Resistance: Erotic Education   178

ACKNOWLEDGMENTS

This book is a very long (love) story. Its first seeds have been planted when I was a postdoc researcher affiliated to the Cluster of Excellence "Normative Orders" at Goethe Universität, Frankfurt am Main, between 2013 and 2015. I thank Rainer Forst, Axel Honneth, and Christoph Menke for having given me the amazing opportunity to be part of that community. The project I submitted with my application for the Cluster was initially about power, normativity, and social critique, but it was only thanks to a conversation with Honneth that it became clear to me that what I really had and wanted to do was to investigate the forms of power, the social norms, and the critical potential disclosed by love relationships. I am grateful for how Honneth's philosophy, and his practical support, have inspired and supported my project ever since.

A very special acknowledgment goes to Dieter Thomä, who has been my mentor during the years I have been working on these pages as a Habilitation in philosophy at the University of St. Gallen, Switzerland, between 2015 and 2022. Besides his constant and useful insights, comments, and criticisms, I want to thank him because he has showed me, with his example, what the sense of a philosophical undertaking should and could be: embracing risks as an exercise of resilience, irony, and self-distance. Staying with the trouble, and enjoying it.

Eva Illouz has offered a fundamental help. While I was spending some months at the New School for Social Research (New York) as a visiting scholar in 2019, thanks to the SNSF grant "Scientific Exchange," I had the chance to meet her in Princeton: she responded to all my theses with deep skepticism, but her bright critical eye managed to bring me to persist in my undertaking, pulling me out of the swamp I had fallen into during that winter.

I owe a great deal to Amy Allen, whose intelligence, sensibility, and philosophical rigor have supported me in all phases of my career, enabling me to figure out my own concepts. She has firmly believed in this book, especially in its latest, more difficult steps. I am also thankful for the precious editorial advice of Wendy Lochner and Alyssa Napier of Columbia University Press, and for the reviews of two anonymous readers, without which the book would have not become a reality.

I have revised the last version of the manuscript during a guest professorship at Freie Universität Berlin, between 2023 and 2024: I thank the faculty members of the Philosophy Department at FU, and in particular Robin Celikates, for this experience, which has been the highlight of my academic career so far. The conversations I have had the pleasure to carry on during this time—especially with Matt Congdon, Manon Garcia, Thomas Khurana, Luise Müller, Esther Neuhann, Karen Ng, and many wonderful students—have been key for refining and bringing to fruition all the ideas defended in the book.

A number of colleagues and friends have delighted and troubled me with great insights, comments and criticisms. Jean-Philippe Deranty, Martin Hartmann, and Andreja Novakovic have read final versions of the book: without their generosity and recognition, I would have not made it. There are others who have offered their precious views on preliminary drafts, related papers and talks: Emmanuel Alloa, Jay Bernstein, Borhane Blili-Hamelin, Marina Calloni, Emanuele Coccia, Lucio Cortella, Paolo Costa, Daniel Cuonz, Maria Daetwyler, Stephanie Deig, Penelope Deutscher, Estelle Ferrarese, Michael Festl, Paul Giladi, Florian Grosser, Michael Hampe, Onni Hirvonen, Heikki Ikäheimo, Roberto Mordacci, Gal Katz, Angelika Krebs, Nora Kreft, Hannes Kuch, Arto Laitinen, Kolja Möller, Lukas Peter, Corrado Pirrodi, Simon Pistor, Emmanuel Renault, Nassima Sahraoui, Matteo Santarelli, Just Serrano, and Dagmar Wilhelm.

ACKNOWLEDGMENTS

Every philosophical inquiry is a difficult and ambivalent journey, that goes through various phases and passions—excitement, anxiety, conflicts, crises, troubles!—which get then somehow crystallized in written words. My warmest gratitude go to the brilliant friends who have accompanied me throughout this voyage, who have given me the conceptual and affective tools to work through it, and who still make me believe and hope this is going to continue: Michela Cappuccio, for teaching me what love and friendship can and should be; Maristella Nigro, for being the mirror that shows me both what I do not want to be and how I could become; Arvi Särkelä, for having been there when the project started, and then throughout many of its phases, and having greatly inspired me; Susanne Schmetkamp, for never being tired to discuss all my ideas and theses; Thomas Telios, for having always pushed me to find my own voice, while often disagreeing with me; and Italo Testa, for the visible and invisible traces in my work, for the patience that has prevented me to give it all up in many occasions, and for the joy (division).

The book is dedicated to my maternal grandmother, who has shown me, from the very beginning, what love is, does not have to be, could be.

LOVE TROUBLES

INTRODUCTION

The Troubles We Desire

When it comes to love, we are all in trouble. We cannot hold to our usual certainties anymore, yet we have never been so certain. We lose orientation and gain a new direction. We feel irremediably weak and exceptionally strong, at the same time. We find ourself bound by new obligations, yet a sense of lightness pervades us. Our minds and bodies spin—how to recognize that we are truly in love, that we are not deluding ourselves? What do we owe to our lovers, and what can we reasonably expect from them? Can we love more than one person at the same time, and how do we do that? These are not theoretical, abstract queries. These (and other) questions do burningly and concretely engage a great number of lovers around the world. Attempts to figure out our life projects, identities, and values are intimately related to attempts to figure out our love lives. In various cultural contexts throughout history, reflections on love have very often channeled inquiries into human nature, and the nature of human associations and creations.

Philosophical inquiries might provide conceptual tools that help both to soothe the chaos and anxiety caused by love and its troubles and to experience them in profound, meaningful, even perhaps new ways—this is, at least, the dare of this book. The branch of philosophy put at work here strives to provide a more specific set of tools: through the lens of critical social philosophy, the book investigates love troubles not as concerning our human condition in general and in the abstract, but in relation to the social, political, economic, cultural conditions that shape our individual existences, and our lives in common. This present inquiry aims at articulating concepts to understand the dynamics and effects of a specific type of love, eros, in our current societies, and why and to which extent erotic love is something that we have good reasons to desire. At the same time, it reflects on those social conditions that are undesirable, as they make love part and parcel of existing habits, norms, and structures of oppression, as, for example, heterosexism, racism, and neoliberal capitalism. Can we figure out what desirable love is, despite the wrongs of our societies? Can we love, in a wrong society? Does eros itself harbor a potential for resisting oppression, and for opening up possibilities for personal and social transformation? The book tries to sketch out some positive answers to these questions.

Troubles of love can be grouped under three broad sets of questions. To begin with: *What is love?* Is it an emotion or a passion, a mode of being in the world and with others, a desire (but for what?), a practice? How can we distinguish love from neighboring phenomena, like infatuation, lust, awe, companionship, a moral duty to care, devotion, gratitude? The book asks in particular about one kind of love, eros, that comprises—maybe counterintuitively at first—both friendship and sexual, romantic love, leaving aside love for parents and children, for fellow citizens, or human beings, love for God and for nonhuman entities. Erotic love is intended here first and foremost as a *social bond*, animated by affective and emotional forces, largely shaped by political, economic, cultural conditions, but not completely reducible to them.

The second set is of ethical or normative nature: *Is love good or bad for us?* When and why can we desire to form bonds of love? Erotic bonds and their troubles can birth magnific joy as well as the darkest distress; they can positively foster and enhance our relations with ourselves and with the world, but also ruin them. The book argues that erotic love is an *ambivalent* social bond that can both enslave and liberate us. We have good reasons to desire love when it is free and makes us experience freedom. Undesirable becomes love when it impairs or damages our freedom, when erotic freedom cannot unfold. This normative distinction is crucial, yet thin and precarious.

The third set of questions opens up a broader social and political dimension: Is love—and, in particular, erotic love—*still actually worth the trouble*? Are the previous two groups of queries meaningful and relevant not only for us individually and personally, but also collectively? What is the sense and role of eros in our societies? This book wants to argue that eros's place in the world should be (continue to be) highly appreciated. And not despite of, but precisely because of, its troubledness, which might bear critical and transformative force.

A quick note on the sense of the pronouns "we" and "our" employed here: I have grown up and studied in Italy, then moved for work to Switzerland, Germany, and, briefly, the United States. My intellectual and academic socialization is the result of a mix of southern and central European as well as Anglo-Saxon, North American influences. The social context that constitutes the critical reference of the book is determined by these coordinates, the ones I know best. Such Western points of reference are not intended in a complacent, justificatory, or self-defensive manner: in fact, the overall aim is to critically reflect on this context and to conceptually elaborate ways to transform it. The positive aspects of the conceptions of love I will draw upon are not meant as strong regulative prescriptions for those who cannot identify with and do not belong to Western traditions and cultures, but just as hypotheses, in need of revision and open to contestation, leading to exercises in critical self-consciousness. Some of the motives might perhaps be found also in different, non-Western contexts, but this is not for me to anticipate and clarify, given my ignorance of other worlds. I can only hope further inquiries into love will want to further contribute to this critical and transformative work, enlarging it beyond its limits, both the visible ones and those I do not see yet.

Let's come back now to the third set of questions, for it is indeed rooted in and emerges from a place of doubt. If we give credit to a long list of recent theoretical and nontheoretical contributions, there are reasons to believe that, contrary to the conviction inspiring *Love Troubles*, love is currently losing its value and appeal. A *loneliness epidemic* (or pandemic?) seems to have been spreading for a while, surely exacerbated during the years of COVID-19. In the last fifty years we have all become more lonely, in different, interrelated senses: our relationships with sexual and romantic partners, with friends, family members, neighbors have become more rarified, less frequent, and less intense. Even if we have significant others, we feel more and more ignored, unseen, or uncared for by them. At the same time, we feel (and are) unsupported by our fellow citizens, our employers, our community, our government. In a recent study, *The Lonely Century*, Noreena Hertz underlines how the separation from other human beings and from ourselves is not accidentally linked to but actually intimately interwoven with political and economic powerlessness.[1]

Hertz's gloomy analysis closely resembles a typical diagnosis of social alienation, that has been often brought up to complain about modern societies. In the nineteenth century, the young Karl Marx develops an influential theory of alienation according to which the modern, capitalist conditions of organized exploited productive (and reproductive) labor have far-reaching consequences also for our psychic and political existences. When we produce, exchange, and try to survive in a system that concentrates capital (and thus material resources, and power) in the hands of a single class, our activities and their products, our fellow human beings and the whole human species, become *alien*, incomprehensible, devoid of any meaning and value for and to us. We are not able anymore to properly understand, respect, recognize, solidarize with other humans because we do not recognize ourselves anymore, what we are doing and why, whether our activities can be meaningful and fruitful beyond our own private, egoist goals, including the goal of survival. Marx understands how the imperatives of the capitalist organization not only of labor, but also of the whole human form of life, are bound to have a massive impact on human love as well. In his *Economic and Philosophic Manuscripts of 1844*, he writes that money has the power to shape and transform individuals' identities, their interpersonal relationships, and their relation with nature. The "creative" or constitutive power of money "confounds" all natural and human qualities and distorts social bonds, thus also swallowing sexual, erotic, and emotional relationships. Money, says Marx, allows, for instance, (ugly) men to form intimate ties with (beautiful) women and can turn love into hate (and, presumably, hate into love). With these sketchy examples, Marx wants to say that capitalism has the power to blur the lines between love and the market. It makes us confused about what truly matters when we engage in love relationships. Only in a radically different society, he thinks, we would experience proper and true love, a love that is not instrumental, and not a "misfortune."[2]

Contemporary social theorists have further investigated the impact of the current economic system on our love lives on the wake of the Marxian analysis. The most famous is maybe Eva Illouz, the sociologist who has dedicated much of her intellectual career so far to the debunking of love troubles. In one well-known study, *Why Love Hurts?*, she declares that her main aim is do to love what Marx has done to commodities—to show, that is, how this human experience, far from being spontaneous and unruly, is shaped and constituted by social relations, how it "circulates in a market-place of unequal competing actors," and that some people (namely, hetero-sexual, privileged men) "command greater capacity to define the terms in which they are loved than others."[3] In her most comprehensive book on this subject matter, which has the even more upsetting title *The End of Love*, she speaks of a gradual and problematic triumph of "negative rela-tionships."[4] Interpersonal relationships are "negative" because we have now developed the capacity and willingness to end them with relatively few regrets and afterthoughts, and we are not ready to commit to long-term, serious bonds. The tendency is explained by describing how an indi-vidualistic, hedonist form of freedom has imposed itself as the major value and goal of present-day societies. This ideology of freedom convinces us that it is fine to pursue our highly individualized whims, wants, and inter-ests, and that we are all entitled to this liberty. Certainly, the right to such freedom is very often not backed up by a corresponding power. Under present-day material, cultural, social conditions, only a very small minor-ity of people have at their disposal the economic and symbolic means to truly realize what they want.[5] Nevertheless, we all tend to look for and choose partners as we look for and choose commodities—namely, to sat-isfy our supposedly momentary needs and wishes. Yet, as soon as our companions' own needs and wishes collide with ours, we start to see them as hindrances on our own paths toward self-realization, as useless encum-brances. In other words, we have all started to act and to feel in our senti-mental endeavors like we act and feel (or are supposed to act and feel) when we seek for a job and financial stability, or want to maintain them.

According to Illouz's picture, the desirability and perceived value of long-term, committed, serious, and deep romantic relationships is wan-ing, but at least we are having a lot of (meaningless, fleeting) sexual affairs (maybe exciting for some, especially for men of wealthy social classes, but mostly causing, especially to women, worries and wounds). But this is not necessarily true: Hertz, as well as other researchers and observers, notice that we are having, at least in the last twenty years, also increasingly less sex. We might be in the middle of a "sex recession" or of a "sex drought," that is affecting especially younger generations—millennials and Gen Z people, that is.[6] Feeling sexual desire for other human beings, finding the courage and the right or appropriate modality to express and convey it, pursuing a sexual connection that might (or not) lead to a romantic commitment: all these experiences raise difficult puzzles and crippling anxieties.

The causes explaining such alleged decline of sexual desire and activity are many and not linear. The chief one seems to lie, again, in the current organization of labor, and, more generally, of the economic system, and in the pervading, colonizing effects that labor and commodities markets have on other domains of social life. The current stage of the capitalist economic, and, more broadly, social system, called "neoliberalism," force people into extremely precarious, fragmented, and demanding jobs that do not only prevent financial stability, but also destroy our capacities to trust other human beings and engage in relaxed, cheerful, hopeful, meaningful interactions with them. A distinctive characteristic of the neoliberal society is how it shrinks the separation between free and labor time. As a result, the majority of us do not have the physical and psychological resources to spend enough quality time with potential or actual sexual partners, or with friends and family, let alone to build up and plan a life together. What is more, in order not to just accumulate wealth, but to survive, we have to conceive of ourselves, to act and to feel in constant competition with others. We are forced to become isolated, independent, self-reliant individuals. Virtues and capacities like emphatic communication (the ability to put oneself from the perspective of the other), care, attention to others' needs and wishes, which are also crucial for satisfying sexual relationships, are not getting us anywhere in life and are not "marketable." If for Illouz such a "neoliberal subjectivity" has become the form of our sexual subjectivity as well, it may also lead to a dismantling of sexual and emotional interests and experiences tout court. It is true, as some have observed and theorized, that "emotion work" and passions have become increasingly valuable on the workplace. Here, however, affects and feelings are viewed in strictly instrumental terms: they have to be finalized to earn a better position, or to avoid layoff, and are ultimately exploitable and exploited.[7] Moreover, the climate disaster, which is felt with alarmed concreteness especially by younger generations, cannot but massively contribute to the sense of insecurity, precariousness, powerlessness, and hopelessness in the future.

New technologies of sex and romance are not a great help. Take dating apps: on the one hand, they can surely allow persons to meet up in contexts in which encounters are impeded by a variety of reasons. In homophobic contexts, for instance, online meeting platforms can help gay people, or persons with queer, nonmainstream, unusual sexual and intimate preferences to find each other and build connections, thus bypassing censure and suspicion.[8] Also, they provide occasions for sex, as well as for love and friendship, when bars, clubs, libraries, schools, and theaters are closed or inaccessible. They can even assume emancipating functions and romantic connotations. Many individuals seem indeed to use these technologies in order to find a long-term partner.[9] On the other hand, dating apps can reproduce and even strengthen tendencies of individualization, hedonism, unwillingness to commit, and, thus, solitude, unhappiness (and, ultimately, unfreedom—if we understand freedom differently from Illouz, as this book argues we should do.) The benefits of these apps are, moreover, advertised on the basis of the promise of "safe," risk-free love. The digitalized process of partner selection is "sold" as more rational than its offline equivalent because agents can broadcast their characteristics, preferences, and aims more clearly from the very beginning.

But is trouble-free love possible or desirable? Very probably not. Take, for example, communication channels like WhatsApp, Skype, Zoom: these technologies open up precious virtual rooms to be together, feel close, share thoughts and affective experiences for people kept at a distance by objective conditions (people who live apart, for instance, for job-related constraints, or people who cannot see each other because of closed borders or quarantine measures). At the same time, digital connection can become a habit that broadens emotional interpersonal gaps and sharpens alienation. The metaverse, alternative cyber realities, technologically enhanced sex dolls or sex robots can be sought and experienced as easier, more controllable alternatives to the complex dynamics of human-to-human interaction, but their effectivity in overcoming our alienation in the sexual and intimate sphere is still highly controversial.[10] It might also be argued that technologies of dating and romance have not really changed their core norms and structures.[11]

The explanation based on a criticism of neoliberal capitalism is not the only one trying to make sense of the current alleged loneliness epidemic. From the 1960s onward—namely, in the post–sexual revolution period, a rich feminist literature has diffusely warned us against the "traps" of romantic passion that vex heterosexual women, but also pose difficulties, in different ways, for bisexual and lesbian women, gender nonconforming people, and individuals who face discrimination on the basis of various social factors, such as race, immigration status, class, religion, ableism, and fatphobia. Recently, the critique pursued by feminist and gender theorists has known an important revival, especially in the wake of the global #MeToo campaign. The aim of the #MeToo movement has been to expose how relationships between men and women, in the family, in private spaces of leisure, in the bedroom, at work, and in political arenas, are skewed by asymmetries of power based on gender, class, and race that harbor abuses and various forms of violence. So, the loneliness epidemic might also be interpreted, optimistically, in light of the fact that more and more people can now find the strength, and have the material possibility, to say "No" to unsatisfying and abusive sentimental and sexual relationships. It might be a sign, for example, of women emancipation: women might be wanting to be independent and mature before committing to partners and family life. There is also an increasing number of people who reject conventional and traditional models (traditional monogamous marriage, or marriage-like arrangements) and embrace some kind of emotional and sexual anarchy and fluidity that cannot be categorized under the label of "love relationship" anymore (or can they?). Have we really entered a "post-romantic age," as Pamela Haag has called it?[12] Maybe yes, and, maybe, if we are committed to gender, economic, and racial justice, this might be good news.

The explanation based on the prospect of gender emancipation is not completely convincing, though. To begin with, it is mostly heterosexual, white, economically, or otherwise privileged women who have the material and symbolic possibilities to rely on themselves alone and to reject marriage. Communities of care, as well as of love and sexual recognition, even in traditional forms, are still viewed as tremendously precious by queer, nonwhite, and economically underprivileged people. Moreover, we can detect a contradiction determining loneliness: on the one hand, the traditional and conventional picture of romance, modeled around monogamous marriage, does still seem a powerful influence on women's feelings and wishes; on the other, the model is in contrast with other influent desires (for example, the desire for a fulfilling, ambitious career), and is difficult to realize under present social, cultural, and economic conditions (for reasons that have been already mentioned). The contradiction turns our search for love into a laborious and painful, if not felt as impossible undertaking.

It is important to acknowledge that erotic encounters do indeed entail a number of risks for certain people, especially in a time where there is a general imperative to be open about one own's sexuality and sexual (or emotional) wishes, and to freely pursue them—except if you are, for instance, a woman, it is very likely that you will get punished for your openness and freedom. In an enlightening critical reflection, *Tomorrow Sex Will Be Good Again*, Katherine Angel sketches the quite anguished situation that women find themselves in as soon as they consider to embark upon some erotic adventure and have to ask themselves, more or less consciously: "In revealing myself, have I forgone privacy and dignity? Will I be pursued, haunted by my own actions? Will I be able to resist the unwanted desires of others?"[13] But are there really good reasons to completely give in to fear, resignation, negativity? In a beautiful essay, "Ballad for Sexual Optimism," Maggie Nelson argues that the historical process of realization of sexual freedom cannot but unravel as a chiaroscuro: phases and experiences of liberation give rise to new forms of oppression; liberties are gained and lost; what appears as freedom at a certain moment in time, and from the perspective of a certain social group, does sometimes shade or even hinder the unfreedom of others. This is true for freedom in general, but the realm of the erotic, where "inchoateness . . . is part of what makes it worthwhile" is particularly revealing in this sense.[14] Nelson encourages us to linger on "gray areas"—on those situations and moments when we do not know what we want, if we should really want what we want, if what is happening or has happened corresponds to what we have truly wanted (and consented to).[15] The present volume moves from Nelson's invitation: gray areas should be explored and interrogated, not removed or "resolved" too hastily. Such a practical and theoretical work should not be viewed as indulgence or compliance with a broken system: proper critical work, resistance, and emancipatory change unfold insofar as we give up on the pernicious dualism freedom versus unfreedom, if we accept uncertainty and ambivalences. When liberated from the obsession of perfect, full freedom, we might then find the courage to spell out some of the things that would indeed make us free.

In her debut novel *Acts of Service*, Lillian Fishman tells the story of a young bisexual woman, Eve, who is in a stable, committed, and loving relationship with another woman, but decides to secretly embark on a passionate affair with a couple formed by another bisexual woman and a heterosexual man (who is an open marriage with another woman). In a sociologically sharp passage, the protagonist reflects on how she has grown up in a world devoid of any normative, substantial, positive orientation (she was referring to her context of origin, middle-class and *white*): no one had explained to her "what mattered," she has never been sure about what "we should dream about," she has been "taught to value love *yet not to rely on it too heavily,* because the world of *excessive freedom* in which we had been made would not foster the long-suffering loyalty that love required."[16] The freedom considered excessive here is precisely the kind of freedom criticized by Illouz: individualistic, negative, hedonistic. As Hertz also notices, in a world dominated by this freedom, duties toward fellow human beings as well as certainties about what is right and meaningful fade away, individuals are left alone, fall into desperation or inertia. The protagonist of *Acts of Service* is convinced that absence of obligations does not make her (and her friends and loved ones) really free. As a reaction, Eve looks for certainties about rules of conduct and feeling in the queer world of New York City. Queerness becomes for her like a faith: in this context, she learns what to want and "what was good to want," what to do with her body and her life, "whom to love, how to love, what to fear so that you might preempt it." Among queer people, dredging up what had been suppressed and interrogating what had been assumed are crucial undertakings: "Openness and sincerity were prized above all else."

Ethical wisdom, self-knowledge, open and therapeutic communication about our own's emotions and identity are desirable and appealing, and, as this book argues, conducive to experiences of both individual and collective freedom. Tellingly, the protagonist of *Acts of Service* cannot realize these values by passively remaining within the moral and social order she has rationally chosen, the queer community of New York, but only by transgressing, lying, behaving in morally and politically questionable ways. She sets out to explore and give in to parts of herself that she is ashamed of (her vanity, superficiality, the desire to be recognized and treated just as a beautiful object). She is not afraid to declare her love for the male protagonist, who she herself presents as a traditionally "toxic" masculine character, an arrogantly self-entitled, dominant man. Toward the end, this male character has to face charges for sexual harassment in the workplace, and Eve is called to testify in his favor. In a passage that is crafted, as I read it, for the purpose to make a conceptual point, the prosecutor asks her whether she identifies herself as a feminist. Eve answers positively, suggesting that the freedom to behave in shady manners, for a woman, contravening alleged feminist dogmas, is part of what a feminist education should be about. (It has to be added that she takes this trial to defend her own choices, not his, as she is not sure about his innocence.) The finale of the novel is ethically and politically ambiguous, if not openly problematic—as love, under present conditions, certainly is.

The present volume seeks to clarify the ambivalence of love and wants to resist those social diagnoses or observations according to which sexual, passionate, romantic love, as well as friendship, would have lost desirability and value. Many recent successful literary publications, some of which will be discussed in following chapters—Elena Ferrante's series known as the "Neapolitan novels," Hanya Yanagihara's *A Little Life*, Sophie Lucido Johnson's memoire *Many Love: A Memoir of Polyamory and Finding Love(s)*, and Sally Rooney's novels—offer proof that erotic love *is still worth the trouble*.[17] These writings work through many interrelated issues, exposing the difficulties to navigate relationships that are in between friendships and sexual love, while vouching for a strong willingness to continue to do so and testifying an openness toward a future that awaits to be rewritten. Friendship and romantic relationships are depicted by these authors not only as a refuge from the harshness and alienation of the present world, related to the dysfunctionalities of capitalist and neoliberal economic markets, of sexist and racist systems, and to the climate disaster, but also as spaces to discuss and elaborate on them.

The claim of this book is that the value of eros is not diminished—rather, we have entered a phase of *deep descriptive and normative uncertainty*: we are deeply unsure with regard to the goodness and desirability of love, and we struggle to comprehend what love relationships exactly are, or have become, what their constitutive rules are. This is acknowledged by Illouz: definitions, evaluations and rules of conduct, in the matters of the heart, have become, she states, "an open-ended question and a problem:" "confusion, uncertainty, and even chaos reign."[18] The rituals, codes, institutions that for a time had regulated and oriented emotional and social habits have lately faded and crumbled. Illouz regards this chaos with bewilderment and weariness, but we do not have to. Can we ardently desire certain kinds of people and want to participate in certain emotional arrangements with them and still regard ourselves as emancipated, independent women? Is the vulnerability that comes with passionate sexual desire always detrimental? Can we love and be free at the same time? Can we romantically and passionately want to be with two or three persons at the same time and claim that we truly love them all? Is it OK and "normal" to consider our best friends the most important persons in our lives? Current social habits, norms, and structures do not provide clear answers to these (and other) questions: confusion and hesitation harbor, however, potential for changes, even radical ones. Social philosophy should be able to help.

Yes, we sometime desire what is bad for us, or are in the dark when it comes to what we truly want. Sometimes it is only neuroses, wounds, and flaws that hold us together. Even the deepest and truest love does not always make us better people; sometimes it does bring out the worse in us. Economic, gender, and racial habits and norms form our desires and systematically make certain people expect or profit from and suffer because of love more than others. Because of economic, gender, and racial structures, certain bodies are regarded as more lovable than others, certain forms of relationships are deemed as more legitimate and worth pursuing then others. Damaging troubles are multiple. This should not come as a discouragement, though, but a plea for being more compassionate and less judgmental with regard to the unruly, messy jumble of our sexual and emotional natures. Also, not all troubles are bad; not everything that is troublesome should be rejected. Some love troubles are desirable: those inviting us to reflect upon and shed light on what we are doing, and why. They solicit and feed philosophical work. As North American philosopher John Dewey has argued, philosophy does not arise from unfulfilled desire, as for Plato, or in wonder, as for Aristotle; rather, it emerges from social confusions, tensions, "when society is disordered and when the normal processes of social interaction are disrupted."[19] Thinking arises, Dewey maintains, "only in the thin cracks of solid habits,"[20] with the aim of dealing "with unresolved situations."[21] A philosophy of love is then needed and is formulated when the habits, norms, and structures regulating our passions, sexual desires, needs for caring and being cared for, and practices of seduction and emotional sharing do not and cannot flow smoothly and frictionlessly. This is the situation we are navigating right now.

Although not thematized as such, the need to address uncertainties around love is indeed felt with great urgency in the academic field: approximately in the last ten years, publications around this topic have grown exponentially.[22] The conceptual work of this book, however, is not aimed at outlining some general, abstract "truths" about love. The question around eros needs to be answered with an ethical, political, and social-critical interest in view. What does eros teach us about society, and even maybe about how to change those social dynamics that we deem wrong and problematic? Such interest is sustained by the fact that, in our societies, not all forms of love appear as troublesome as erotic love. The loves for our children, family members, and members of our community seem to still retain solid value.[23] Critics have rightly argued that neoliberal mechanisms have shrunken the space and the time for family love, for communal solidarity, and for nonintimate forms of affection. However, capacities and possibilities to love the people around us in nonerotic ways do not appear as ambivalent goods per se, but rather as precious resources that are sadly under attack. On the contrary, erotic bonds of love—and, in particular, sexual passion and romance—can not only be structurally impeded; they themselves become means of problematic social mechanisms. They can be complicit with oppression and domination, with the ways our societies make us miserable. For this reason, a focus on erotic love is particularly needed. In such acute troubledness, we might find seeds for a cure.

The book develops an account of erotic love as a problematic endeavor and at the same time as a space to elaborate on it in critical and transformative ways in five chapters and an excursus. Chapter 1 traces an initial, provisional map for our exploration of love. It reviews and problematizes the most influential "models" that seek to describe love's nature in the contemporary philosophical panorama: love as *union* or *fusion*, love as *care* or *robust concern*, and love as an ensemble of *collective or shared actions and emotions*. Such accounts of love, we will see, seem to have problems sticking to a mere descriptive level of inquiry: they "naturally" call for a reflection on love's goodness and desirability. Chapter 2 expands the map by proposing an account that tries to overcome the limitations of the previous models, by at the same time consciously assuming and reflecting upon certain limits that are inherent in a conceptual discourse on love. The ambition of this chapter is not to pinpoint love's essence, but to shed light on several *dynamics* and *consequences* that constitute the process of erotic love. First, eros is prompted by and sustained by a particular type of interpersonal *recognition* that consists in bodily, sensual awareness and consciousness of the beloved as a special, unique, singular *vulnerable* being, triggering a practical interest in becoming a factor in their self-experience and self-realization. Secondly, the dramatic interplay between dependence and independence at stake in the process of erotic recognition gives rise to a complex series of *power plays*. Third, such process unfolds by forming, undoing, reforming erotic collectivities. A particular emphasis is put on the *transformative* consequences of such dynamics, both on individual selves, on the collectives they form, and beyond them as well. The chapter draws upon the theoretical resources, read as mutually illuminating, of Hegelian recognition theory (Simone de Beauvoir, Axel Honneth) and ethical perfectionism (Stanley Cavell). These approaches allow accounting for love's complexity, as well as its ambivalence: it is supremely difficult to say when this experience can be good for us. On a philosophical level, however, at least, we can say when love can be free and make us free. And this is what—so the main thesis of this book, which this chapter starts to delineate—makes love (troubles) desirable.

Why narrowing down the perspective to one type of love only, though—namely, just to erotic love? In an excursus, I specify the reasons for this focus, expanding on the senses and boundaries of the adjective "erotic." Differently from commonsensical understandings and practices, eros includes both passionate, sexual love and intense forms of friendship. Moved by eros, lovers and friends usually go through very similar experiences, as a vast array of literary and real-life examples demonstrate. Erotic love, I argue, is particularly interesting, as it is placed at the threshold between intimate, private, and public, political domains of social lives. Eros is, on the one hand, detached, free from broader social rules, norms, structures and habits; on the other hand, it is profoundly shaped by them. This slippery, liminal position makes it into a surprising and efficacious critical-theoretical tool, even though not in immediate and direct fashion. My understanding of erotic love is inspired by key figures and motives in the historical Romantic traditions of philosophers and poets, but it questions present-day beliefs and practices determining what I call "romantic ideologies." Many love troubles can be overcome by questioning such ideologies.

Casting erotic love at the threshold between the public and the private, between sociopolitical and intimate life, pushes us to think *critically* about erotic love. For this reason, a critical social philosophy—not just an ethical, moral, or political philosophy, or a metaphysics (or social ontology) of love—is required. Thinking critically about erotic love means to develop a double perspective, which matches eros's ambivalence. While love relationships and their mechanisms are taken as object of social critique (chapter 3), erotic bonds are studied as intersubjective and collective spaces where critical and transformative resources can potentially be found (chapters 4 and 5). Contrary to what the majority of contemporary critical theorists of society and social philosophers tend to think, love is an interesting and relevant subject matter for projects that want to detect rules, norms, structures, and habits based on and reproducing neoliberal, sexist, racist, and other social pathologies (forms of oppression, injustice, powerlessness, invisibility, exclusion) and think about ways to resist to and to transform them.

The book delineates answers to the three aforementioned sets of troubles, which are interconnected. The attempt to figure out love's nature is not an objective here per se. Rather, this attempt is conditioned by and premised upon the interest in grasping whether, how, and to what extent love might be desirable. I am not, however, interested in love's general, abstract desirability: the point is to decide whether eros can still be desirable for us, in our societies. If we cannot theoretically decide with certainty when erotic relationships are good, what we can do is try to establish the objective, structural intersecting conditions that impede or damage lovers and friends and their bonds in different ways. It is the intent of chapter 3 to develop this critical perspective; the chapter aims at showing that, far from being an autonomous social sphere, as modern social theorists (Niklas Luhmann, Anthony Giddens) have theorized, love is deeply conditioned and shaped by larger social structures, habits, and norms that can have two types of pernicious impact. Social conditions can either *impede* the formation and unfolding of erotic bonds, or make them into mechanisms that reproduce and strengthen forms of oppression. Love can be damaged and damaging in three different modalities: it can be complicit with larger structures of oppression (complicit love), as well as put certain people in the position to dominate (mastery love), and exploit others (exploitative love).

Chapters 4 and 5 overturn the perspective of chapter 3, tracing ways in which eros can actually (partially) liberate itself, offering instruments to detect and overcome impediments and damages. Chapter 4 looks for these resources in the affective and emotional dimensions of erotic bonds. By considering some contemporary discussions around affects and emotions and bringing them in a dialogue with Romantic voices and some early critical theorists in the Frankfurt school tradition (Theodor W. Adorno and Herbert Marcuse), the chapter argues for a critical and transformative conception of affects and emotions in three steps: first, this is a conception that questions cognitivism and praises a certain kind of (temporary) affective confusion; second, the conception rejects social constructionism and embraces a particular type of naturalism (*critical naturalism*); third, affects and emotions should be thought of as deeply shared, also on bodily, precognitive, and prediscursive levels.

Finally, chapter 5 develops an account of erotic love more decidedly on a sociopolitical level. By relying on a series of exemplary stories, told by movies and novels, and especially on Audre Lorde's illuminating insights on eros and social oppression, the chapter argues that bonds of erotic love might represent private, small-scale experimentations in which capacities for critique, resistance, and political agency are cultivated. Erotic bonds' experiments can contribute to movements in which oppressed groups struggle for gaining what John Dewey calls "public recognition," but they can also exhibit actions and emotions or affects that rather *attract* public recognition from society at large. Moreover, erotic experiments can open up spaces for building critical and transformative subjectivities. The erotic thus becomes a space for education: not only for individual selves, with regard to their individual desires, identities, and projects, but also for oppressed and oppressing social groups.

What do we learn, what does society learn, thanks to erotic (experimental) bonds? In one word: freedom. The *fil rouge* that traverses *Love Troubles* consists in the relation between eros and freedom. We cannot understand erotic love if we do not understand how erotic bonds are moved by recognition, unfolding through power plays that have to do with our dependence on others and on the necessity for independence and, as such, open up a space, in between the private and the public, in which individuals learn how to be free. We become free when we are not coerced, forced, oppressed by other human beings or by social habits, norms, and structures, when we are led to experiment with our selves, to pursue our desires and projects. But who are we, and what are the desires and projects that really and truly matter to us and are worth pursuing?

Other human beings, as well as the habits, rules, norms and structures that shape us, and that we contribute to shape, are there to help us find out.[24] Many times, our desires and projects can only be pursued together, shared and realized with other human beings, in small collectivities and in larger social groups. Contrary to Illouz's understanding, freedom is not exercised against others, for both individual and collective exercises of freedom are communal enterprises. Sometimes, realizing freedom requires that we liberate ourselves, individually and collectively, from certain damaged social bonds, and from their damaged and damaging conditions. Being overwhelmed by, letting ourselves dive into, articulating, understanding our affects and emotions, are key moments in such processes of liberation. Sharing affects and emotions, cultivating them collectively and considering their effects on collectivities beyond ourselves is also key. On a broader social and public level, as especially the last chapter shows, freedom corresponds to a collective, social process in which troubles become visible, are detected and addressed. Troubles arise because some invisible, marginalized, and oppressed groups become aware of their situation, grow impatient and exasperated with it, and engage in actions aimed at changing it. A society learns to address and (somehow) overcome troubles when oppressed groups develop critical capacities, accept their dissonant affects, and decide to do something with them, find the courage to display their emotions and thoughts. The oppressing groups, more or less directly responsible for the damages, have to learn critical and transformative capacities as well, to assume the perspectives of the others, find the courage to become inspired and moved by the representatives of, as María Lugones put it, different and alternative "worlds of sense."[25]

Erotic love and its troubles teach us about all the different facets of freedom, and their dark sides. Lovers and friends are there for us when we are going through personal transformation; they are part and parcel of the transformation. We realize freedom collectively, moved by the affects and emotions that our lovers and friends spark in us, sharing and trying to understand such affects and emotions with them. Social troubles might become visible, and unbearable, and solutions start to delineate (also) when we feel and see them from within erotic bonds, with the help of our lovers and friends. Love troubles might appear as problematic, risky, overwhelming, but erotic bonds also promise an experience of freedom that discloses possible alternatives that we want to and must build up together.

Chapter One

SOME KINDA LOVE
A (Provisional) Map

Every human being, in every corner of the globe, has experienced love somewhen, in some form, and has probably faced troubles because of it. This should be safe to say. But what is love? Answers to this query are far less safe. Ideas and practices of love vary substantially across cultures, epochs, social contexts. Our gender, sexuality and sexual preferences, race, social class, wealth, religion, individual upbringing, and life phase exert an undeniable influence on our ideas and practices. Most of the time, we hold contradictory, confusing, misleading, or even dangerous beliefs. Most of the time, we have no idea what we are doing when we are in love and making love. To tell *the truth, or at least some truths*, about love seems extremely hard. Can philosophy come to the rescue? Philosophers themselves are undecided. Some of them do believe that philosophy can be indeed helpful to assuage our minds and even give practical orientation. Others think that usual philosophical methods cannot but fail in this undertaking.

Carrie Jenkins is one contemporary authoritative philosopher of love who firmly believes in the power of her discipline to bring conceptual and practical clarity to our emotional lives. With analytically rigorous and at the same time politically engaged spirit, she has made (romantic) love into a legitimate object of metaphysical study. In a seminal article that intends to launch the metaphysics of love, Jenkins asks about the *reality* and the *nature* of love.[1] She specifies the paradigmatic metaphysical question—*what is love?*—by formulating it in narrower fashion: *What does it mean that x is in love with y?* This phrasing casts love as a relationship between two single individuals, at one moment in time, and concentrates solely on the perspective of x, the subject of love. But the formulation does not exclude and, on the contrary, invites to consider that x can be in love not only with y but also with z, and others, at the same time. According to the map that Jenkins sketches in the paper, these are some of the metaphysical options that pick up the meaning of x's love:

- *Eliminativism*. What does it mean that x is in love with y? Nothing. There is no such thing as (romantic) love;
- *Quietism*. What does it mean that x is in love with y? We cannot know, and we should drop the question (although we do not have to give up on love altogether);
- *Identity theories*. What does it mean that x is in love with y? Many things. There are different concepts (e.g., sexual desire, union, care) that allow us to identify x: x might be in love with y when x sexually desires y, or desires to form an union with y, or cares for y. When adopting a pluralist position, moreover, one can combine different identity theories;
- *Functionalism*. What does it mean that x is in love with y? It means that love brings x to "realize" a "functional role";
- *Social constructionism*. What does it mean that x is in love with y? x is in love with y in the ways in which social institutions, traditions, practices, and norms dictate;
- *Natural realism*. What does it mean that x is in love with y? x is in love with y in the ways in which natural (biological or neurochemical) processes dictate.

According to Jenkins, identity theories of love are too variegated and messy; they do not allow for precise and clean metaphysical thinking. For her part, she presents arguments in favor of the *functionalist approach*, which, in her view, should be able to accommodate both *social constructionism* (or constructivism) and *natural realism*. She calls her version of functionalism "constructionist functionalism." Constructionist functionalism affirms that the relation of love between x and y is metaphysically characterized in terms of the functional role(s) that the love relation plays in people's lives. In simpler words: *love is as love does*. In romantic love, a role refers, for example, to practices of courtship, dating, and family for-mations, romantic ritualized expressions of feelings (heart-shaped letters, roses, love songs, hand-holding), evaluations (the beloved is valued very highly; their interests are treated as one's own), institutionalization (mar-riage), and norms of monogamy.[2] The role of romantic love consists, hence, in prompting x, to a sufficient degree, to engage in sufficiently many of these activities with respect to y.

Jenkins argues that a wide range of the functions fulfilled by love are a product of a certain society and a certain culture: this means that, for her, functionalism implies social constructionism. However, this position does not maintain that *everything* about love is social. An inquiry into the role of love implies also inquiries into the ways in which love, especially roman-tic love, is played or realized. And the role of romantic love can then be played or realized by mental states that can be best understood by study-ing psychology or cognitive science, by brain states and processes best understood by studying neurophysiology, and by drives best understood by studying biology and evolutionary history.[3] The social constructionist view is then compatible with a kind of natural realism concerning the realizers of the role of love. Brian Earp and Julian Savulescu, two ethicists who have written extensively on the neuroscience of love, draw on Jen-kins's dual account and suggest that love is to be studied from two differ-ent standpoints at the same time. We can, namely, interpret it *either* as a cluster of biological factors experienced subjectively and shaped by vari-ous social constraints *or* as a cluster of socially mediated subjective experi-ences, shaped by certain biological constraints. Love is not just one or the other: it is both.[4]

Questions concerning the social and natural dimensions of love are key, but what does "both" exactly mean? What is the interrelation between the two dimensions? How are our brains and bodies in love and our social practices interrelated? Are these just two separate epistemological per-spectives that must then be somehow held together, or is there something more to them? These are quite thorny questions, which concern in nuce the divide between culture (or society) and nature: a central and long-standing problem in the Western philosophical tradition, that Jenkins, Earp, and Savulescu do not fully address. As I will show in chapter 4, an inquiry into love needs to face the problem and hazard answers. As a whole, Jenkins's metaphysics, in spite of its sharpness, provides a rather dry and gaunt picture that leaves us hungry for more: Is love just a role or function in our lives that can be realized either on the basis of natural or of social prompts? Can we really understand love if we self-obsessively assume just the perspective of an individual person, x? Can we achieve clarity by cutting the matter to the bone? Both our lived, everyday experiences, and a huge pile of artistic and philosophical references in the Western tradition (and beyond it) suggest negative answers to these questions.

At the opposite end of the philosophical spectrum, there is Paul Kottman's book *Love as Human Freedom*, written to show how philosophy should avoid general, abstract theories that drastically reduce the shimmering complexity of the phenomenon, that flatten and homogenize its cultural and psychological manifestations and disregard its historical ramifications. Kottman rejects the metaphysical approach, arguing that its distinctive question—*what is love?*—is misleading and unhelpful. For his part, he raises an alternative question: What does love help us to explain? Love is not a "thing" *to be made sense of,* Kottman contends. Love does, rather, help us *making sense of* a number of events that shake and trouble human beings, like death, the passing of time, and biological reproduction.[5] In the course of human (Western) history, our practices and related conceptions of love have changed—yet we make love, fundamentally, for one reason. Thanks and through our love practices we try to "make sense of our world and each other"; love is "a practical form of self-education"; love is not a specific entity (an emotion, a desire, a function), but, more generally, the "expression of our desire to understand," and thus, ultimately, of human rationality.[6] Kottman's strategy is intriguing, but it is clear that it cannot completely avoid the *what is* question. The book does indeed define love *as* something—namely, as a learning process, that comes to correspond, in Hegelian fashion, to the historical progressive realization or actualization of human freedom. This idea reminds of one of the most ancient theories of love, conveyed by the dialogue between Socrates and Diotima in Plato's *Symposium*. The exchange famously illustrates love as a ladder, a process of ascension, through knowledge, toward the highest good. This is the process through which we gradually come to better understand or grasp and realize ourselves and other human beings, artifacts, scientific and political laws, and ideas about what is beautiful and right.[7]

If love is a form of knowledge, can love be *only* about knowledge? When we are in love and make love, we try to make sense of the world, of others, and of ourselves, but we also do other stuff: for instance, we play with and take care of others. What does love knowledge, then, amount to, exactly? Is knowledge only about something we *do,* or is it also about something we *undergo,* by which we are *undone*? We'll see possible answers to these and related questions in the chapters to come.

Jenkins's and Kottman's antithetical approaches do both entail important insights. Taken together, despite their methodological divergences, they reveal that, if we do not want to embrace eliminativism or give in to quietism—that is, to drop love, or the project to understand it—we cannot but try to understand *what love is.* Contrary to Kottman's attempts, this is an unavoidable question, though a question that, contrary to Jenkins's attempts, can hardly be bridled by clear-cut categories. Metaphysical and philosophical-historical approaches do not suffice. A more encompassing and varied range of conceptual instruments should be mobilized with the aim to say *at least something* substantial about love. I hence propose a different map of love, that track *some kinda love,* as the title of the Velvet Underground's song suggests, especially those too quickly dismissed by Jenkins as "identity theories." Three theoretical models, in particular, are worth considering: love as fusion or union, love as care or robust concern, and love as a bundle of shared or collective actions and emotions.

WE ARE ONE (BUT ARE WE THE SAME?)

According to a very popular, influential model, love is the desire to be *deeply united, fused,* even, with the beloved one. The archetype of this kind of love is to be found in one myth narrated by the character of Aristophanes in Plato's *Symposium.* It is not by chance that *The Symposium,* one of the key texts marking the genesis of Western philosophy, is dedicated precisely to the multifaced and contested nature of eros. *The Symposium* is one seminal philosophical text precisely because it practically shows, and not only explains, what philosophy is: a series of *conversations between friends,* circling around one troubling issue, held in an intimate space at the threshold between the private and the public (a "dinner party," whose cultural and political relevance is made clear in the opening of the story).

The animated, not always calm and peaceful conversations stage different, even incompatible, positions that oscillate between ironic levity and dramatic intensity, rely on storytelling, poetry and myth, and do ultimately not lead to any agreement.

The dialogue opens with a group of Socratic devotees who want to remember and pass down the narrative we are about to hear. Apollodorus, a disciple of Socrates, in response to a request of an anonymous friend, accepts to recall the events that took place many years before during a famous dinner party hosted by the poet Agathon to celebrate his first victory in a dramatic competition. Apollodorus had not participated in the Symposium personally, but heard its report from Aristodemus, another lover and follower of Socrates, who was himself present at the party upon invitation of his mentor. After dinner, two participants, Eryximachus and Phaedrus, protest that Eros has not yet got his fair number of poems, hymns, and paeans illustrating his goodness and invite the other guests to fill this gap.[8] Phaedrus, Pausania, Eryximachus, Aristophanes, Agathon, and Socrates offer in turn their views by trying, at the same time, to contradict and ameliorate the theses presented by the previous speakers. Contrary to his friends and followers, Socrates does not speak directly in his name, but reports Diotima's doctrine. (Diotima, the only female voice, defender of the most ambitious philosophical view of eros of *The Symposium*, is an absent character.) In the end, a visibly drunk Alcibiades shows up unexpectedly after the other guests have delivered their speeches. He joins the conversation by doing something else: exposing his dangerous liaison with Socrates, his passionate amorous sentiments for him, and the disruptive, derailing, and transformative effects that these feelings have on him.

In this intricate and intriguing context, eros is not only the object of inquiry but also a force driving the guests to speak and confront themselves. In this chapter, I reconstruct only Aristophanes's well-known narrative. Aristophanes is a comedian, and his speech is anticipated by the suspicion that he is just going to entertain his commensals with silly jokes. His contribution is probably meant as a parody of the previous one: Eryximachus's speech about the healing and harmonizing power of eros. In spite of the fact that his intervention was perhaps not meant to be taken very seriously by his commensals, Aristophanes's description of the "power of love" will have remarkable consequences for the theorization and practices of love of the subsequent 2300 years.[9]

The comedian articulates his reflections as a mythological genealogy of the human species. In this story, human anatomy has undergone a change that has made human beings weaker, needier, and more vulnerable than they were before. Once upon a time, narrates Aristophanes, persons were round beings, with back and sides making a circle, and extraordinarily strong and ambitious. Their insolence was not tolerated by Zeus and the other gods, who decided to humble them by cutting their round bodies in half, thus considerably downsizing their power. From that moment on, human beings needed to find their missing halves in order to reconstitute their original wholeness and feel complete again. Eros, intended both as a god and its interiorized version (as "inborn" in every of us), is the force that pushes human beings to look for and rejoin their designated lovers and thus to lessen their individual vulnerability. Love helps to "restore us to our ancient state by trying to make unity out of duality and to heal our human condition."[10] Since the genders in the original condition were three—entirely male, entirely female, and both male and female (i.e., androgynous), each human being can be reunited with a same-sex person or with a person of the opposite sex. Only the two halves of the original androgynous can procreate and continue the human species. Complying with ancient Greek social norms, however, the most valuable connection corresponds to a reunion of two men. Regardless of their gender connotations, every reunion is nevertheless the source of endless joy. What do lovers want? According to Aristophanes, they do not know exactly, or they cannot put their feelings into words. But in the case in which someone like the god Hephaestus would make the offer to join them together and "fuse" them until "instead of two," they "become one," "no one . . . would admit to wanting anything else."[11]

Aristophanes's metaphorical narrative has heavily influenced the construction of the modern idea of Romantic love. In the most iconic novel of German Romanticism, Friedrich Schlegel's *Lucinde*, the male protagonist Lucius tells his beloved Lucinde: "There will come a time when the two of us will perceive in a single spirit that we are blossoms of a single plant or petals of a single flower."[12] Only with her, he sees himself "complete and harmonious,"[13] and cannot distinguish between the love he feels and the love she feels, for the two emotions "are identical and perfectly united."[14] Another example: in the most dramatic letters that the English Romantic John Keats writes to Fanny Brawne, the separation of the lover from the beloved, the breaking of the union, appears as unsustainable: "I cannot exist without you." He declares desperately: "You have absorb'd me. I have a sensation at the present moment as though I was dissolving."[15] The self is nothing if not merged with the beloved one.

As the philosopher Robert Solomon testifies in his book *About Love: Reinventing Romance for Our Times*, the fascination and influence of Aristophanes's myth is largely felt in our days as well. Love corresponds, he writes, to the emotional process of "merging" or unifying "two souls," giving rise to a "shared self" that (re)determines the individual ones.[16] His actualization of the fusion or union model of love is characterized by three main ambivalent moves. First, love is regarded as both an eternal, essential idea as well as the product of historical circumstances. While the essence of love, pinpointed as fusion or union, has been first revealed in *The Symposium*, it has blossomed properly only in modern times, thanks to the modern emphasis on individualism.

As a matter of fact, the second paradox concerns the ontology of the individual. On the one hand, modern human beings strive for independence and autonomy and look for confirmation and exaltation of their singularity, also in love. On the other, they want to overcome the isolation and coldness that come with individualistic independence (and solitude) and look for a love that "breaks down all distance and denies the integrity of the isolated body. Love invades and occupies the body, subverts it with its own needs."[17] For this reason—and here comes the third ambivalence—love is both the source of the most radiant joy, when the union is achieved, and of the most exquisite pain, when lovers are necessarily divided again. Necessarily, because modern lovers cannot not be(come) independent and autonomous, even if they have to suffer because of that. One can also say that lovers cannot *really* be merged: in certain moments (especially in sexual intercourse) there is just an illusion or a symbol of merging. Solomon, in fact, speaks more precisely of the *desire* to be united, not of the full realization of a union, a desire constantly frustrated. This frustration leads to conflicts and disharmony between lovers, but also to the desire to overcome the conflict and reestablish peace. The dynamic, according to Solomon, has profound transformative consequences for lovers: one never remains unaltered by erotic encounters.

The theory of love as union or fusion has been defended by another philosopher, Robert Nozick. Love, for him, is the desire to form a new entity in the world, a loving *"we,"* a desire that, also in this view, has paradoxical form.[18] On the one hand, lovers want to completely possess the other, as they desire to have an influence on their identity. On the other hand, lovers do need the partner to be an independent, nonsubservient, autonomous person. Nozick believes that respect for the partner's autonomy as well as desire for "complete possession" can be conciliated "in the formation of a joint and wondrous enlarged identity for both."[19] Each individual has to transfer the right to take independent and unilateral decisions to a sort of joint pool or venture. Human beings in love relationships do take decisions together. As a result, their individual identities do not stay the same as before.

Contrary to Solomon, Nozick does detect gender-based differences with regard to the ways in which individuals regard and relate to the love bond. Both men and women, Nozick remarks, see the *we* as crucial for the formation of their selves. Men, however, "draw the circle of themselves containing the circle of the *we* as an aspect within it, while most women might draw the circle of themselves within the circle of the *we.*"[20] Men tend to love by incorporating the other, women by alienating themselves in the other. Nozick does not comment further on these differences.

Another theorist of love as union or fusion, rarely discussed in the analytic debate on the topic, is Eric Fromm, a psychoanalyst and critical social theorist. Helpfully, he provides an argument that defies Nozick's phrasing of the desire of union as possessive desire. In his popular book *The Art of Loving*, Fromm argues that the willingness to grasp, to "penetrate," to "know the secret" of one's 'own' lover, would correspond to their *reification*—namely, to the transmutation of the partner into a *mere thing*.[21] This is not necessarily morally deplorable, just incompatible with an union theory of love.[22] If the partner is perceived and treated as a thing, it would be impossible to create a shared identity with them; the love bond would not allow an expansion of the boundaries of the self.

The starting point of Fromm's conception of love is a human anthropology that closely resembles the mythical one illustrated by Aristophanes. Like those ancient human beings who have been harshly punished by the gods for their hubris, human beings are and feel desperately alone, helpless and separated from others. They would do anything to be liberated from the prison of loneliness and reach out, unite themselves with their fellow human beings and the external world. Diverse are the options for over-coming separateness—orgiastic fusion (!), conformity (which, in modern capitalist times, is achieved through and thanks to commodities), produc-tive and creative work—but the most efficacious one is, according to Fromm, precisely the achievement of interpersonal union in love. The desire for this kind of union is the fundamental passion that keeps the human species together. Fromm admonishes, however, not to think of the union in symbiotic terms. In "mature love," love is not a force of self-annihilation, but an active power that allows individuals to break the walls that, in a modern, ego-centered and individual profit-oriented world, keep human beings separated.[23] The social diagnosis according to which contemporary society condemns men and women to desperate loneliness, as mentioned in the introduction to this book, is at the very center of Fromm's analysis. In his eyes, erotic love represents an impor-tant resource of resistance and transformation. Love is a power—a power, we might say, quoting the (post)marxist theorist Michael Hardt—that "generates social bonds," a force that binds people together, thus fostering their particular capacities and qualities, their senses and singular human powers.[24]

The fusion or union theory has attracted complaints. Let's consider the major ones. For instance, some critics regard with suspicion the idea of love as a force of change. Irving Singer, for example, argues that lovers should not want to alter their beloved. Lovers should, rather, accept their partners exactly the way they are, love them for whom they are. This lov-ing acceptance "is an interest in the other as one who is unique in her totality."[25] This observation sounds about right: Can I really feel loved by someone who sends the signal that I am not OK the way I am, that I need to change, maybe in order to meet their expectations and fulfill their wishes? Hardly. Rather, I would feel loved if someone would tell me, by invoking Augustine's formula *Volo ut sis: I want you to be.* The problem with Singer's proposal, however, is his underlying conception defining the individual. He tends to see lovers as independent, sovereign individuals who are in control of themselves, endowed by stable and fixed identities that are not fundamentally conditioned or shaped by and within interac-tions with others. Lovers would then affirm and attend to the "sheer autonomy" of the other, but would not have any influence whatsoever on each other—which sounds phenomenologically not quite correct.

Alas, as Bennet Helm sharply notices, the central argument of union theorists, according to which a loss of individual autonomy is inevitable, acceptable, and even desirable, when it comes to love, does not properly challenge the atomistic, individualistic view of human beings. While professing the intention to overcome the individual perspective, the union model does ultimately and ironically remain trapped within a self-focused point of view and an egocentric conception of intimacy. The blurring of the distinction between my beloved and myself is often pinned down to an "appropriation of my beloved's interests."[26] Moreover, while the loving experience corresponds or aspires to a unity that supersedes individuals, such an experience is always regarded and reflected from the point of view of the singular lover. Keats, in the letter to Fanny quoted earlier, was painfully aware of that: "My love has made me selfish."[27] Not every union theorist, however, is affected by this criticism. Nozick does explicitly argue that lovers, by building up and sharing diverse activities and even an identity, need to actualize their autonomy in a collective way. For him, what is most salient to lovers is "*what holds between the two of them*," and not the self as an end point of the relation.[28]

The second line of criticism expresses concern for the blurring, or even vanishing, of the boundaries of the lovers' selves. In the sexual union, individuals are apparently not able anymore to clearly perceive (and respect!) the boundaries of their reciprocal selves: "They occasionally whisper to one another, in the act of love, that they can no longer tell where one flesh ends and the other begins, can no longer be sure whose gasp of pleasure belongs to whom, foo all flesh and pleasures are shared."[29] Outside the bedroom, a shared identity of this sort is realized in multiple ways: for instance, the lovers' career choices are to be understood as the outcome of their extended conversations and confrontation; one's ambitions, successes and failures come to correspond to the ambitions, successes, and failures of the partner. In Roland Barthes's words, the lover who seeks and rejoices in loving fusion would say: "I am engulfed, it is because there is no longer any place for me anywhere, not even in death. . . . I am no longer *gathered together*; opposite, neither you nor me, nor death, nor anything else *to talk to*."[30] Both the self and the other are "annulled by love."[31] Doesn't this sound alarming? Why do lovers stop to desire to see, touch, converse with one an*other*? Don't they fear the possible disappearance of their beloved?

The risk is exacerbated and becomes more alarming for those individuals who already tend to underestimate themselves, to sacrifice their own wishes and aspirations for the sake of their fellow human beings, who have lower self-confidence and self-esteem and are not trained to make their voices heard in public spaces, their presence noticed and respected. That is to say, the union theory of love is more risky for women who comply with traditional gender identities. Simone de Beauvoir has famously debunked and criticized the "dream of ecstatic union."[32] The dream is a promise to save woman, to rescue her from the insignificant, unsubstantial, boring reality to which an oppressive social life condemns her. For women have difficulties in realizing for themselves a concrete, meaningful, rich reality; they believe they can find a magic reality by merging with their beloved (male) partners. This makes her, however, even less real: by becoming him in the erotic fusion, she loses herself.

Such worries are legitimate. They do not consider, however, those theories of love as union that have already anticipated and addressed difficulties of the sort. Fromm, for example, has put forward a version of the union model that strongly criticizes the dissolution of the selves in what he calls a symbiotic merging. He firmly rejects self-loss and self-abnegation and rather advocates for "mature" love, a connecting (not fusing) force that should empower individuals, regardless of genders, instead of weakening them. What Fromm does not consider, however, is the severe hindrances posed by gender inequality, injustice and oppression to his conception of nonsymbiotic, "healthy" union.

One relevant shortcoming of the union theory, not enough discussed by its critics, consists in the shabby distinctions drawn between romantic love and friendship. The most obvious one, as Solomon maintains, is that romantic love, but not friendship, depends and thrives upon sex and relies on sex as its medium. Sure, he admits, we might even have "sexual friendship," but the occasional overlapping does not eliminate the differences.[33] We are attracted to friends for motives (loyalty, intelligence, shared interests, personality) that differ from those explaining the attraction to lovers (sexual charm, fantasies, looks); lovers have more demands and expectations than friends; friendship is supportive but love is "something all-embracing but therefore restrictive and exclusive too."[34] But the most important difference lies in the problem of identification: friends "circumscribe" our identity, while lovers define it. Friends can share, for example, food, happy occasions, football games (!), worries, conversations; lovers in romantic relationships can do the same, but they, additionally, can share an identity, which is the most "central and intimate thing" we could share.[35] As Nozick also believes, we cannot be part of more than one loving *we* at the same time, because our personal identity cannot be determined by more than one love union. It would be too confusing—"schizophrenic," even. Since our friendships are not so decisive for the formation of our identities, we can, however, have more than one friend.

Why should sexual attraction be triggered by look and fantasies, and not (also) by intellectual qualities? Why is romantic attachment to be necessarily conceived of as exclusive? Why should friends have less expectations than lovers? Why can our identity be transformed and (re)defined only by one romantic partner? Why cannot friends have the power to determine who we are, and who we want (not) to become? Why is a strong identification possible with one romantic partner only? Solomon and Nozick do not offer proper philosophical arguments to answer these questions. Unfortunately, their views about the distinction between romantic love and friendship seem mainly sustained by prejudices and commonsensical opinions rooted in their social and cultural contexts.

Union theorists seem, moreover, to forget how certain friendships have been sometimes depicted precisely in the terms of union or fusion. The most famous one is probably Michel de Montaigne's depiction of his own (nonsexual?) friendship with Étienne de La Boétie. In this relationship, friends would be able to "mix and blend one into the other in so perfect a union that the seam which has joined them is effaced and disappears."[36] A bond between such friends, maintains Montaigne, brings them to forget about their duties and to banish from their thoughts everything that would imply and require separation and difference. Everything is in common between them ("will, thoughts, opinions, goods, wives, children, honour, and life"); their "agreement" is "that of one soul in two bodies."[37] Very revealing, in this respect, is Nancy K. Miller's recounting of her friendship with Naomi Schor: in the "collective memoire" *My Brilliant Friends*, which is also an essay on female friendship and mentorship, the literary scholar speaks of the blurring of the boundaries between she and her friends (especially when they come to share similar sentimental situations) as a process of "over-identification:" "We loved being two in one, two as one," she writes. Nancy tells about her desperate need for Naomi.

She sees her friend, following a central motive in Elena Ferrante's very fortunate series of novel (the first volume has the title *My Brilliant Friend*), as her double.[38]

WITH A LITTLE HELP FROM MY FRIENDS

According to the second influential model considered here, all forms of interpersonal love consist in a *robust concern* for the beloved's well-being. The concern is expressed through the attempt not only to actively contribute to but also to participate in the others' well-being—to actively care for them. On this account, we *care* for our loved ones *for their own sake*, and not with the aim of fulfilling our own wishes and desires (if only the desire to be merged or simply reunited with them).

This conception is indebted to Aristotle's discussion of love in books 8 and 9 of *The Nicomachean Ethics*. The term prevalently used by Aristotle for referring to our subject matter is not "eros," as for Plato, but "philia." "Philia" should be a more encompassing and polysemic term than "eros," as it refers to a multiplicity of social relationships: sexual love, passionate love, long-term companionship, asexual friendship, affective bonds between family members, relations of esteem, and respect and solidarity between citizens. Aristotle, in the spirit of his time, was not much interested in clear-cut distinctions between more or less private or public species of philia. His social context was one in which the boundaries between emotional, familial spheres and the political arena were much more porous and worked according to different rules than modern ones.[39] At the same time, Aristotle makes the effort to articulate a taxonomy that distinguishes between different kinds of philia, especially on the basis of their motives (pleasure, utility, goodness), and of the relational status of the friends (they can be similar or dissimilar because of virtue, or of social or biological status.)

The Nicomachean Ethics is mainly a theory about the good life, and friendship is essential for a good life, for human happiness and flourishing (eudaemonia). Friends are deeply needed both in richness and poverty. In bad times, they are a refuge; they fulfill educational purposes for the youth, and for the elderly they are a fundamental aid—in the prime of life, they inspire noble deeds.[40] Aristotle distinguishes between three kinds of philia. The first type is when a bond of friendship is formed to seek pleasure. The second kind of philia is when friends seek advantages ("utility"). The third kind is formed when good men want to wish their companions well not for their own, but for the other's sake. The last type of philia, which brings together virtuous men who are equal,[41] amounts to a *perfect* form of friendship.[42] In a perfect bond, the concern for the others' well-being is reciprocated, and those involved in the relationship must know about it: "To be friends, then, they must be mutually recognized as bearing goodwill and wishing well to each other."[43] This does not mean that, if A loves B, and wishes them good, A must expect or demand that B loves them in return. Furthermore, A's love is not made conditional upon B loving them back. A's sentiments for B, and B's for A, are unconditional; they solely depend on A's and B's good character and on the fact they have both found good matches. However, Aristotle argues, persons can have perfect friendship only when their concern for the other's well-being is mutual.[44] Similarly, persons who are virtuous and find each other would end up reciprocating their concerns for the other, thus forming perfect friendship. A and B can enormously enjoy each other's company and profit from it, although the cause of their bond is to be found neither in pleasure nor in more or less mutual advantage.[45]

Perfect friendship requires time and familiarity. Although intensity and desire play a role in these intimate bonds, a concern for the friend's well-being is not much the result of a feeling, but is rooted in virtuous character and disposition. In virtue-based friendship, the good we seek is our friend's good; in pleasure-based and utility-based friendships, on the contrary, the good we seek is our own good. Moreover, activity rather than passivity is paramount for bonds of philia: we form friendship not because we have been "hit" by certain emotions and are passively driven by them, but because we chose to care for and spend time with friends. Such choice springs "from a state of character."[46] The things that friends do together are not just abstractly described in terms of care and concern. Aristotle refers concretely to those activities (e.g., athletic exercises and hunting, drinking, or the study of philosophy) that friends share as they spend their lives together. A good, happy, flourishing life is a life shared with the persons we love. But "living together," thus fully realizing, with friends, human beings' political nature, amounts mostly to a "sharing in discussion and thought."[47] Not only actions but also emotions are shared, for a friend is one who "grieves and rejoices" with their companions. As we will see in the next paragraph, Aristotle has introduced not only the care model of love, but also the idea according to which love amounts to a collectivization of actions and emotions.

Aristotle's reflections on philia do generally apply to sexual love as well. However, there are a couple of passages in which Aristotle tries to distinguish erotic passion from nonsexual friendship. He defines the former as "excess of friendship" or as "a sort of excess of feeling."[48] Furthermore, it is in its nature to be felt toward one person only, whereas we can be friends with more than one person at the same time (but not with too many of them, as each friend requires a lot of time and energy). Aristotle considers passionate love a pleasure-based friendship, and, as such, not very meaningful or stable. In the case of the relationship "between lover and beloved," pleasure does not derive from the same source: "For these do not take pleasure in the same things, but the one in seeing the beloved and the other in receiving attentions from his lover."[49] Aristotle seems to believe that sexual love is characterized by a fundamental asymmetry, where there is always one who loves more, while the other does just enjoy being the object of such loving recognition. However, when the two lovers become familiar with each other and start to love each other's character, this type of relationship can grow into perfect friendships.[50] Persons who love each other sexually, in other words, can have a perfect friendship: for them, sexual pleasure or the advantages provided by sex are not the driving motor of their bond, and what they share is more than just sexual bliss and passion.

Harry G. Frankfurt is one of the contemporary philosophers who has most significantly, and controversially, expounded upon this model of love as care—or, to use another tag, as robust concern.[51] Love is, for Frankfurt, "disinterested concern for the existence of what is loved, and for what is good for it."[52] Love is characterized mainly by the desire for the beloved's own flourishing and absence of harm. The lover harbors this wish not for the sake of promoting some further goal, for the good of the beloved is a goal in itself. The value of love for the lover derives from his unconditional dedication to the beloved, to her intrinsic well-being. The lover's activities are *subordinated* to the interests of the beloved. Their primary goal is not to receive benefits but to provide them.[53]

This dedication or even subordination is not problematic, according to Frankfurt. On the contrary, it is precisely what bestows the highest value to the activity of loving. Love matters greatly to us *because* it is a devotion to the well-being of our love objects. When we love and dedicate ourselves to our loved ones, we are serving our own interests as well. Why? Because, according to Frankfurt, in genuine love there is an identification between lover and beloved.[54] The well-being of my beloved coincides with my own well-being. This move reminds of Aristotle's thesis of the entanglement between self-love and love for the other. In *The Nicomachean Ethics*, self-love is important for friendship to work. Loving a friend means assigning the greater good to oneself, and vice versa.[55] Each lover must "perceive the existence of his friend together with his own, and this will be realized in their living together and sharing in discussion and thought."[56] In perfect friendship, spending time with friends, sharing activities, thoughts, and emotions, is motivated by an altruistic concern. The other is, however, not experienced as radical alterity, but rather as "another self."[57] The observation of the actions and emotions of my friends helps me to better know myself as well. If my friends are good and virtuous, I can come to see and know myself as good and virtuous as well. We need our friends to develop self-knowledge, which is the highest good. Our relation with ourselves is mediated by relationships with our friends, and our relationships with them are mediated by self-knowledge and self-esteem.

Frankfurt, however, wants to have identification of the lover with the beloved without taking on board the conditions of self-love, reciprocity, and equality. Lovers do yearn for reciprocity, but the fulfillment of this desire is not essential for love, he thinks.[58] Our interests and well-being coincide with the interests and well-being of our beloved also in the case that they would not reciprocate our feelings, would not care for us, would consider us, more or less consciously, not worthy. This notion, admits Frankfurt, does not apply well to romantic or sexual love, which is, in fact, defective and disappointing. Romance and sexual passion are usually linked to experiences of infatuation, lust, obsession, possessiveness, and dependency, which risk to make selfless and unconditional care or concern rather rare or impossible.[59] The purest instance of love is rather, for Frankfurt, the love of parents for their children.

There other philosophers, however, who do equate love *in general* with care or robust concern. Philipp Pettit, for example, starts from the assumption that every form of love, including romantic love, is a good that robustly demands care. His work on this subject matter does not intend to demonstrate or discuss this assumption, but, rather, to illustrate how and to what extent robust demands are imposed on those who are intimately, even romantically, attached to other people: "If you love me, then on any actual occasion where it is appropriate you have to show me care," he writes.[60] I love my partners; hence I care for them. This care is not contingent or random: what I cherish when I cherish my partners' love, according to Pettit, is a disposition to provide care that is resilient enough to survive situational shifts in the inclinations and pressures that affect them.

The care or robust concern account of love have attracted criticisms as well. The first shortcoming of this model is that it does not manage to precisely capture the specific kind of intimacy that occurs only in close, interpersonal love relationships (between friends, parents and children, or sexual partners). Neera K. Badhwar argues, quite convincingly, that the display of selfless concern for and devotion to the well-being of fellow human beings is not a sufficient indicator for love to be in place.[61] We can selflessly and devoutly dedicate ourselves to the other not necessarily because of love, but just on the ground of duty, or because this attitude and behavior toward the people who are close to us (e.g., family members, acquaintances, husbands and wives) is part of our identity—because we have been socialized, educated, and trained to become caregivers of this sort. Women have, for example, been socialized and trained to excel as caregivers. Indeed, within the Aristotelian framework, the need to distinguish intimate, "private" relationships (between close friends, parents and children, sexual partners) from less intimate but still friendly relationships (e.g., among fellow citizens) was not very pressing. One might argue, as Frankfurt does, that what differentiates a loving from mere compassionate, nonloving concern is that, in love, the interests of the lovers are strongly identified with those of the beloved. This solution does inject more intimacy and closeness into the care model, but it also makes it draw dangerously near to the union account, thus eliciting the same problems that its critics have detected.[62] A second criticism concentrates on the egocentrism that seems to affect the care model as well. Ironically, while the lover is said to love their beloved for their own sake, to be outward-looking, projected and concentrated solely or predominantly on another person's good, the act of loving is described only from the lover's perspective. As the German philosopher Angelika Krebs sharply notices, although the lover is ready to sacrifice herself for the beloved, it appears as if there would be no real exchange or dialogue between them.[63] The identification between the "I" and the "You" is constructed from the former perspective, on the basis of the motives of "I" alone. The other's views, interests, wishes are not seriously taken into consideration. The objects of love play just a passive role: they are the receivers of love, and they do not get to speak, decide, act.

According to David Velleman, lovers might desire to care for their beloved sometimes, but care cannot define the nature of love tout court. When we think of, feel, or relate to the people we love, we do not necessarily feel that we want or have to care for them, to do something to improve their well-being. We might also feel profound admiration or pride for them; we might be in awe in front of their virtues. Less nobly, we might also feel envy, or some kind of resentment.[64] If we were compelled to care for our beloved most of the time, we would very probably end up in "unhealthy" behaviors; our care would become oppressive.[65] More generally, Velleman criticizes conceptualizations of love that proceed in terms of "aims" to be achieved, intentions to be pursued. He proposes instead to view love as an attitude toward the beloved as a person, and not toward any result, including, namely, the result that consists in the promotion of their well-being. This attitude is conceived of by Velleman as "arresting awareness" in front of the value of a human being envisioned as an end in itself. The loving awareness, as he beautifully puts it, arrests "our tendencies toward emotional self-protection from another person, tendencies to draw ourselves in and close ourselves off from being affected by him."[66] When we love someone, we become vulnerable, exposed to the sheer presence of another person who, like us, is an end itself. But what does follow from this awareness? This is a crucial question, which is not answered by Velleman.[67]

Following one of the central Aristotelian theses, love must be conceived as a good, as one necessary component of the good life. But what about the case in which love for another person would amount to plain suffering, which does not promote or imply any good? This is not an infrequent case—on the contrary. Jonathan Lear is not convinced by Frankfurt's idea that disinterested love for other persons is a blessing per se. He puts forward the following example: Abelard loves Heloise, but he is in prison and knows that she will never know of his feelings and thus benefit from them. That is, Abelard is actively in love but cannot care for his beloved, and because he cannot do her good, yet continues to love her, he suffers.[68] In this case, neither of them would accrue some benefit from Abelard's love—a love that nevertheless can hardly be put into question.

Another striking example along this line is the case in which a slave falls in love with their master. The condition of slavery is the paradigmatic case of lack of freedom, or of domination: the slave's will is entirely subservient to the will of the master. It could happen that the slave falls "actively, autonomously, selflessly" in love with the master, and makes the master's ends their own ends, not for any selfish benefit, but simply for the sake of the master.[69] This, according to Lear, cannot represent any good for the slave, as it only reaffirms and strengthens domination.

Frankfurt disagrees with Lear. When the slave serves the master's end out of love for them—and not, say, out of fear—they are acting, in a certain sense, autonomously. The exercise of autonomy, Frankfurt says, improves the slave's life. Admittedly, this might be a source of trouble when the master is evil, but it could amount to a good if the master is a decent person.[70] The slave can, of course, also achieve autonomy by emancipating from the master; in this case, however, autonomy would not be rooted in love. To be sure, at this point, Frankfurt admits that love is not always to be regarded as a good or as aiming at the good.[71] In some circumstances, the preferable thing to do would be to resist "the authority of love," to disregard the reasons that love gives us to act, and hence to disunite the will. This contradicts, however, what Frankfurt says elsewhere: that the interests of the lover coincide with the interests of the beloved, that selflessly pursuing the beloved's good is a good in itself *also for the lover.*

The love story between master and slave is not just a thought experiment: real-life conventional or traditional love relationships under conditions of patriarchy are not dissimilar from Lear's master-slave examples. Krebs argues that Frankfurt's idea of love as selfless and disinterested care makes room for the exploitation of the "weaker" participant in the love relationship—traditionally, women.[72] There is indeed a long tradition of feminist critical theory problematizing the role that care has played and continues to play in traditional families and heterosexual relationships, as well as in society at large.[73] In principle, both the one who provides care and the one who is cared for are in a position of turning care into a means of exercising power over the other. The caregiver is in a position of power because the recipient depends on her, more or less urgently, for the fulfillment of needs and wishes. The caregiver may exercise power or not, more or less intentionally, by actually denying or giving care. At the same time, the one who is cared for is also in a potential position of power. If one manages to attract and secure as much care as possible, the benefits might significantly empower him. An unwillingness to reciprocate care might further strengthen this power position. The gendered language is not accidental here: traditional gender identities have been criticized precisely for asymmetrically reifying the roles of caring and being cared for in a relationship between two people. Conventional love relationships today are still affected by such asymmetry.

It has to be remarked that, while such feminist critiques seem to be very well placed against Frankfurt and other contemporary proponents of the care or robust concern model, they might find a precious ally in Aristotle. *The Nicomachean Ethics* does in fact convey some useful insights for critically addressing imperfect or problematic intimate relationships. The problem, one might indeed argue from an Aristotelian standpoint, is that traditional heterosexual relationships are not based on equality, reciprocity, and self-love. While this did not trouble Aristotle, who envisaged women as naturally inferior to men, the issue does of course solicit a critical philosophy of love today.

LOVING IS SHARING

The third model, which can be called "collectivist," is based on the conviction that we cannot understand love if we concentrate solely on the point of view of the singular person who loves or is in love with another person. On the collectivist account, on the contrary, love is something bonding two or more people who, more or less intentionally, do and feel something together. Lovers cannot be understood solely as separated and independent beings, but also, and more importantly, as integral members of a (small) collective entity, in which actions and emotions become profoundly shared. Love, as Krebs puts it, "is not about each partner having the other as his or her object; it is *between* the partners."[74]

This model is not completely new for us. Nozick has been listed as a union theorist, but he can be regarded also as precursor of the collectivist model. Collectivists, however, do stress more strongly than others that in order for these shared actions and emotions to occur, the boundaries of the lovers' selves cannot disappear. The loving *we* is not described as the result of the fusion of individual entities, but it is not their mere addition either. Aristotle as well offers precious indications for the collectivist model, for which the activity of care is not however fundamental.

One of the first and most detailed account of the collectivist model is provided by Marilyn Friedman, alongside the detailed and refined feminist critique of the fusion model that she pursues in her influential paper "Romantic Love and Personal Autonomy." Her point of departure is Neil Delaney's intuition, according to which lovers' desire to form a romantic *we* would resemble the "wish among sovereign states to form a republican nation."[75] While one of Delaney's goals was to reconcile the union with the care model, Friedman puts forward an alternative. She recasts Delaney's image by reflecting on the characteristics of a "federation of states" and its meaning and implications for a conception of loving collectivity. In such a collective, two separate states retain some of their individual powers and capacities while forming a joint venture that generates shared goals and purposes. As a result, a third entity emerges, one that involves "the lovers *acting in concert* across a range of conditions and for a range of purposes."[76] Lovers remain separated and separable; they continue to have chances to act on their own, driven by their individual wishes, following their individual purposes. However, when A and B form a romantic *we*, their being together is something more and something different than the mere sum of A and B (and, in principle, C, D, etc.) They have in fact formed a third entity.

For Friedman, lovers come together on three different and interrelated levels. First, they form a new *subjective* entity, a novel subject of experience that feels joys, sorrows, moments of ecstasy, insight, contentment, doubt, fear, anxiety, and even loneliness. Second, lovers come together on the level of *agency*: they engage in joint enterprises for various purposes and toward various ends. Third, lovers form a collectivity in what Friedman calls "objecthood": their objects of attention or concern are shared too. Unlike a federation of states, the loving collective is not entirely formalized and stable—or at least not always; it does not follow fixed, clear, predictable rules. It can be dynamic, shifting, in need of continuous renegotiations and reaffirmations. What is more, lovers can form a collectivity in some respects but not others, and the modalities of their togetherness shift over time. Two lovers might attend to the same need or interest (e.g., going to the concert of their favorite band) as a couple (they go to the concert together) or individually (they go alone). Lovers can act together as a collective agent, but focusing their attention and resources on meeting the needs that only one of them has (e.g., they read and critically discuss the paper written by one of them). Or, they can deeply share certain activities (e.g., they coauthor a paper) but not others (e.g., sport).

The issue of personal autonomy is, in the work of Friedman, paramount both for understanding the nature of love in general and for distinguishing between bad (harming, oppressive) and good (fulfilling, empowering) kinds of relationships. Personal autonomy is a good and is defined, roughly, as self-government. In order to autonomously act, choose, and commit, one has to be able to make "more deeply and truly hers those dimensions of her biography that constitute or manifest her agency or her identity."[77] Autonomy requires both the capacity to reflectively consider whatever is at stake in one's actions, choices, and commitments, and a relative freedom from influences and constraints. One cannot, however, do this alone: autonomy is a social competency that can be acquired, nurtured, and expressed only through certain social practices. Now, practices of love, including romantic love, can both *enhance or diminish* personal autonomy. According to Friedman, romantic, heterosexual love entails a risk of reducing or even erasing individuals'—and especially women's—autonomy, especially of those women who go for the fusional experience of love. If, however, relationships' patterns manage to escape the traditional gender order, love bonds could develop potentials for promoting individuals' autonomy insofar as they foster self-understanding, self-esteem, mutual learning, and capacities to act (alone and in concert). Being for a while the less autonomous party of a romantic *we,* moreover, does not necessarily preclude one from growing more autonomous.

Bennett W. Helm offers another account of collectivist love that builds upon Friedman's work. According to Helm, not only we can better understand personal autonomy if we conceptualize shared or joint actions and emotions (or "felt evaluations"); a reflection on intimacy is also paramount to conceptually grasp collective agency and personhood in general.[78] A conceptualization of friendship and love shows how we build up a *plural personhood*, and how autonomy is enhanced by sharing individual autonomous exercises.[79]

Similarly to the theorists discussed in the previous paragraph, Helm's point of departure is a definition of love as care for another person for their own sake: this implies caring about the things the beloved cares about and responding emotionally to things affecting their well-being. The mere reference to robust concern, however, fails to provide an adequate account of intensely intimate relationships, for, as we have seen before, it is too comprehensive. The type of care specific to friendship and love, Helm argues, implies the *sharing* of interests, evaluations, and personal identities. Sharing in love amounts to an intimate identification, which does however not require, cause, or imply any disappearance of one's own self. Love, in Helm's view, is "a matter of intimate identification in which you come to have a concern for the identity of your beloved that is the same in kind as your concern for your own identity." This identity-sharing is paramount for an understanding of the relevant *emotionally evaluative* attitude that characterizes intimate bonds. Lovers come to share their partners' emotions, or "felt evaluations," as result of their valuing the things and activities that constitute their partners' identities and thus represent for them objects of value. Emotions, including loving ones, are, for Helm, felt evaluations that entail commitments: commitments have to be received and attended to because they are felt as important—that is, as having an import, as worth pursuing, because conducive to a good life.[80]

Consider, for example, the emotion (felt evaluation) of pride that the author experiences because of her wife winning a bagpipe competition. (This is Helm's example.) This pride includes desires that motivate the lover to act on behalf of the beloved. Moreover, desires and actions provide occasions for the lovers to feel pride or shame about themselves. For example, if the author fails to support his wife's commitment to bagpiping, he might be feeling ashamed. Friends and lovers do not simply assume and share their partners' emotions and values. Their reciprocal engagement in each other's lives allow them also to influence and shape each other's personality in rational ways. As Aristotle has already claimed, the intimate identification, the sharing of felt emotions and the mutual shaping of them do, moreover, require that friends and lovers take actively part in the same undertakings. If, for example, antiracist political engagement is of great import for my partner's identity and life, I cannot just limit myself to assign a value to their activism or to encourage them to be involved in the planning and realization of various antiracist actions. I should also come to appreciate them, and even to participate, at least to some extent, in such actions myself.

Note an important difference between the collectivist model and the union model: while the love unity seems to be predominantly a physical, sensual, if not a sexual one, or, at least, to necessarily rely upon a bodily component, the former has a broader notion of unification. The identification with the beloved, for the collectivists, is not (first and foremost) a merging of fleshes, but a convergence of minds. Collectivists underline that it is not (necessarily) an intensively passionate, derailing experience, but a sober, rational one.

Like Friedman, Helm advocates for a social conception of autonomy: "the rational influence that close friends can have on each other in determining their shared sense of what is important in life" does not undermine their autonomy—it is not, for example, a delegation of responsibility—but, on the contrary, can be "central" for its proper exercise.[81] Relationships of friendship and love, according to Helm, show how autonomy can be exercised as a *joint enterprise*. Friends and lovers, who are able to shape each other's thoughts, feelings, and lives, form not simply *a plural agent* but, more intimately, a *plural person*. A plural person is formed when persons who love each other transform their shared cares and values into joint cares and values. Moreover, they cultivate a joint conception of the kind of life they want together, and in this sense they form a joint identity as a (plural) person.

Isn't this model vulnerable to the same problem that critics, Helm among them, impute to union theories? Helm admits that his notion of intimacy accommodates occasions for the lover to quite heavily intervene and try reshape the beloved's perspectives. However, if lovers and friends were not individually autonomous, they could not exercise the capacity to coordinate their efforts to generate their collective identity as a loving bond and their collective understanding of a life worth living. Moreover, since lovers and friends deeply care about the well-being of their partners, they do not only respect and thus preserve their autonomy as individuals, but even encourage and foster it. Plural personhood consists in an extension of our individual autonomy, which is expanded to include the autonomy we exercise jointly with others. Helm does not speak only of autonomy, but also of freedom, a "new freedom of joint action," which extends also onto the social realm: plural persons do always act in a complex social domain, together with other plural persons, and not simply as individuals.[82]

Angelika Krebs presents yet another account of collectivist love that she names "dialogical." More decisively than Helm, she stresses the distance between the collectivist and the care model: "love is about sharing and not about caring," she declares.[83] The "curative" element can certainly happen within the loving *we,* but does not need to be much emphasized. As discussed earlier, it can sometimes even damage (romantic) love. The most important thing to grasp when it comes to love, for Krebs, is the ways in which lovers come to share not only actions but also, significantly, feelings or emotions. Joint actions are something different, more encompassing and complex, than simply aggregations of individual deeds. While each agent tries to continuously adjust their individual inputs to the collective undertaking, it is the latter that orient and give meaning to the former. Joint action can be performed for obtaining some further goal or for its own sake. An example of the former, of "extrinsic" joint action, is when a group of friends walk together in order to reach a restaurant where they want to dine; an example of the latter, of "intrinsic" joint action, is when a group of friends walk together just for the pleasure of walking. Intrinsic joint action is usually accompanied by positive sensations and feelings. Some further goal might be reached as a result (e.g., a fitness goal); often, the result is the flourishing and personal enrichment of those involved carrying it out. Such goals, however, are not the motivators for intrinsic joint actions.

Joint actions can moreover be both "impersonal" and "personal": while in the former the agents come together and join the group on the basis of their characteristics and willingness to contribute to the action itself, in personal joint actions individuals are bound together because of their personalities, of what matters to them the most. Consider a students' reading group on Hegel's *Phenomenology of Spirit* (my example). Take the case in which the students do not know each other well, but only know that they are all talented and motivated students, and that their only aim is to understand the philosophical text in order to pass the exam: this is a case of impersonal joint action. If, on the contrary, the students decide to meet up and read the *Phenomenology,* a book they all love, because they appreciate and enjoy each other's company and take advantage of this occasion even for deepening, with each other's aid, not only their philosophical knowledge but also the knowledge of themselves, they are taking part in a personal joint action. Love corresponds, according to Krebs, to an ensemble of joint actions that are intrinsic and personal.[84]

Lovers and friends are, moreover, capable of joint or shared emotions. Lovers and friends, on Helm's view, can infect each other and shape and influence each other's emotional life, but the emotions are felt individualistically. I can come to feel pride or sadness because of my partner's successes or failures, if these have import for their identities and lives, and their identities and lives are shared by me as well. The pride or sadness I feel remain *my* pride and sadness, though, for Helm, and my partner's pride and sadness are different and separated from mine. Krebs's view, on the contrary, suggests that, sometimes, lovers are able to take part in the *same emotion.* As members of a loving *we*, individuals find themselves in an emotional, affective state that transcends their own particular, singular feelings. They are *in the same pride, or sadness, together.* If I come to share my partner's activities in their anti-racist group, what happens is that I can come to participate in their emotions (rage, or hope) as well. Again, a joint feeling does not (or should not) amount to a form of fusion or merging of the selves: individuals share an emotional state while at the same time retaining their own particular, singular feelings. Each affective experience does contribute to the emergence of the collective emotion; the shared or joint feeling has, in turn, an impact on individuals' emotions (and, more broadly, on their lives and identities).

To sum up, we can say that we form a *dialogical we* with our lovers when:

- we become emotionally affected (*betroffen*) by the same situation in similar ways;
- we perceive that our lovers are experiencing similar feelings;
- we jointly evaluate a certain situation;
- we express our joint emotions in a collective emotional narrative;
- we generate a collective language, a collective world view and collective emotional patterns and schemes, and collectively arrange and organize our lives on the basis of such language, view, patterns and schemes;
- we produce a common self, or a common identity, by being interested and paying deep, intimate attention to our lovers' particular singularity;
- we act together on the basis and as a result of the collective emotion we have generated.

The capacity and possibility to share feelings in these ways depend, according to Krebs, on shared action. In an Aristotelian vein, lovers and friends develop the capacity and disposition to collectively feel while, and because, they are participating in common activities.[85] Falling in love and maintaining love relationships is a process that develops through time and requires the active, ongoing engagement of individuals.

Krebs calls her account "dialogical" because love is like a conversation: of bodies that not only speak but also act, feel, are affected by each other. Within a conversation, individuals' (communicative) actions, gestures, and signs do directly rely on the others' actions, gestures, and sign, and depend on the others' contributions to acquire sense and direction, to unfold, to be specified, clarified, or even rejected. In order to be able to express themselves and thus participate in a (bodily, emotional) dialogue, individuals must retain their singular voices, perspectives, more or less justified points of view. More decidedly than Helm, Krebs intends to overcome a rationalist and cognitivist account of collective love: her favorite examples for illustrating the ontology of the loving *we* are dancing (a waltz) and making music together.[86] In these activities, the coordination, interplay, and amalgam between agents exceed the verbal dimension and include affects, bodily sensations, and reactions.[87] However, Krebs is careful in stressing the rational, active, autonomous aspects of such forms of being together. This should ensure that participants in intimate collectives could at any moment back out from it, regain their separateness and individuality. Krebs, unfortunately, does not expound more specifically on the role and import, on the dangers but also on the potentialities of bodily, pre- or nonlinguistically articulated sensations and interactions for the unfolding of the loving dialogue. But, as we will see, collective experiences, including dances and conversations, do also entail moments of self-forgetfulness and self-loss that might have noncontrollable, ambivalent effects, also potentially disruptive and derailing.

The last version of the collectivist model that I want to mention, because it belongs to a different tradition and conception of philosophy from those mentioned before, is Alain Badiou's. The French philosopher sees (romantic, sexual) love as a *perspective* on the world "from the point of view of two and not one."[88] Lovers form a collective subject that regards the world in a certain way; through the eyes of the subject of love, which resembles a "prism," the world appears as the same world to both lovers. For this common experience of the world to become possible, the differences characterizing the two lovers cannot be erased; on the contrary, they have to be cherished. This is why the love perspective corresponds to the point of view of "difference," not of "identity." Importantly, the collective activity of *looking at* does not amount to a representation of the world, but, rather, to an active construction and transformation of it. Badiou's conception is worth mentioning because it signalizes, alongside Helm's reference to freedom as joint action of plural persons, an aspect often neglected by contemporary philosophers of love—namely, love's generative, creative openness to a worldly, nonprivate, almost public dimension, to that social, political context inhabited by lovers and friends.

The model of love as ensemble of collective actions and emotions presents two main advantages in comparison to care and union identity theories: first, it explicitly calls for and accommodates a critical attitude and interest (i); second, its ontological presuppositions are more elaborated (ii):

(i) *Critical interest.* While their primary aim is understanding what love *is*, the representatives of the collectivist model do, furthermore, make concrete efforts to distinguish between somewhat good and somewhat bad practices. Although Helm consciously presents his account of friendship and love in ideal terms, he acknowledges that love relationships can unfold in less than ideal terms. He singles out two criteria for identifying failed love relationships: first, the respect for the beloved's autonomy, and, second, the concern for the beloved's well-being. It follows that lovers behave badly when they act paternalistically, disrespecting or not sufficiently taking into consideration and care for the beloved's autonomous sense.[89] But lovers can also fail their beloved when they are too indulgent and detached and do not intervene to protect them from harm and to promote their well-being. Krebs, for her part, sees respect for the partner's autonomy as the basic criterion for distinguishing bad and good love too: without respect, relationships cannot properly work out. Respect, for persons' autonomy and for moral laws in general, is not only a moral standard but also a constitutive rule for proper, successful, and happy relationships.[90]

Friedman as well criticizes romantic relationships insofar as they are asymmetrically structured with the consequence of reducing the autonomy of women. Differently from Helm and Krebs, her criticisms are not directed toward those individuals who, for personal, psychological, subjective reasons, fail to respect their lovers and friends. She is much more interested in the larger structural, objective, social conditions that put men and women in asymmetrical positions and shape their interactions in ways that have harming, oppressive effects. Differently from union and care theories, hence, such a collectivist social ontology goes beyond the private dimension. The "collectivities" of love and friendship must be thought as intimately interconnected with broader material, political, economic dimensions of social life. As Aristotle's philosophy of philia had already envisaged, it is the political context that sets up the conditions for intimate relationships of friendship and love to thrive.[91] In the following chapters, the social embeddedness of love and its troubles will be further investigated.

(ii) *Ontological rich articulation.* The collectivists intend to overcome the simplified atomistic perspective, that focuses solely on the scheme *x loves or is in love with y* (Jenkins). The collectivist model invites to adopt a *threefold view* on love bonds, which comprises: first, a *subjective* or *individual* perspective, that takes into account lovers' and friends' individual emotions, attitudes, dispositions, wills, intentions, actions, and so on; second, a *communal* one, according to which the love bond forms an acting and emotional entity on its own, different from the mere sum of individual actions and emotions; and, third, an *intersubjective* one that considers relationships between lovers and friends that constitute themselves and unfold in various ways, with various outcomes, on the basis of both individual and collective actions and emotions. In the following chapters, a fourth dimension, a *social* one, will be introduced: as we will see, individual and collective loving acts and emotions, as well as relationships between lovers and friends, are shaped by social norms and structures of different sorts. At the same time, social norms and structures can be shaped by what lovers and friends do and feel.

Alas, collectivist theorists tend to largely uphold a harmonious, stable and stabilizing, conciliated view of the social ontology of intimacy. Tensions, discrepancies and struggles—between individuals and between individuals and their *we(s)*—are not denied, but also not systematically explored. Disagreements and struggles seem to solely represent mere inconveniences that have to be avoided or overcome as quickly as possible for the sake of a smooth, well-functioning love bond.

Margaret Gilbert, one of the first and most acute theorists of collective or joint agency, has dedicated some interesting pages to marital love. This particular type of collectivity, she believes, is characterized by a high degree of "stability" that is at the basis of husband's and wife's shared views, values and principles and that is needed to sustain long-term projects. In order to reach stability, compromises must be made: as a result, "personal preferences will pale or get converted. The couple's practices may . . . so *predominate* that the individual has no countervailing tendencies any longer."[92] This observation does indeed accurately capture the dispossessing and self-transcending character of intense forms of love, especially if embedded in long-term, committed, and official relationships. However, in this scenario, disagreement, separation, and conflict are disapproved of. This fear of troubles, so to say, seems problematic, as the collective entity, not only in the fusion but also in the collectivist model, might end up suffocating and obliterating individual selves.[93] If lovers and friends were brought to cultivate wishes (and fantasies) for harmony, integration, frictionless interaction and attunement, they would risk to hide or foreclose who they really are and desire, thus ultimately jeopardizing the loving *we* itself. As a corrective to this too harmonious and static view, the next chapter outlines a more dynamic, *agonist* idea of love.

Chapter Two

"HE HAS KISSED HER WITH HIS FREEDOM"

Bound by Ambivalence

So, *what is love*, then? In the previous chapter, we went through a map that illustrates three different models: love as (desire for) fusion or union with another human being; love as desire and care; and love as the realization of an ensemble of shared actions and emotions. Each model has virtues and vices. The aim of the map was not meant to be exhaustive, to settle controversies, to endorse or reject the one or the other model. In order to understand at least something of what love is, we need to learn from the impasses and difficulties we encountered while crossing the mapped landscape, to bring together and further develop some of the lessons learnt.

Are we still in the business of mapping definitions and accounts of love, though? Hasn't our interest somehow shifted? Both present-day and ancient discussions, while trying to pinpoint love's nature, end up almost inevitably asking about its goodness or desirability as well. Whichever definition or conception we choose, troubling issues are hardly avoidable: Is falling and being in love good for us? When and under what conditions should we become wary of love? It seems that a normatively neutral, or a strictly descriptive, approach to this phenomenon won't do.[1] To ask *What is love?* is not enough. But trying to decide when and to what extent love is something that can enrich us and make us thrive, or else damage or even destroy us, is as tricky as choosing a definition or conception. Many philosophers circumvent the issue by casting love as a good thing, as something that cannot be bad: love and domination, oppression, or injustice, are mutually exclusive, they say. When there is (true) love, people cannot harm each other.[2] But such a bright, positive view seems like an easy way out of the uncertainty, one that reduces the complexity of the phenomenon rather than help to thoroughly understand it. It seems more realistic and instructive to admit that not only love can be many things, it can also be either good or bad for us—good in some respects and bad in others. Many times, we cannot practically disentangle the good from the bad. For this reason, it is important to sketch out some normative and critical guidelines for a discussion of love.

In the last chapter, we gathered some precious insights that help to identify love relationships gone astray. From the criticisms against the union model, for instance, we have learnt that love becomes problematic— unacceptable, even—when individuals' independence and autonomy are impaired: when the boundaries of the selves risk becoming blurred or even disappearing, and when individuals' actions and emotions are heavily conditioned, influenced, or not respected by their partners or friends. Autonomy counts as the main criterion in the collectivist account as well. Tellingly, this criticism closely resonates with a worry raised by critics of the care model: feminist thinkers, in particular, have drawn attention to the ways in which the demands of care can put lovers and friends in problematic, asymmetrical positions. The persons who feel compelled to care more, usually women, run the risk of falling into a position of oppression, crushed under the burdens of care duties and responsibilities. However, the receiver of care can also become oppressed. Provision of care can serve as a tool to manipulate and control the other. Care might become a mechanism of oppression and an impairment of autonomy, in both directions.

But should we try to be autonomous and independent all the time, even in the bedroom and with our most intimate companions? Are autonomy and independence so desirable in every domain of our lives? The experience of love seems to teach us precisely how pleasurable and generally important it is to let go of or loosen up the obsession with the individualism and separateness implied in the imperatives of autonomy and independence. It feels good to be taken care of, to rely on our trusted loved ones, to lose control over ourselves and over others and external circumstances, not to be "in charge" all the time. Yet such prospects can generate anxiety and worries, and for good reasons.

Let's try to navigate these troubles. Towards the aim of distinguishing between *desirable* and *nondesirable* forms of love, this chapter wants to expand and transform the criteria of independency and autonomy into the broader, multifaced normative and critical category of *freedom*. I suggest that desirable love allows individuals to "kiss each other with their freedom," to employ the metaphor of Joni Mitchell's song "Cactus Tree" quoted in this chapter's title. Freedom seems a pretentious and heavy concept, and it is indeed quite a troublesome one. Borrowing from the title of one of Angela Davis's books, we can say that freedom is a process, and a process of *constant struggle*. Moments of both dependence and independence, heteronomy and autonomy, are to be cast as parts of this struggle. The difficult, normative idea of freedom should be helpful for better figuring out the ambiguity or ambivalence of love, which will be thematized in the first section. In order to shed light on this double face, I expound, in the second section, on a model of love that promises to bring together some of the most distinctive features presented in the previous chapter. This is a *recognition model of love*, inspired by a Hegelian notion of recognition in the sense of *Anerkennung*. Love relationships as relationships of recognition are, as I argue in the third and fourth sections, dynamics or interplays of various forms of power. Power—a certain practice of power—births *self-(trans)formation*, or at least this is what I try to show in the fifth section, with the aid of Stanley Cavell's perfectionist ethics of marriage and divorce. At the end of the chapter, we will finally have a first outline of the kind of freedom that is promised by bonds of love. An understanding of erotic freedom will be helping us, then, in chapter 3, to reflect upon what we might and should *not* want in love.

THE DOUBLE FACE OF LOVE

One of the most influential feminist theorists—and icons—in Western culture and history, Simone de Beauvoir, gives voice to a conflict with regard to love. Her thoughts on this matter oscillate between a radical critique of what love, under the present social conditions of patriarchy, *is*, and what love *could be* or *become* once women and men have managed to liberate themselves from such conditions. One of her most famous books (or, probably, the most famous one), *The Second Sex*, includes a chapter dedicated to the figure of the "woman in love," which ends with the following words: "The day when it will be possible for the woman to love in her strength and not in her weakness, not to escape from herself but to find herself, not out of resignation but to affirm herself, love will become for her as for man the source of life and not a mortal danger."[3]

These lines encapsulate, dramatically, the very core of love's ambivalence. On the one hand, love represents a social tool for reproducing and justifying women's position of subjection, their disadvantageous emotional and economic dependence on men, their incapability to affirm independence and autonomy. As a consequence, women involved in erotic relations may face dangers and ("mortal"!) risks. On the other hand, however, love can be imagined and conceptualized as a space for powerful, creative, spontaneous self-expression and self-affirmation, where individuals can thrive and mutually acknowledge, affirm, and celebrate each other in their vulnerability and singularity.

In her work, Beauvoir conveys the ambivalence of love from two angles. On a first level of analysis, she speaks of love relationships both from a descriptive-critical and from a normative-imaginative, almost utopic, standpoint. When she adopts the former, she proceeds to investigate love practices and discourses (e.g., in novels) in order to show how they are involved in the constitution and reproduction of harmful gender identities. When in love, women tend to devote themselves completely to their men. As a matter of fact, men expect their female partners to offer themselves as a gift; they are disappointed or even angry if they fail to do so, but are not ready and willing to reciprocate. What is more, women mostly desire to be merged with their companions, while men desire to absorb their female partners in their lives and projects, thus achieving "narcissistic exaltation."[4] In this way, women are brought to assume the other's identity, while men tend to forge women's inclinations, views, values according to theirs. This is not, notes Beauvoir cleverly, completely lacking rationale. The reasons of their—free?—choice are bad, but there are reasons nevertheless. Female submission to their lovers appears to them as a smart, feasible way to achieve, through their participation in the sexual or romantic union, some of the characteristics that men possess but are denied to them. At least in the society described by Beauvoir, women, *as women*, cannot be really active and free; they find difficult to engage, by themselves, in meaningful economic, intellectual, artistic, or political endeavors. As part of a love union with the man they have allegedly freely chosen, they could, however, acquire some desired "manly" characteristics; they could become, transitively, so to say, active, free and engaged. A woman can thus shine through reflected light, and this might be better than no light at all.

However, Beauvoir does not pursue this negative path of denunciation. Even if until now we have never known a different scenario than unequal love, we can (and must) try to imagine how things could be otherwise. A new and better love would be, then, a form of relationship in which two individuals, man and woman, "recognize" each other reciprocally *as equal*, and as *free* beings. "Authentic" love, as Beauvoir calls it, occurs when lovers see and treat each other as free to give and receive love as they feel it, but also, more generally, to pursue their wishes, desires, and projects as they see fit. As a result, both female and male lovers would really learn, thanks to each other, what exactly such wishes, desires and projects amount to, what their real purposes and values are: "For each of them, love would be the revelation of self through the gift of self and the enrichment of the universe."[5] The final sentence of *The Second Sex* suggests that authentic love could also work as forerunner for a more general model of relationality between the sexes. Beauvoir employs here the infelicitous term "brotherhood," which we can better understand as friendship. This model would help to "make the reign of freedom triumph."[6]

Beauvoir's take is fascinating because it suggests that love is both a highly private experience, one that contributes to the formation and transformation of the self's personal identity and interiority, and a worldly activity, one that contributes to the formation and transformation of our world in common. The French philosopher does not explain the connection between the two forms of (trans)formation. One possible link, which I will further explore in the final chapter, might consist in the fact that education and development of the individual is not simply an inward activity, but has to do with the discovery and the knowledge of the world "out there." In love, suggests Beauvoir, "through another person, a new world is revealed and given to you."[7]

Equality between the sexes is intimately connected with women's emancipation and freedom. Realization of equality does not mean overcoming or neutralizing, or being blind, to individuals' differentials related to gender or sex (or race or age). On the contrary, recognition in love does allow one to perceive and cherish the loved one as a unique and special being, different from anyone else. Lovers are (made) equal, rather, because they are both equally free. The freedom of individual lovers, for Beauvoir, does not mean detachment and independence from material, bodily, affective, and social conditions; other human beings should not be and are not necessarily felt as potential threats to one's freedom—on the contrary. While figuring out what love *could be* in a better society, we realize that desire, attraction, and emotional and bodily needs put everyone in a condition of dependence that cannot be ignored or erased—a condition, though, that does not have to *necessarily* be source of anxieties and fears. The vulnerability that comes with dependence can give rise to forms of oppression, yes, but it can also be the basis for joint adventures, some of them enabling individual flourishing and joyous self-expression.

Beauvoir casts the ambivalence of love not only on the level of social theory, but also from a more general, existential, and metaphysical perspective. Even in an ideal world that would follow principles of equality and freedom (between the sexes, but, crucially, not only), we would have to accept and live the "ambiguity" of our condition. We are fundamentally ambiguous beings because we strive for transcendence (we look into the future, build up and change our worlds) and are contemporarily doomed to immanence (we find ourselves heavily embroiled in the present condition, conditioned by the past, including past traumas): we are both flesh and spirit, subject and object, activity and passivity. As a matter of fact, the erotic experience is the one that most poignantly reveals to us such a condition, as well as the one that promises to bring together, almost to reconcile, the two sides of the ambivalence. The promise is precious, but is never really fully realized. In the chapter on "Sexual Initiation" in *The Second Sex*, Beauvoir claims that in a "blossoming" erotic life, the loved one remains an "other," distant, like a foreign country, but without hostility.[8] In this combination of and oscillation between distance and vicinity, eros cannot be regarded as a peaceful endeavor. Among the forms that the "human couple" will discover once "the slavery of half of humanity is abolished," Beauvoir enlists "joy," as well as "rivalries," "tension," "suffering," and the "failure" of human existence.[9] Love is an adventure; it entails promises that are often not kept, and also risks.[10]

To recap, the ambivalence of love appears as twofold: to begin with, if we want to conceptualize the good of love, we cannot do it without taking into account those social, objective social conditions that hinder or enable human flourishing. But a second meaning of love's ambivalence cuts deeper, on a more general and existential level, and is difficult to dispel: even if we were able to liberate ourselves from damaging social conditions, we would have no guarantee that the troubles of love would be "worth it.'" Freedom, in love or otherwise, is not a given, but hard and painful enterprise that does not always succeed.[11]

ADVENTURES OF INTERDEPENDENCE

We wanted to know what love is; we have encountered freedom, several times. In order to better understand what love is, or something about it, we should, then, try to better understand what and to what extent love has to do with freedom. Helm and Krebs, if you remember, had framed autonomy not just as an external normative criterion, but as constitutive for love. For both philosophers, (personal) autonomy means capacity of *self-determination*: the possibility to realize and the actual realization of what one decides to want to do and to be. On the one hand, friends and lovers are uniquely able to shape each other's thoughts, feelings, and lives; on the other, individuals' autonomous actions and evaluations are fundamental for enjoying joint autonomy. Lacking respect for autonomy, love relationships cannot be properly formed, or risk to flake apart. Since lovers and friends deeply care about their reciprocal well-being, they do not only respect the other's autonomy; they also encourage and foster it. Helpfully, Helm extends the meaning of "autonomy" to include collective exercises: we come to decide what we want to do and to be not only as individuals, and alone, but also as a couple, a family, a small collectivity of friends. In Beauvoir's picture, the idea of freedom (that does resemble Helm's and Kreb's autonomy, but it is not identical with it) is intimately connected with an idea of "reciprocal recognition." We are *in* love, and we are *making* love when we engage with each other through acts of a certain kind of recognition. What does it mean?

Beauvoir's notion of recognition is largely inspired by G. W. F. Hegel's philosophy. As Hegel and a group of his contemporary scholars have conceived it, recognition (in German, *Anerkennung*) consists in a particular act of affirmation or confirmation of and of attendance to another person or group of persons. Axel Honneth, the most influential contemporary theorist of recognition, distinguishes between three dimensions of interpersonal Anerkennung: love, respect, and esteem or solidarity.[12] In esteem, persons recognize others as having particular qualities and capacities and as able of achievements that have broad social and political ramifications. Recognition as respect takes persons as capable of rational self-determination (autonomy) and bearers of rights and duties that follow thereof. Love stands for the most corporal, material, and immediate mode of reciprocal recognition, which represents the first necessary condition for the formation of individual subjects and for a successful development of their selves. Following a psychoanalytical inspiration, Honneth's conception of love is modeled mostly on the parent-child relationship, but it can be generalized to include love between adults as well. Some of his passages are indeed particularly apt to understand Beauvoir's authentic love as a relation between free persons that are not ashamed of and do not fear their shared bodily, psychological, material vulnerability, but who are drawn toward each other and can thrive together exactly because of and through it.

According to Honneth, lovers "mutually confirm each other with regard to the concrete nature of their needs," thus recognizing each other as "needy creatures." As such, persons "know themselves to be united in their *neediness*, in their *dependence* on each other."[13] In love relationships, our constitutive exposure to and dependence on others is what immediately bonds us and drives us to reciprocal recognition. When becoming the object of recognition, we are treated and (should) feel as "infinitely unique."[14] While I do not love everyone and everything I recognize as a needy and vulnerable creature, when I love someone I am drawn precisely to the specific, unique characteristics that make *them* in need of the kind of recognition and care *I* (I think) can uniquely provide.

This idea is, to tell the truth, not a prerogative of the Hegelian tradition of social philosophy. A similar motive can be found, for example, already in the final episode of Plato's *Symposium*, when Alcibiades is abruptly entering the scene. This part tells about the particular kind of knowledge that corresponds to love's knowledge. When showing up wasted at the party, Socrates's younger lover joins the round of encomia that I have briefly recapitulated in the previous chapter. He does not try to expound upon the general essence of eros, as his friends did before him. Alcibiades decides, on the contrary, to recall his singular experience, his own passion for Socrates, a personal story of bewilderment and fascination that has had, he thinks, an educational impact on him. If we want to understand eros—this seems to be the sense of what Alcibiades is telling us—we cannot understand it in universal, necessary, essential terms. And yet Alcibiades *is* telling us a sort of general truth about love. He is showing, with his example, what love as a form of practical knowledge consists of—namely, as Martha Nussbaum puts it, in a "keen responsiveness of intellect, imagination, and feeling to the particulars of a situation: an ability to pick out its salient features, combined with a disposition to act appropriately as a result."[15] Through love, we learn how to grasp, understand, and relate to the unique singularity of an object—the singular, unique bodily, affective, emotional, psychological, intellectual determinations of another human being.

Aristotle, introducing a thought that will later be developed by Hegel and by the Hegelians, claims that, under particularly felicitous conditions, lovers find ways to reciprocate such loving recognition.[16] (Does Socrates reciprocate Alcibiades's love? Hardly.) Importantly, this is not first and foremost a moral or more generally normative imperative: we do not *ought to* deliver loving recognition—we are not morally obliged to reciprocate someone's love. Rather, mutuality of recognition is constitutive for a certain kind of love: in order to constitute ourselves fully as lovers, we cannot but recognize each other. To put it in other words: if the person who recognizes me in a loving way is not recognized by me in a loving way, their love and recognition for me cannot count much. And vice versa: if the one I recognize in a loving way does not recognize me in a similar way, my loving recognition will not be important and relevant for them either. For sure, I might be in love with someone who, sadly, does not love me back. Unrequited love is not excluded in this scenario. A recognition theory of love shows, however, that only *mutual* or *reciprocal* loving recognition can open up the experience of a fully constituted love *bond*.

Although contemporary theorists and critics of Hegelian *Anerkennung* (or other senses of recognition) are not primarily interested in crafting a philosophy of love on its basis, I believe that recognition theory offers precious tools for our inquiry. Let us further dive into this theory, although things will get a bit technical from now on. Recognition theory highlights, in particular, the following characteristics of love bonds: the interrelation between activity and passivity (i.e., between the experience of being an object and of being a subject of recognition); the (troublesome) interrelation between dependence and independence; the the bodily dimension of this interrelation; the mutuality of self-experience enabled by these bonds; and, finally, the transformative consequences of eros.

Activity and Passivity

First of all, note that, by being recognized—by becoming an object of recognition—I become an "attractor of recognition" myself.[17] As an object, a passive receiver of loving actions, gestures, and words, I am not only passive, because I have the (often unintentional) capacity to make the other into a giver of recognition. And vice versa: the person I lovingly recognize is actively contributing to make me a recognizer. There emerges a mutual dynamic in which loving attitudes and behaviors are enhanced and grow together—not just because lovers do something, but because, simultaneously, they are made into something and are the recipients of what others do to them. The recognizer does actively recognize, insofar as they are attracted or moved to give recognition; the recognizee is object of recognition, but they are at the same time able to attract others' recognition too.

The interrelation between being recognized and recognizing—the fact that being recognized lures recognition, and that the activity of recognizing implies being an object of recognition—defines relationships of *Anerkennung* in general, but is most strikingly visible in erotic dynamics. According to Hegel, the most primitive form of recognition is that of passivity, of being immediately recognized (*Anerkanntsein*), and is manifested clearly in phenomena of sexual (both human and animal) intercourse, as well as in other and more complex forms of love.[18] Consider how (some) nonhuman and human animals initiate sexual intercourse, aimed at sexual reproduction, by "naturally" (through, for instance, smells, sounds, chemical signals and enticements, gestures), and, without much deliberation, attracting the attention and arousing the appetite of another organism of the same genus or species and of opposite sex. From a Hegelian point of view, the most natural and immediate form of difference between lovers or sexual partners, and hence the first moment of their individuation, corresponds to sexual difference. But human beings' individuation, difference, hence capacity or power to attract, depend on other, equally important factors. The mutual dynamic of attracting recognition, then, should also be valid beyond the Hegelian limited heterosexual configuration, especially if sexual intercourse, as part of erotic love, is conceived as disentangled from the aims of sexual reproduction and caring for the offspring.[19] This emphasis on the passive side of recognition allows to stress the nondeliberative, nonintentional, spontaneous features of love interactions: being attracted to someone—being drawn by their recognition and moved to recognize them—happens to a great degree (not completely though) inadvertently, according to dynamics that bypass reasons and deliberation, that cannot be controlled or steered. This can be problematic if we want to realize our freedom in love. Yet, maybe counterintuitively at first, it might also contribute to the unfolding of the (troublesome) process of freedom—as I will try to explain in chapter 4.

Interrelation Between Dependence and Independence

Taken more generally, Hegel's passages explicitly dedicated to the topic of adult love (*Liebe*) exhibit some continuity with the union or fusion model of love, but develop it further in some important respects. Hegel depicts love as the sensuous and emotional process of overcoming lovers' independent selves, thus constituting a unity, a *we*, that absorbs all differences and particularities, including material ones, and the things that lovers own and with which they identify. This process, however, is never accomplished. Singularity is never annihilated: by letting themselves be absorbed, lovers do realize themselves as true human beings, as what/who they really are. Moreover, as mentioned in the passage on sexual and loving attraction, one needs to be an individuated, separated entity in order to have the power to attract and give recognition. In the *Philosophy of Right*, Hegel speaks of *Liebe* in these terms:

> Love means in general terms the consciousness of my unity with another, so that I am not in isolation by myself but win my self-consciousness only through the renunciation of my independence (*Fürsichsein*) and through knowing myself as the unity of myself with another and of the other with me. The first moment in love is that I do not wish to be a self-subsistent and independent person and that, if I were, then I would feel defective and incomplete. The second moment is that *I find myself in another person*, that I count for something in the other, while the other in turn comes to count for something in me.[20]

In *The Spirit of Christianity and Its Fate*, Hegel writes, similarly: "In love man has found himself again in another."[21] This experience of being-with-oneself-in-an-other (*Bei sich selbst sein in einem Anderen*) can be rendered also as a *being-at-home-in-an-other*. This translation is justified by the facts that *bei*, in German, commonly means "at the home of." Hegel himself sometimes speaks explicitly of being "at home" (*zu Hause*) in the other.[22]

Hegel suggests something more, something potentially troubling: in order to find *myself*, really, in concrete terms, thanks to and in the bond with my loved ones, a bond that we can call "home," I have to leave who I am now. I have to lose myself first, who and what I think I am or I have been—or maybe just realize that, until now, I have just been a shadow of what I can really be—in order to be able to embrace transformation and reach a higher, more fulfilling substantiality. In order to find the "truth" of one's personality, says Hegel, we have to give up its "particularity," or, more precisely, we have to give up an "abstract" (generic, elusive, nonconscious) particularity in order to "win back" a "concrete" (solid, rich, conscious) one. This succeeds, both in romantic love *and in friendship*, if we dare to "immerse" ourselves "in the other."[23]

The process can be painful. In his early writings, Hegel says that love "recoils if it senses an [exclusive] individuality in the other."[24] Independent individuals are portrayed as unhappy, restless, anxious, incapable of "integration [or completion]."[25] Later on, in the *Philosophy of Right*, the tension between individual independence and merging with the other is called a "tremendous contradiction:" the lovers do desire to go beyond their limited selves and embrace otherness in the blissful erotic union—yet this is ultimately impossible.[26] But should we necessarily embrace the gloomy, desperate view according to which differentiation, opposition, and the impossibility of symbiosis are to be thought of and experienced as a failure of eros? Shouldn't we, rather, regard lovers' relative independence and ultimate "unavailability" as a resource for flourishing and empowering intimate bonds?

Love troubles may be desirable.[27] We form ourselves concretely precisely as result of actions and passions of recognition.[28] The recognition-based framework, I believe, allows us to overcome the worries generated by the fusion or union theory of love. Hegel's contradiction does not have to be "tremendous": it can be reinterpreted, more softly, as a "precarious balance between independence and attachment."[29] The intertwinement between dependence and independence, heteronomy and autonomy, separation and merging, is certainly precarious: love relationships, even happy ones, entail risks, maybe constitutive ones. Misunderstandings, disillusions, certain forms of distance, and even aggressiveness are factors in the unfolding of relationships of recognition and, hence, of love. The desire to be close in some sort of union, connected to the feelings of dependence on the other, is continuously, inevitably, and painfully broken by the affirmation of individuals' independence. Separation and self-affirmation are needed in order to establish a real intersubjective connection—namely, a relation between different, singular agents who are able to continually reestablish their boundaries and thereby acknowledge and take care of each other's particular needs and wishes.

Needy Bodies

A recognition theory of love emphasizes the bodily dimensions of our love encounters more decisively than the models analyzed in chapter 1. Freedom itself is (also) a sensuous experience. As Honneth puts it, love relationships set free "our inner nature" through mutual confirmation: "Each person is a condition for the freedom of the other by becoming a source of *physical self-experience* for the other." In intimate bonds, we recover our "natural neediness," "without fear of being humiliated or hurt."[30] "Natural neediness" refers to those needs profoundly felt as newborns and through further phases of growth that are recollected in erotic encounters between adults—of being firmly but tenderly held, sensibly and knowingly touched, truly heard and seen, adequately (not suffocatingly) protected. Such needs are scary: other persons are not necessarily always there to hold, caress, care for us; they might not know what to do, or bring themselves to do it. We cannot ever force others, the persons we love and who love us, to satisfy our needs, as the provision of this kind of physical care, which is at the same time affective and emotional, can only pour out as an act of freedom. We are at the mercy of others: in desirable forms of love, this does not feel like a huge problem. The passage resonates with Beauvoir's idea that free love means a partial, temporary overcoming of the fears aroused by the experience of excruciating human vulnerability. Better said, intimate relationships disclose human beings'

vulnerability, implied in and revealed by our physical, affective, material dependence on others, while at the same time encouraging us to cope with its risks and dangers. The courage and force to deal with vulnerability and the risks of interdependence is provided by the effective, ongoing care, attention, and presence that lovers and friends are capable of giving.

The Mutuality of Self-Experience

Mutual satisfaction of sensuous needs and wishes, for which we deeply depend on others, is one face of love. The other face is the fact that such caring interdependence enables, or might enable, independence. On the recognitive model, in good, successful love relationships we develop and reinforce self-confidence and self-reliance: we become able to figure out, build up, and realize our desires, purposes, and projects. By being dependent on others, we make self-experiences that allow us to affirm ourselves as autonomous. Here, as well, there is a double directionality. In adult love, each lover's positive relationship to oneself ("self-experience") *is conditioned by the other's self-experience.* Pursuing the others' self-experience also has positive effects on one's self-experience. In other words: with my lovers and friends I feel free to disclose my weaknesses, failures, fears, worries, aspirations, and desires. I sense that these persons, contrary to superficial friends, colleagues, strangers, and the like, will try their best to deeply understand them in their specificity, without consciously and instrumentally using them to control or hurt me. Thanks to such recognition, I am put in the condition to experience myself—to see myself anew—from novel standpoints, with heightened (self)consciousness. But this succeeds only if I am at least partially able to do the same for my friends and lovers.

Transformative Effects

We do see but also touch and smell each other as vulnerable creatures. The gestures of loving recognition try to disclose and sometimes succeed in disclosing the most secret weaknesses and unspeakable desires of our loved ones. Confronted with, moved, and aroused by my beloved's vulnerability, I feel awe, admiration, sometimes bewilderment; this special person is in the position to attract my recognition. If I can attract their recognition too, we might form a bond of love based on mutual recognition. But this bond is not stable, static; rather, it solicits deeds and passions that shake and make our individual selves unfold as well as the bond itself. Recognition, that is, entails a solicitation to go beyond the given situation. In recognizing my lovers and friends, I do not simply establish a bodily relation with them, acknowledge and confirm the qualities and talents that make them who they are (now). In loving them, I am also able to perceive (mostly confusingly, vaguely) how they would be able to develop and actualize some of their traits beyond the present situation and identity, in ways that might, arguably, make them flourish (further), make them (more) free. This is not something that lovers and friends do on purpose; they do not pursue the intention to change the other. Transformations, however, are very often the result of recognitive dynamics.[31]

One of the most brilliant, detailed and complex illustration of the process of recognition in love bonds is provided, I think, by Elena Ferrante's much celebrated series of novels, the so-called Neapolitan novels.[32] Lila and Lenù, the two protagonists, are best friends. Ever since their childhood, Lila has been, for Lenù, the person whose recognition of her matters the most. Lila acknowledges Lenú's "brilliance," her intellectual and literary talents, and pushes her to bring them to fruition. Without her friend, and without a lifelong, intensely close confrontation with her, Lenù would have probably not found the strength to go to middle and high school, attend a prestigious university, publish novels, and become a public intellectual. Lila's capacity to understand her best friend does certainly depend on their shared vulnerability, rooted in sexist social norms that prevent women from studying while forcing them to emphasize their bodily attractiveness instead, to their economic disadvantage, in many forms of symbolic and physical violence. The two women come from the same socioeconomic background, in a poor, working-class suburban neighborhood in southern Italy, controlled by dangerous Mafiosi hitmen. More specifically, it is Lila's love that brings her to deeply understand Lenù's internal and external blockages and to elaborate an efficacious response to them. It is their love bond that allows the former to grasp, not always consciously, the particular suffering of the latter and to figure out the tactics she and only she can enact to become the person that her social context would not allow her to become.

The fact that the love bond does not suppress, but, on the contrary, does emphasize, bring to the fore, even create individuals' unique characteristics is well conveyed by Ferrante. Over the four volumes, she tirelessly shows all the commonalities between Lina and Lenù: they live in very similar homes; they are both prodigiously gifted in school; they play with the same doll; they both despise and love the same people; they even share the love for one man, Nino; and, toward the end of the series, they become pregnant at the same time. They are, simultaneously, very different: Lenù copes with the suffering and the violence by being tolerant and accommodating, Lila by aggressively challenging her enemies and securing tactical alliances. Lenù continues with her studies, while Lila stops after elementary school and becomes an entrepreneur; Lenù leaves the neighborhood and then eventually Napoli, while Lila stays. In a Hegelian fashion, their relationship unfolds following a double movement: they are drawn impressively close to one another and then drift apart, they become one, separate, one and then the other, again and again. Lila's capacity to help Lenù, to foster her academic and literary career, is based in their shared lives as well as in their mutual differentiation. Their bond has spectacularly transformative consequences—at least for Lenù, who manages to liberate herself from the class and gender constraints that have shaped her identity, choices, and feelings.

The Neapolitan novels constitute a helpful example for us, among other things, because they clarify the meaning of reciprocity in recognition theory: Lila's recognition of Lenù's brilliance is so valuable, for Lenù, because Lila represents the most valuable recognizer in Lenù's eyes.[33] If, at the end of the first volume, Lila explicitly calls Lenù her "brilliant friend," the whole narration in the four novels is moved by Lenù's ongoing attempt to describe, make sense of, keep up with her friend's extraordinary intellect and artistic gifts. Who is the truly brilliant friend among the two? Clearly both. Had Lenù failed to see, inspire, and solicit Lila's genius, Lila's recognition of Lenù's potential would have not brought about the same transformative effects. Such fundamental reciprocity, however, does not necessarily correspond to an ongoing reciprocation of recognitive acts. For example, Lila often does not show interest in her friend's important life events. More importantly, and troublingly, reciprocity does not necessarily amount to equality: Lila's brilliance can be testified to only thanks to Lenù's literary and essayistic works, as only she, as a professional writer, is in the position to make her own voice heard. This is maybe what most clearly proves Lenù's more "successful" transformation. Lila's life has been harder and darker; she has enjoyed less social recognition, and her many projects have systematically failed (yet the undecided finale might be read as suggesting otherwise).[34] Such discrepancies open up an agonist field between the lovers.

PLAYING WITH POWER

The process of recognition in love is not peaceful and harmonious, but troublesome. The interrelation between independence and autonomy on the one hand and dependence and vulnerability on the other gives rise to power dynamics. Lovers exercise power over their partners, empower them, and are at the same time subjected to their powers. A recognition theory of love must then include a theory of power.

Exercises of power can be of different sorts.[35] Power, to begin with, is *power to*—to do certain things, to be, but also to feel in a certain way. In this sense, power is an ensemble of capacities and resources that individuals can rely upon for differentiating themselves from others, affirming themselves as independent, autonomous agents and being recognized as such. Lovers are powerful when able to independently and autonomously figure out and affirm their needs, desires, goals, and projects. *Power to* is both passive and active. It is both a "kind of *doing*," but also "a kind of *becoming* and *being*"; it is both "the power of initiating, producing a change, and the power of undergoing a change."[36] It is not solely an individualistic exercise: capacities and resources are embedded in and cultivated through the interaction with others and their positive (recognizing, caring, affirming) responses, and they can be shared.

Dependence on others (in this context, on their loving recognition) opens up the possibility of exercising power in a genuinely intersubjective and social sense: we are powerful not only insofar as we can do something or be and feel in certain ways, but also if we do something *to* our fellow human beings, if our ways of being and feeling move, influence others, signify something for them. We exercise *power over* others.

Power to and *power over* are interconnected. My *power to* happens to depend on, among other things, the power my loved ones have over me. *Power over* can be defined as the power to affect the partners' self-experience, self-realization, thus their *power to*. One's self-experience may be affected insofar as it is simply acknowledged, or positively approved and confirmed. Crucially, it can be also motivated and shaped as a result of exercises of *power over*. A plausible way to think of *power over* is as *seduction*. It is not only and not primarily the seduction that brings a person close(r) to another person and that convinces the potential lover or friend to initiate a love bond with the seducer. It is, furthermore, the seduction in which one manages to shake, inspire, shape different aspects of their lovers' and friends' lives. Power hence provides the material, so to say, for self-experience. Exercises of seductive *power over* bring lovers to better understand, formulate, and realize needs, desires, and projects. The relation between *power to* and *power over* might result in forms of individual and, as we will later discuss, collective empowerment.

For example, let's go back to Simone de Beauvoir—more precisely, to a phase in her biography.[37] Consider how, after World War II, Sartre tried to persuade her to participate in the many political activities in which he himself was involved. In the very beginning, Beauvoir was reluctant and skeptical, as her main desires and projects were to be found in the literary and philosophical fields, and she did not see how she could ever find satisfaction and self-fulfillment in politics. Nevertheless, she did follow her companion's suggestion and eventually find her own way, different from Sartre's, to act politically: she became involved in feminist struggles. We may say that Sartre's power over Beauvoir, that moved her to engage in activities alien to her original idea of self-realization, was a factor (one among many others) in bringing her to find a new powerful and autonomous way of self-expression and engagement. At the same time, Sartre's career, especially as a philosopher and as a writer, was largely possible because of Beauvoir's shaping, inspiring, and sustaining power over him.

There is an important condition for *power over* to be really empowering: it cannot suppress or block the others' *power to*. One lover's shaping and constituting *power over* the other is empowering as it does not prevent, or even as it allows, the possibility for the partner to *resist* such power. The seduction, in other words, must always leave open the possibility of failure, and of a counterseduction. If reciprocity works, each lover's exercise of *power over* the other empowers both the other (i.e., contributes to the other's *power to*) and the self at the same time. To reformulate in the terms of power a thought formulated in the previous section: me seducing my lovers and friends (to do, think, and feel certain things) is constitutive for their self-experience; vice versa, my lovers and friends seducing me are constitutive for my self-experience. Lovers' self-experiences depend on their exercises of power and counterpower.

The recognitive process in love bonds is crossed and animated by a power play that includes and implies a series of tensions, conflicts, struggles—especially when one feels the need to counteract the others' power, to resist seduction—but might also lead to a process of empowerment that is more or less reciprocal. Love exhibits a sort of agonist nature.

Recall our two friends from the Neapolitan novels. Both Lenù and Lila—especially the former—are deeply dependent on the other's recognition, which empowers them to further develop their talents and discover and pursue their goals. The seduction game between the two is subtle and multifaceted. Lenù becomes a writer as the result of Lila's influence: already as a child, Lila had discovered and shared with her friend Louisa May Alcott's *Little Women*, deciding that one day she would become rich by writing a similar novel. And this is precisely what she will make Lenù do in her place. Lenù, however, does not gladly and peacefully submit to Lila's power. In a desperate attempt to revendicate her own independence from her friend, for example, she decides in the end to tell the only story that her friend had forbidden her to write: Lila's own story. Paradoxically, Lenù affirms her own independence by entangling her life and work even more tightly with Lila's. In general, she succeeds in affirming her power over Lila, by becoming a powerful intellectual, while Lila remains an unknown commoner. Lila does not easily accept Lenù's growing power either, although this is the power she has herself contributed to bestowing upon her. As response to each of Lenù's educational or professional achievements (being accepted in middle school or university, a new publication), Lila flaunts a scornful distance from her friend's intellectual milieu and launches a new innovative business idea. And, every time, Lila's brilliance succeeds in overshadowing Lenù's (at least in Lenù's eyes).

Probably nobody better than Lila and Lenù could embody Nietzsche's idea of agonist love, according to which a best friend is actually a sort of *best enemy*. To love someone is to be close to them, while simultaneously opposing, contradicting, and resisting them. Both Lila and Lenù could easily cry out to each other the words uttered by Nietzsche's Zarathustra: "I love you thoroughly, I am and I was like you. And I am also your best enemy."[38] Similarly, Ralph W. Emerson has suggested to see and treat your best friend as "a sort of beautiful enemy," someone we cannot control (someone "untamable") but at the same time devoutly revere.[39] The "enemies" we love are those who challenge us to go beyond our limits, to become a version of ourselves that flourishes beyond given social expectations, roles, and pressures. As Emerson declares, "Better be a nettle in the side of your friend than his echo."[40] How can we prod and challenge our friends and lovers without overpowering them? To formulate the worry with Nietzsche: "Can you step up to your friend without stepping over to him?"[41] Is it possible to care and warmly welcome our loved ones' needs and wishes and simultaneously treat them as beautiful enemies? Positive and nonambivalent answers to these question cannot be given once and for all.

The power-based, agonist picture of loving recognition sketched in this section is aimed at illuminating the chiaroscuro of dependence and independence, the complex interplay of seduction, the whirlwind in which we lose ourselves and have at the same time to establish our own's individual boundaries. Relationships of recognition, and of love, do not solely consist of generous and benevolent cooperation. They are in themselves ambivalent processes that include the negative, antisocial, irrational, aggressive, egoistic aspects of human psychic and social realities.[42] The reconstruction of the agonist dynamic inherent in love bonds allows the disclosure of a whole range of difficulties and puzzles: the feeling that one is on the brink of a self-loss, for example, can be both a joyous, exhilarating feeling and a source of anxieties and fears; affirming one own's singularity and resisting the other's seduction can have both the effect of reinforcing the *we*—by, for example, (re)establishing equality between the partners—and of deeply challenging the value and sense of the whole relationship. Loosening or breaking (part of) the dependence knot might be both liberating and devastating. Lovers' individual *power to* can either jeopardize the collectivity or help to shake it in productive, creative ways, preventing the bond from becoming suffocating (or boring). Lovers' *power over* their partners can become excessive and disproportionate, generating, as we will see in chapter 3, forms of domination, oppression, exploitation, and even violence. Even the most desirable outcome of agonism, mutual empowerment, cannot be thought of as free from phases of misunderstandings, tensions, painful negotiations, concessions, and surrenders.

ME AND YOU, AND WE

Until now, I have depicted bonds of love as intersubjective relationships between individual persons. But the insights from the collectivist theories are not forgotten: some of the most meaningful dimensions of love arise when we stop to feel and act as separate persons and start to feel and act as part of a collectivity, *as a* collectivity ourselves. Now we should be able to reread these insights from within a recognition-based, agonist account of love. As a matter of fact, recognition theorists are well versed in discussions around collective action and social groups.[43] Some have argued, for instance, that paradigm cases of group agency or of acting (and feeling) together are among the paradigm cases of interpersonal recognition. Mutual recognition seems, moreover, to represent a pivotal condition for lovers to partially let go of their individuality and separateness and thus to become able to share emotions and activities without the fear of being obliterated and disappearing in the *we*. Although not every social group formation presupposes genuine mutual recognition, it is hard to see how lovers' collectivities would not.

We can illustrate the link between recognitive attitudes and the functioning of (small) social groups by starting with a rather minimalistic example brought up by Margaret Gilbert. The scene is this: the author is reading in a library in Oxford, when she notices someone who comes to her table and sits in front of her. She looks up and gazes at him until he too looks up. The two look at each other. She nods toward him and briefly smiles, and he returns the grinning gesture. Gilbert describes this interaction—which does unmistakably resemble the opening of a flirting scene—not simply as one of mutual, very basic intersubjective recognition. The reciprocal gazing and smiling at each other amount to a "joint commitment"—namely, to the recognition that "as a body" "he and I were co-present."[44] The remarkable point here is that these two persons' recognition of themselves as "co-present" corresponds to the emulation of a single, embodied individual that recognizes itself in a certain moment in time and space. In their "public actions with respect to one another" (actions of mutual recognition) both she and the stranger "must act as if they are literally 'of one mind' with respect to the recognition that p."[45] There is then, between Gilbert and this man, an entre nous, a scene of togetherness that cannot be broken down to their individual points of view. Their encounter in that space and time is not about either of them taken singularly; it is about the two taken together. What they are and have together do not entirely correspond to (the sum of) their individual perspectives and acts of recognition yet are, of course, constituted by them in their particular relationship. It should not be difficult to translate this minimalist model to bonds between two (or more) lovers, although these are much more intense, complex, extended, and conflictual than just looking and smiling at each other. As Sophie Lucido Johnson puts it: "Relationships are collaborative chemistry; they're always at odds with the sum of their parts."[46]

In one letter to her North American lover Nelson Algren, Beauvoir offers a very insightful picture of a loving *we*, where the individual selves are both strongly united and yet separate, able to see and recognize each other in their differences. In the letter, Beauvoir recalls her ten-days' visit to Nelson's apartment in Chicago, at the beginning of their romantic affair. On the one hand, she writes: "*You* saw *me* loving you, and I, *you* loving *me*, so anyway we were both present to both of us—and it was *our* love." The bond has an intense collective dimension ("*our* love"), and yet the you is not the me, or I, and vice versa. In fact, writes Beauvoir, there is a "difference" between them. The difference consists in the fact that, on this occasion, she has entered his "home," "town," "life," which for her is a "faraway place, a wonderful, strange foreign place," "as remote and stupendous as fairy land and yet as true and sure" as her love for him. As such, Nelson's home cannot be as precious to him as it is for her. They share, they both are in, the same happiness, yet they are happy in their own "peculiar way."[47]

As we have already seen, a collective of love is not only made up by what its members do, but also by what they feel. As pointed out by Ronald de Sousa, individual emotions are constituents of a collective emotion while at the same time are constituted precisely by the fact that each individual is a member of that particular group to which the collective emotion is attributed. Collective emotions can thus acquire a sort of life of their own. Shared or collective emotions may emerge in various ways out of multiple individual states. In the case of a sexual bond, "each lover's desire is enhanced by perceiving the other's desire, which is simultaneously enhanced by perception of his own."[48] It follows that not only individual lovers have or can exercise power over their partners; *the we itself exercises a certain power over its participants too.* My self-experiences, and the range of emotions they elicit (e.g., the joy and fear aroused, often at the same time, by the possibility of self-loss) are shaped and influenced not only by my partners' self-experiences and emotions, but also by the fact of finding themselves together in love, acknowledging and recognizing the fact of being there.

Not only individual power over others, but also the power that the love bond exercises over the individual lovers, can amount to a form of empowerment—collective empowerment. In the literature on power theories, collective empowerment may be referred to as "power with," as "the ability of a collectivity to act together for the attainment of an agreed-upon end or series of ends."[49] Together, and only together, lovers and friends are able to initiate projects, to pursue shared goals. Importantly, though, *power with* has also an affective and emotional dimension, and acting *and feeling* together can be, and is in fact often, pursued without any further end. A sense and taste of playfulness, that is, does inherently belong to such bonds. Even if an end is indeed in view, a precious value of the experience of sharing lies in the unforeseeable consequences that exceed the end.

It is significant, in this respect, that Gilbert stresses the genuinely public character of recognitive relationships that build up a collective entity: when there is mutual recognition, the acting together cannot but be public, cannot consist only of private thoughts, actions, and feelings.[50] Hence, love relationships have always, in a certain respect, a public dimension: they are integral part of broader social, cultural, political contexts, and they cannot be insulated from them. The *power with* of love, then, signifies something also with regard to and in relation to such larger contexts, as we will explore in the last chapter.

Alas, the collective dimension may also block individuals' self-experiences, molding and steering their actions and emotions in ways that suppress their *power to* and have harmful consequences. This is why *power to*, as power to resist, can (and sometimes should) be exercised not only in response to other lovers' exercises of power, but also with regard to the collectivity. Agonism, that is, operates horizontally as well as vertically. *Power to* includes all the operations individuals can perform in order to reconsider, renegotiate, challenge, even (temporarily) break their *we*: for instance, reflecting upon the ways in which their emotions have been intensified, amplified, or even maybe distorted by collective emotions, concentrating on and trying to reconnect with their own individual emotions, leaving the partners "alone" and (re)gaining a distance from them, reconsidering how they want their *we* to go on, and to be publicly recognized.

The agonist interpersonal dynamic—how lovers exercise power over each other—reverberates in the *we* as well. As long as the bond exists, the results of renegotiations and challenges contribute to undo and recreate an ensemble and its *power with*. Amélie Rorty speaks, poignantly, of a "dynamically permeable" love.[51] Individual lovers are changed as result of the interaction with their partners, and these changes generate further changes that interest the details, the form, the habits and routines, the scopes, the values, the identity of the *we*. The intensity and frequencies of these changes vary from lover to lover, from relationship to relationship, and from phase to phase in the same relationship.

In part 5 of *Many Love*, an essay and memoir on polyamory, or polye-ros, we find a textbook example of collective activity and emotionality. The author, Sophie Lucido Johnson, tells about her relocation from New Orleans to Chicago with her partner, Luke. While carefully describing their distinctive individual contributions to the action (she organizes the route, he drives, she rents the truck, he remembers to pack the mattress and the wineglasses last), she stresses at the same time the collective nature of the undertaking: neither of them could have succeeded alone, physically, logistically, or emotionally. As we learn afterward, the shared project of moving will have empowering consequences for both of them, and especially for her. In Chicago, Sophie starts a master's degree in creative writing that leads her to write and publish her first book. This collective series of actions (packing, lifting furniture and boxes, cleaning, driving) is sustained by and elicits an emotional dimension that both lovers experience as new and unprecedented. The writer conveys the novelty and special intensity of the experience by observing how such a project required "a lot—a lot of . . . emotional energy, a lot of emotional time," whereby emotional time designates the time that "expands inside the space of real work."[52] The day of the moving becomes the longest one of her life. Such emotional expansion is not simply functional to the accomplishment of the project, but it brings about a series of unexpected side effects that have heavy implications both for the lovers and for their bond. First, it is the inextricable entanglement of both positive and negative emotions unleashed by the move that leads Sophie to fully realize the value of the particular friendships she is leaving behind, and of friendship more generally for her life. Second, the move puts Luke and Sophie in the physical and emotional condition to take a crucial decision with regard to the structure of their loving *we*. In the end, after a long conversation that unfolds during the trip, explicitly portrayed by Johnson as crossed by a subtle yet unequivocal power dynamic, they both decide to start a polyamorous project.

BECOMING WHO YOU ARE, BECOMING ANOTHER

One characteristic of love bonds has strongly emerged in the previous sections: transformation. Transformation of the individual selves in love, transformation of the relationship, and of the loving *we*. Engaged in agonist dynamics, lovers are pushed to interrogate themselves, gain a better grasp on whom they are, on their needs and desires, on who they desire to become, alone and together. This aspect emerges powerfully—and, hopefully, more clearly—if we read another author who might appear at odd with the philosophical context of our map: Stanley Cavell.

Cavell does not identify himself with the tradition of our Hegelian recognition theory, and he does not have a proper philosophy of love. In a book dedicated to a special genre of movies that he calls "comedies of remarriage," he does however develop an array of fundamental reflections on marriage, intended not as an institution but as a paradigmatic and exemplary community of love and friendship.[53] Comedies of remarriage are movies made by Hollywood filmmakers in the 1930s and 1940s. Cavell discusses the following seven comedies of remarriage: *The Lady Eve* (Preston Sturges, 1941); *It Happened One Night*, (Frank Capra, 1934); *Bringing Up Baby* (Howard Hawks, 1938); *The Philadelphia Story* (George Cukor, 1940); *His Girl Friday* (Howard Hawks, 1940); *Adam's Rib* (George Cukor, 1949); and *The Awful Truth* (Leo McCarey, 1937). These films belong to a historical phase in which, according to Cavell's peculiar and original reconstruction, the United States had the opportunity to (re)define their own cultural and political identity, while struggling to emerge from a devastating capitalist crisis and confronting themselves with the European continent lacerated by World War II. The vicissitudes of the exemplary couples of these comedies, and especially of their female parties, would help to figure out the role, for such cultural and social redefinition, of ethical and political virtues, as well as of philosophical conversions taking place in everyday private and intimate contexts. But Cavell's analyses manage, I believe, to shed light on erotic dynamics that go well beyond this specific context and can be easily read from within the conceptual coordinates of recognition theory.

The main drive of the comedies' plots is to get the central pair back together: the leading lady and her male companion must deal with and overcome the concrete possibility of a separation, a divorce. These films are not interested in depicting the first phases of a love affair; they do not dwell on the emotions and dynamics marking the moment of falling in love. Mostly, the protagonists have known each other for a long time, and they are well aware of each other's vulnerabilities and powers, weaknesses and strengths, flaws and virtues. Even when they have recently met, a playful familiarity characterizes their exchanges from the outset. The comedies unfold by depicting the series of adventures—games, travels, gigs, parties, conversations, and disputes—in which the couples are engaged, trying to cope with the difficulties and frustrations of everyday life in common while inventing novel and unexpected ways to be together.

Two main philosophical questions, in Cavell's eyes, guide the characters' actions and words: What are the conditions of human happiness, of a form of life worth pursuing? And can intimate relationships based on sexual love and friendship form a social space in which such conditions can be actualized? "Marriage" is the name that Cavell gives to intimate relationships of the sort. In two cases—*It Happened One Night* and *Bringing Up Baby*—the two protagonists are, significantly, not actually married, although they act as if they were. This circumstance represents an opportunity, argues Cavell, to ask what indeed could count as and constitute a "real" marriage. The answer is: a community of love between persons who need and want an *education*: they need and want, that is, to find and create who they are and want to be, both as persons and as an erotic *we*.[54]

Cavell's movie stars are constantly, almost obsessively, involved in profound conversations aimed at establishing the conditions and the meanings of their being together, romantically and as friends. Confrontations and dialogues are the means to determine "whether we can live together, accept one another into the aspirations of our lives" and presuppose a conception of the self as "always becoming, as on a journey, always partially in a further state."[55] At first, it is the female protagonist who appears as more in need of and willing to pursue this journey, which is intended by Cavell as a learning process. In the sexist context of the 1930s and 1940s in the United States, women craved that education that would allow them to finally fully become human beings, leaving behind or escaping the social roles of "just" wife and mother. The leading ladies of Cavell's comedies come to realize that their husbands and former husbands (or husband-like companions) are indeed apt to take up the role of educator.[56]

This interpretation, although perhaps accurate with regard to the movies, can certainly raise the suspicion that it reproduces and reinforces the sexist framework it intends to question. Yet note that the process of education for some of these women includes the selection of the right man for the job. In *The Philadelphia Story*, for example, Tracy (Katharine Hepburn) finds herself torn between three men: her former husband, C. K. Dexter (Cary Grant), wealthy yacht designer and heavy drinker; her fiancé, George (John Howard), self-made man and aspiring politician; and Mike (James Stewart), tough journalist by day and romantic writer by night. In the end, she chooses to *remarry* Dexter. He is the only one, it appears, capable of helping her to disclose the real nature of her desires. He teaches her how to accept other human beings' weaknesses and flaws, leading her to embrace her own vulnerability, to step off her pedestal and turn from a cold, marmoreal goddess into what he calls a "first-class human being." The human being one has to become, according to Cavell, is not an alleged ideal, perfect, flawless figure, but a person made of flesh and blood, able to be affected and to suffer, to receive and hold others' emotions, a person who commits mistakes and learns from them, animated by the hunger to discover her own desires and how to realize them in concert with others. Interestingly, Cavell's ethical theory has been called "perfectionism," whereas the sense lent to this term does significantly diverge from our commonsensical meaning of perfectionism. We have not to become "perfect" according to some external, general, allegedly objective standards of perfection, neither according to too demanding self-ideals. On the country, we have to figure out what truly works for us and learn to accept our flaws and failures.

In *His Girl Friday*, Hildy (Rosalind Russell) has to similarly choose between her former husband, Walter (Cary Grant), a whirlwind of a journalist and her former boss, and her new fiancé, Bruce (Ralph Bellamy), an easy, relaxed, somehow naive bourgeois. In the end, she too chooses the man who pushes her to acknowledge her true desire to work as a reporter, who offers her a life of adventures in a harsh, morally ambiguous world, far from the dull comforts of domesticity (again, this is the character played by Cary Grant!). In order to gain access to experiences that teach the power to act on behalf of a world we can actually desire, contends Cavell, we must recognize ourselves as drawn beyond our present repertory of inclinations, toward an "unattained but attainable self."[57] Recognizing and giving in to our (erotic) attraction to other human beings and to the power they have over us—to seduce, to change us—is one central exemplification of Cavell's perfectionism. Irrationality, in this context, amounts to the failure to act on one's desire, or to act in the absence of sufficient desire, or to accept a confusion about desires without doing anything to clarify them.

Are women the only ones who need to learn about their true desires? No. This erotic education must be, according to Cavell, mutual. For sure, the woman's education, or the "creation of the new woman" (a woman who knows what she wants, who is autonomous and independent, who has a fulfilling life outside of the private sphere), constitutes the central drive of the plot. However, the leading man's task is not simply to prove he can take on the teacher's role; he must at the same time show his willingness *to be himself educated* by his female companion. In other words, the woman's education—or, in Honneth's terms, self-experience—*cannot work if it does not attract and bring about the man's education and self-experience as well*. The process of acquisition of self-knowledge, just as in recognition theory, must be reciprocal. In order for change to really happen, both men and women must be able to learn and undergo change. This is illustrated, for example, by the series of adventures and misadventures that Dr. Huxley (Cary Grant) goes through after he meets Susan Vance (Katharine Hepburn): in *Bringing Up Baby*, it is the male protagonist that has himself to be "brought up." He must learn not to take himself too seriously, to combine the pleasures of the intellect with the pleasures of the senses, to reconnect with the dimension of play and magic—in other words, to be a good partner. In *It Happened One Night*, Peter (Clark Gable) takes very seriously his task to lecture Ellie (Claudette Colbert) about a number of things, transforming her from a spoiled, ingenuous girl into an autonomous, independent woman able to take her fate in her own hands. However, in a crucial moment of the movie—in the proverbial hitchhiking scene—the roles of teacher and pupil are reversed. Cavell thinks that an essential feature of this genre, which he calls also "comedy of equality," is to leave ambiguously open the various questions concerning gender difference.[58] What constitutes female and male identities is precisely what is at stake in the process of creation both of the new woman and of the man who deserves to (re)marry her. One of the emancipatory qualities of these movies is given also by the openness and uncertainty characterizing the (re)elaboration and transformation of gender difference.

These stories are all adventurous ones, as exemplified by the fact that the central pair is often shown "on the road" (*It Happened One Night*, *Bringing Up Baby*, and, toward the end, in *The Awful Truth*), traveling together by boat (*The Lady Eve*), or engaged as a team in some worldly undertaking (*His Girl Friday*, *Adam's Rib*). And, as in any adventure, obstacles and difficulties arise and must be faced. In remarriage comedies, the main hurdle corresponds to and is symbolized by divorce, or by the threat thereof. "Marriage is always divorce," contends Cavell, "always entails rupture from something, and since divorce is never final, marriage is always a transgression. (Hence marriage is the central social image of human change.)"[59] In order to enjoy the good of a genuine, "authentic" marriage or love bond, falling in love and being together (caring, sharing, desiring) are not enough. Separation happens, and then the bond must be reconstituted and reaffirmed.

Divorce, to begin with, serves as reminder that the transformative process—"becoming the one you are, and as becoming one in marriage"—is a painful one.[60] Creating the conditions and opening a space for the discovery and realization of one's true desires require a modification of encrusted habits, and thus a sacrifice of some of the familiar modalities to relate with others and with oneself. The consequences of such process are difficult to foresee; benchmarks are in short supply. Separation is furthermore tightly linked to the power struggle that Cavell's characters find hard to avoid. If both man and woman aspire to being the partner's educator and recognize the importance of the education that the other can provide them, they must both be able to forgo, at least for a while, their autonomy. This cannot but create hostility, as exemplified by the heated yet witty disputes that all of these couple are staging. Commenting on *Adam's Rib*, Cavell does indeed speak of a "a struggle for recognition," in which both Amanda (Katharine Hepburn) and her husband, Adam (Spencer Tracy), enact a series of strategies with the aim of inducing their spouse to acknowledge the soundness of their position in the trial they are both working on.[61] By pushing Adam to see the reasons behind the decision to defend Doris Attinger, a woman accused of the attempted murder of her unfaithful husband, Amanda seeks to be recognized in her profession as well as in her public role as a defender of women rights. By insisting on prosecuting Doris, Adam seeks to be recognized as a man who has not given up his authority, but is nevertheless committed to gender equality, and to equality and reciprocity in his marriage. Cavell depicts the struggle also as a "dialectics of remarriage," which consists of an interrelation between mutual independence and intimate threats to independence, between the capacity to "notice one another" and to be strangers to one another.[62] But the movie is not only about *individual* recognition and its struggles: Amanda wants in fact *her own marriage*, based allegedly on equality and reciprocity, to be recognized as the kind of marriage that is worth pursuing. She wants her erotic collectivity to be recognized in its specificity and in its exemplarity, as a model that bears public, political relevance.

The genre of remarriage constitutes a striking example of the ambivalence of love that I have introduced with Beauvoir: Does Adam of *Adam's Rib* genuinely respect his wife? Is he genuinely committed to equality in marriage? Was his aggressiveness just a farce? Does Tracy choose Dexter, in *The Philadelphia Story*, because he is really able to disclose for her the true nature of her own desires, or does she fall into his arms again out of habit and class conformism? On a theoretical and on a practical level, these and similar questions cannot but remain undecided. Cavell's work is relevant for us since it casts the question of love not with the aim of defining an universal essence; rather, it helps to reveal potentials that might or might not come to fruition.

EROTIC FREEDOM: A FIRST SKETCH

In traveling again through our map, we have come to trace a new path that delineates love as a kind of education: a process in which we learn about ourselves, about others, and about love itself. We learn that our lovers' and friends' learning processes are the condition for ours, and vice versa. This education in and through love can be both an individual path we have to travel by ourselves with the help of our lovers and friends, and a collective undertaking, in which mental processes, actions and emotions are genuinely shared.[63] We learn by becoming one with our loved ones, and at the same time by separating ourselves from them. We learn by caring, by receiving care, and we learn to resist care when it is not empowering but suffocating.

In other words, this is a process through which we realize freedom. Various conceptions of freedom have emerged, implicitly, in the depiction of love bonds in this chapter. Individual freedom is meant, first, in the sense of self-determination or autonomy. It comes to the fore when lovers are and become able to figure out who they are and what they want, and try to realize it. In this, reasons and emotions are deeply amalgamed: to be autonomous means to have the capacity to give reasons explaining our own's preferences, decisions, and projects, to show, that is, that we have not been coerced and manipulated by external forces, and that we are able to practically follow such reasons. It also means that we have a fairly good grasp of the emotions that might have motivated, influenced, or shaped such reasons, and also that we are able to "own" them and "stand behind" them. When we, as adult human beings, enter love relationships, we are obviously already autonomous in some ways, and we desire those relationships that seem to enhance our autonomy, thus making us thrive. Individual realization of freedom can thus be accompanied by positive emotions, but it does not have to.

Individual freedom cannot be obtained independently, or, worse, at the expense of others. Relationships with others—in this case, with lovers and friends—are necessary for freedom. Two attitudes are particularly relevant here: first, taking into account, enjoying, admiring, engaging with, on various bodily, sensual, and cognitive levels, the particular being of our loved one *as they are*, and, second, soliciting it to go beyond their present situation and limitations. In free bonds, lovers make each other feel seen, touched, held, encouraged in their own irreplaceable particularity. The well-being and self-assurance produced by these acts create the conditions for further explorations and experimentations in view of new achievements and disclosure of new possibilities. Lovers do not simply assume to be valued for their current constitutive qualities and talents, but also for the inclinations and interests they "might develop at same point in the future."[64] Lovers do support each other's development, even when it takes unforeseen directions. As Emerson strikingly put it: "A friend is Janus-faced: he looks to the past and the future. He is the child of all my foreign hours, the prophet of those to come, and the harbinger of a greater friend."[65]

In the lines of Joni Mitchell's song "Cactus Tree," there is a man—a sailor, an explorer, a climber, a soldier, an adventurer: in Beauvoir's words, a man of "transcendence"—who "kisses" his woman with "his freedom." The sexual, intimate connection between these two makes freedom a *transmissible, shareable* condition and activity. Unlike Beauvoir's woman in love, who cultivates a mere illusion of freedom by participating in the alleged freedom of the man, Mitchell's woman learns what freedom is thank to this man, and she then goes out in the world by herself and learns to enact it on her own and in her own ways: she is "busy being free," it seems, far from and without him. She travels, makes him wait for a reply to his letter, and falls in love with other people. If she is like the leading ladies in Cavell's comedies of remarriage, she will kiss him with *her* freedom too, in return—and both their individual freedoms, and their freedom together, will be increased.

In order to be free, alone, and together with their partners, women like those in Cavell's, Mitchell's, and Ferrante's exemplary tales must learn how to exercise power. Power is pivotal in lovers' education into freedom—provided it does not degenerate, as we will see in chapter 3, into domination, mastery, exploitation. Seduction means shaping and influencing the partners' preferences, emotions, choices, convictions, beliefs. Resistance to seduction is part of the process. Revisions and transformations both of lovers' self-conceptions, identities, and emotions, and of their *we*-conceptions, *we*-identities, and *we*-emotions result from such mutual exercises of power.

If we take into consideration the agonist nature of eros, it becomes evident how lovers have to regularly put up with a series of imperfect, shameful, unvirtuous, or even morally questionable traits displayed by themselves and by their partners. In free bonds, it might happen that individuals' cultivation of their personality and character end up in a morally or ethically "higher" self. Following Cavell and his perfectionist ethical position, lovers become "better" when they gain a better grasp of their "true" desires and of their power(s) to realize them, and when such a self-knowledge and self-consciousness is authentically and deeply shared, conducive to the others' self-knowledge and self-consciousness. This is important for communities too, according to Cavell. To be sure, coming to know oneself, one own's emotional landscape, wishes, and desires, how (and if) to translate them into actions and projects that are worth pursuing, is an extremely challenging and demanding undertaking. It is not, however, an unattainable, merely regulative ideal. It is, rather, a *process* that develops through (self-)experiences and goes through various phases—also ambiguous phases, as we will see in chapter 4, of confusion, self-derailment, even of nonfreedom. The North American philosopher John Dewey captures this point exactly when he writes that freedom consists in "something which comes to be, in a certain kind of *growth*; in *consequences*, rather than in antecedents. We are free not because of what we statically are, but inasfar as we are *becoming different from what we have been*."[66]

Erotic freedom, then, is an individual learning process. But erotic freedom is also a collective, shared enterprise. In romantic love and friendship (like in more complex processes of political, democratic will-formation), argues Honneth, freedom must be understood also as a "common practice," which realizes something valued as a good by the participants in this practice.[67] The good has a collective character, because it can be realized only by the united efforts of all those participating in the group. This freedom is "not something an individual subject can perform on his own, but rather something he is only able to achieve in regulated collective action with others."[68] The collective realm of erotic freedom has also to be seen as an expression of *power with*. Lovers come to understand and realize what they are and desire to be and to do not only as individuals, but also as a *we*: as a couple, a triad, a network of friends/lovers, they figure out what their identities or characteristics as a collective are, what works best for them, what is for them worth pursuing and realizing, how they want to be seen and considered by others. The process is set in motion and sustained by capacities to appraise and become aware of the emotions collectively shared, the emotional burdens and difficulties they face as a group, what makes them, for instance, happy or sad, euphoric or calm, proud or joyful.[69]

The process of freedom is an ambiguous one, a chiaroscuro, and itself a process of change (and it could include changes for the worse.) The process, moreover, can always reach a dead end, or stop. Lovers can easily become blind in front of their blockages, fail to see the moments and phases of unfreedom or unilateral power. They can more or less consciously decide to avoid the possibility of a Cavellian divorce, of a break of the interdependence that would allow them to reconsider and reenact their true desires, as individuals and as collectives. In chapter 3, we will explore the dark regions of the present map, analyzing the ways in which love turns into a mechanism that impedes and blocks the realization of freedom. But, before turning to the dark sides of love, we need to specify, and justify, the *type of love* that specifically constitute the object of the present inquiry: erotic love.

EXCURSUS

Why Erotic Love?

Many readers might feel excluded from the picture that has been taking shape so far. The boundaries of our map have indeed been drawn by focusing on certain images and scenes of love at the detriment of others. A lot of space has been given to turbulent, inquisitive, and dramatic dynamics. What about the peaceful and stable bonds between persons who accompany each other with loving support on a daily basis, and who have been doing that for a big chunk of their lives? Eva Illouz, most notably, scorns the instability and fleetingness exhibited by the current model of romantic and sexual arrangements. Present-day love is indeed haunted by the specter of its ending: divorces, breakups, ongoing problematization have become quite widespread. This is the sign and the expression, in the eyes of the sociologist of love, of the pernicious triumph of the isolated, self-centered, and egoistic individual over communities of care. The value of heated sexual and romantic passions tends nowadays to trump other values and expectations promised by long-term companionship, like solidarity, mutual trust, commitment. The certainty that my partner is going to be there for me no matter what, the safety of knowing and feeling that personal identities and life projects are an integral part of a larger *we*, the comfort and pleasures of shared habits: in our accelerated, highly competitive, ultraindividualistic societies, these goods do not seem very appealing anymore.

It is now time to better specify the kind of love that is the object of this inquiry, and why it "has to" be this kind and not others. I suggest to refer to the figures and modalities of love that have been the protagonists of the last chapter neither as "romantic" nor "passionate," nor "sexual," but rather as *erotic*. I have nonchalantly used this adjective already, but it needs now to be pinned down and justified. It is true that the account of eros pursued in our map does consciously put a lot of emphasis on the freedom to break the bond: in Cavell's terms, on divorce. This freedom entails the crucial possibility to affirm individuals' autonomy, to resist the partners' power, as well as the power of the whole bond, to find out who one really is, to become someone else. The argument here, in disagreement with Illouz, is that free love is not based on a simple definition of individualistic, negative, hedonist freedom. Free love does amount to a complex process of realizing *freedom together*, a process that unfolds through various phases, including, as we will see, moments of liberation or emancipation from oppressive social conditions. Erotic relationships are not necessarily short term, superficial, and egocentric—quite the contrary, in fact, though they are indeed agitated rather than calm, open and shaky rather than stable and firm, "fallible" rather than quietly resting on solid certainties. These are ambiguous features, whose value rests in need of further elaboration. To be clear, the claim that has to be explained and justified is not that eros is more valuable than other forms of love, but that it has its own peculiar import, not only from the perspective of the individual but also from social and political standpoints.

The particular value of eros, I argue, lies in its capacity to bring to the fore the bright and the dark sides of human freedom. The boundaries of our map have been traced—we might now come to realize—not with the final aim to understand *only* what love is, and the conditions under which we might consider love desirable. Through a discussion of free and unfree erotic bonds, this is the dare of the book: we should instead come to grasp human freedom (and unfreedom) more generally, which, in turn, should allow us to come to a better grasp of our form of life. In particular, it is the *transformative* dynamics of our individual and collective practices that a theorization of erotic love and of erotic freedom helps to illuminate. Eros is taken here as a sort of magnifying glass to better discern and conceptualize how broader processes of education and change, not only on personal but also on social and political levels, come to the fore and unravel.

Obviously, eros is not the only transformative factor in our society, nor the most important one. The broader social and political impact of erotic love is certainly limited, but in its limitedness it is precious: it shows how private and intimate affairs, while remaining private and intimate, can stretch beyond these limits. I do not deny that other forms of love—for example, stable companionship, bonds of solidarity and care between people who we do not know themselves intimately, love for one's own people or community—can harbor critical and transformative force too. On the political reverberations of these other, less intimate, less intensively emotional and sensuous forms of love, much has been written already, in the wake of diverse theoretical and political orientations, from liberal[1] to post-Marxist[2] to spiritual ones, most notably those inscribed in the tradition of African American civil rights movements.[3] The intent of this work is to concentrate, rather, on something different: on a form of love whose social and political impact has been largely overlooked, or even openly questioned, mostly by feminist critics.

One of the objectives of this work is to explore if, how, and to which extent the entanglement of eros with problematic habits, norms, and structures—for example, with sexist or racist ones—can actually make eros into a good resource for critically detecting and calling into question precisely (some of) these problems. Our learning about love would correspond to learning about social troubles, and what we can do to face them. The complex process of freedom, as I have begun to say in chapter 2, seems to have intimately to do with the troubledness of love, and of our societies more generally, as well as with its potential to fruitfully, although partially, deal with them.

Not only lovers in long-term, stable bonds might feel excluded from the present account, but also people who truly and deeply love their parents, grandparents, children, siblings, and other family members. The freedom to leave, interrupt, or end the bond is out of place in parental and family love. Surely we can in principle decide to break any contact with parents or family members, even to abandon our children, but this prospect does (and should) arise less frequently, and it requires a great deal of justification. Breaks have to be prevented for moral reasons or reasons of duty, when the bond includes one or more persons in strong need of care, and where the relationship of care is asymmetrical (paradigmatically, care for young children and for the elderly). The freedom to leave, however, is only one component of erotic freedom. Consider, moreover, how in our contemporary (liberal, democratic) societies we do not "choose" our parents, children, and siblings, but we do in some way "choose" romantic or sexual lovers and friends. According to the legal and cultural rules and habits of our form of life, we tend to choose the latter predominantly on the basis of intense individual affective experiences. The emotions we feel toward certain people, that is, can be accepted, assumed, or rejected in order to form, reform, avoid, or end romantic relationships or friendships with them. It is different with family members: I have a bond with my siblings or with my parents not in virtue of what I feel for them, or not only.[4] Strong feelings are also not taken as a determining factor in the more diluted forms of love bonds we might feel toward the members of the larger collectivities to which we belong (extended families; political, religious, or artistic groups; social classes; urban, regional, national, transnational communities; even humanity in general).

In our social contexts, we do recognize the power and even the right of such an intense, overwhelming affectivity even on institutional levels: nobody can force anybody else, at least *in principle*, into an erotic relationship. It is regarded as a modern achievement in Western societies that marriages or marriage-like relationships cannot be imposed (anymore) by family, social or religious groups, or politics. This might remain a mere ideal, but as an ideal it is indeed acknowledged and cherished. It counts as a matter of fact as the principle that leads social struggles for cultural and legal recognition of homosexual and queer couples, tribes, and families. Similarly, there are no moral, legal, or political rules dictating our friendship bonds. Only individuals' *emotions* and affects—not costumes, economic imperatives, political motives, traditions—must count, at least in principle, *as reasons* to form and maintain this kind of relationships.

The fact that individual emotions have or should have this social weight goes hand in hand with another assumption: lovers and friends do exercise power over each other. They try to seduce one another, in both sexual and nonsexual ways, and nevertheless they cannot force or manipulate someone to fall in love or to continue loving them, or to bring them to become a true friend. If we have the suspicion that our loved ones are in a relationship with us without having given their free consent or without wanting it truly and full-heartedly, the relationship loses its allure. We cannot force ourselves either to develop feelings or desire for someone.

Love is free also in the sense that it is something that happens, freely, spontaneously. We cannot take the decision to fall in love or to develop and maintain this sort of relationships on the basis of reasons that are not "reasons of love," as Harry Frankfurt famously call them.[5] Imagine that I start to suspect that the person I love is with me out of a sense of duty, or because I can provide them a serious of goods (money, safety, various forms of help), or just because I am good looking and sexually attractive, or only because I remind them of their mother or father: in all these cases, the value of the relationship with this person would get inevitably spoiled. I would suffer, probably recoil. If I love this person, I desire a bond with them on the basis of love itself, and for no other reason. But, as a *result* of love, says Frankfurt, I would then acquire reasons to act and feel in certain ways: it is the love for this person that gives me reasons to, hence motivates me to, spend more and more time with them, become interested in what they are interested in, get to know their loved ones, etcetera.

If it cannot be explained on the basis of "exterior" reasons, reasons alien to the "essence" of love, is love irrational, hence inexplicable? Not necessarily. In his beautiful *Love: A New Understanding*, Simon May has made an impressive effort to delineate the overarching reason that lead people to seek love in its many expressions: romantic love, love for children, for God, for one own's country, for art, and so on. May submits that love corresponds to a promise of rootedness in a world that we supremely value, the promise to find and build up an ethical home in it. This is not a predetermined home, in an already given world, but either a completely novel home that we still have to find, and that we can reach only by leaving behind the known one, or a home that we have to retrieve from an individual or collective past and reshape. In both versions, the home or habitat opened up by love is not a final and perfect one, not a consoling shelter, and is at the same time uncannily familiar and excitingly unfamiliar. It has the effect to deepen our sense of existence, to intensify our reality and vitality, to give us resources for becoming who we truly are. May harshly criticizes Frankfurt for its obscurity when it comes to explain exactly what grounds love.[6] When I fall in love with someone, suggests May, it happens not mysteriously, in ways "impossible to define," but for a specific reason—namely, the fact that I perceive that this person is promising me a home in the world.[7] Also on May's account, however, this reason of love is not explainable on the basis of exterior reasons. May does not really put in question the most interesting point made by Frankfurt in his work, concerning the autonomy of love, even though his explanation of love's nature sounds more compelling than Frankfurt's model of love as care, sketched in chapter 1.

Let's now linger on one peculiar and rather upsetting implication of the idea of the autonomy of love. If our motives of love are independent from exterior reasons—for example, moral ones—these might become uncontrollable, wild, in problematic ways. My conviction that my love will give me a home in the world might very well be accompanied and sustained by affective forces that carry me away and overwhelm me. And these forces might become dramatic or dangerous, especially if the promise of rootedness is not kept, or it is, but at great costs, or if I am deluded about it. Reasons of love can overpower other orders of reasons; paradoxically, they might bring us to irrational, and thus *unfree*, behaviors. This seems a fairly common experience when it comes to love, especially sexual love. As Ann Carson puts it, "Love is something that assaults or invades the body of the lover to wrest control of it from him," in the vocabulary of ancient religious experiences: a "struggle of will and physique between the god and its victim" occurs.[8]

In order to prevent such paradoxical, even dialectical, turns of reason into unreason, it might be argued that love cannot have to do with such irregulated passions, and that it should be indeed conceptualized as responsive to moral or normative reasons. The autonomy of love, it might be argued, needs to be curbed. In chapter 3, we will as a matter of fact address some limitations exhibited by the idea of love's autonomy on the wake of sociological and social-theoretical reflections. However, my argument is not that disruptive, seemingly irrational moments do not belong to the erotic experience. Chapter 4 will try to show that the experience of being overwhelmed by affective powers that seem, at least for a phase, uncontrollable and not submitted to reason, the experience of a "crazy reason" of love, is valuable precisely in view of the process of liberation and of freedom (hence of reason!). Affective self-control and cultivation of our emotions are surely part of an *education to love,* but the education that love consists in is not reduced to rational, disciplinary moments. Going through affective experiences in which we feel that *something, in some moments, at least,* has power over us, in which we lose control and lose ourselves, being carried beside and beyond our usual identities, patterns, habits, and that can have a crucial learning effect. In the words of Carson: "A mood of knowledge floats out over your life. You seem to know what is real and what is not. Something is lifting you towards an understanding so complete and clear it makes you jubilant. . . . To address yourself to the moment when Eros glances into your life and to grasp what is happening in your soul at the moment is to begin to understand how to live. Eros' mode of takeover is an *education*: It can teach you *the real nature of what is inside you*."[9]

It is not that we can be free, in love, *despite* this element of unfreedom (confusion, passivity), but (also) thanks to it. The educational part of the process of love would not happen if we were unable to relinquish (a bit of) control, to accept that there are aspects in ourselves and in our lives that are unknown to us, and that as such provoke uncanny and unsettling affects, not entirely reducible to our will, rational plans, well-formed reasons—not for a while, at least.

There is much that awaits to be explained: how love bonds can unravel as mechanisms of unfreedom, crushing erotic freedom (chapter 3); how certain moments of submission and passivity because of erotic affects contribute to the overall process of freedom (chapter 4); and how from unfree love can we shift to free love, thus opening up ways to envisage and practice free social bonds more generally (chapter 5). In the remainder of this excursus, though, we should further dwell upon the adjective "erotic," and on the features it entails.

Should erotic love be conceived as a "home" in the world? The metaphor represents the very core of Hegelian *Liebe*, as seen in chapter 2, as well as in May's account.[10] Like Hegel, May claims that roots in the world in which we yearn to be grounded, thus finding our home through love, are necessary for growth and change. More decidedly than Hegel, May also claims that roots themselves are dynamic, that they involve growth and change: "In order to (re)discover our true home we must lose our accustomed habitat—our habitual mode of living. We must, in a certain sense, experience ourselves as being displaced, and even in exile"—uprooted, in fact.[11] In my inquiry, the experience of the erotic is not much that of effectively finding and building up a new world, or of the effective rebuilding and reappropriation of an old one—practices that are certainly pivotal, as May rightly argues, for human existence. Rather, I contend, love designates a more limited, liminal, but crucial experience: the passage from the

present, given, known home, to a future one that is still to be properly fig-
ured out and realized.

A variety of philosophers and theorists have offered intriguing and
insightful definitions of eros. Plato's and Carson's insights have already
become part of our map. My conceptualization of the erotic is moreover
indebted, albeit somehow reluctantly, to both British and early German
Romantic philosophical and literary traditions—"reluctantly," since the
legacy of these traditions, in our contemporary Western societies, is contested and ambiguous, on philosophical and on cultural grounds. While
the sociocritical interest of this book requires a criticism of current *romantic ideologies*, some of the conceptual resources for criticizing them are
provided precisely by historical Romanticisms.

In chapter 1, I have mentioned some Romantic passages in continuity
with the union theory, which were problematic. Yet, in unsystematic and
fragmentary ways, navigating through a constellation of observations
about metaphysics, epistemology and aesthetics, early German and British
Romantics have provided insights to think of love beyond union theory.
Let's briefly review the most important of them:

(i) *Love is (sensual) education*: romantic love amounts to a process of becoming
oneself, of self-knowledge and self-transformation. For example, "only through
love and the consciousness of love does man become man," writes Schlegel.[12] In
this process, the phases of passivity or receptivity are crucial: we learn about ourselves insofar as we let ourselves undergo experiences involving the senses, if we
remain open to what we can receive from the environments, including other persons, and also if we "trust" our nonrational or not completely rational faculties.
Only such sensual, intuitive, imaginative experiences can reveal to us aspects of
the world, of other people, and therefore of ourselves, that we did not know before.

(ii) *Love is a dynamic, lively relation*, an ongoing becoming: the capacity to
remain sensible to what can surprise and bewilder us, not necessarily in positive
ways, requires a resistance to the temptation to idealize, immortalize, fix, and
reductively objectify our loved ones, reducing them to closed and unchangeable
identities. Although some Romantic authors give in to idealizing tendencies, reit-
erating motives and patterns of previous, courtly traditions, one central commitment of Romanticism does lie in the attempt to portray the nonperfect or imperfect,
flawed, "real" object of love, to sense the beloved's mutability and contradictory
nature, to stay away from artificial constructions.[13]

(iii) *Freedom and equality are inherent to love's nature.* Some Romantic authors, especially Friedrich Schlegel and Percy Bysshe Shelley, have explicitly and enthusiastically endorsed, at least in words, the equality between men and women, as well as the necessity of women's freedom. For Shelley, women's freedom, the liberation from "a great part of the degrading restraints of antiquity," is even considered a sort of material condition for the production of the "poetry of sexual love."[14] Women, Shelley seems to suggest in his essay "A Defence of Poetry," cannot become the object of lyrical expression if they are not themselves subjects, agents of the stories told about them. In the "Dedication" that introduces the poem "Laon and Cythna," his wife, Mary, is represented as a "free" woman, walking "as free as light the clouds among," and as a nonconformist one, able to "burst" "the mortal Chain of Custom" and "rend" it "in twain."[15] (This is, by the way, Mary Wollstonecraft Shelley, whose masterpiece *Frankenstein* has achieved more fame than any work ever written by Percy Bysshe.) In his scandalous novel *Lucinde*, a portrait of the unconventional marriage between Lucius und Lucinde (partially unconventional in our days as well, given the hints at a possible polyamorous finale), Schlegel claims that lovers of different sexes have to mutually recognize each other as equal and free.[16] Recognizing each other as equal and free is also recognizing the irreducible singularity of the beloved.[17] Manfred Frank, one of the most influential scholars of German Romanticism, understands love in the work of an array of Romantic authors as a "cosubstantial relation between beings that are equal in rank and autonomy, a relation that excludes servitude and domination."[18] For Frank, it is this basis of equality in freedom that allows lovers to shift their "center of gravity" beyond their individuality and reach a transformative unity. The young Hegel testifies to this commitment when he writes that true love "exists only between living beings who are alike in power and thus in one another's eyes living beings from every point of view."[19]

(iv) *Love is disruptive.* The internal requirement of romantic lovers to reciprocally recognize themselves as free and equal, although in their singular variations and uniqueness, is explicitly connected to the disruptive, critical power of love to challenge, or even destroy, moral and social norms—"reason and morality," in Schlegel's terms.[20] Romantic love claims the right of a "charming confusion" against a given ethical, cultural, and political order.[21] Certain romantic lovers, like, for Schlegel, Lucius and Lucinde, seem to put into question, with their example, the reality of a gender order that has not yet de facto realized women's freedom and equality. This is an order, in Schlegel's vision, that does not allow men to feel and acknowledge in themselves their own feminine capacities and virtues—in particular, passive and receptive powers. Love's logic seems, moreover, to be substantially at odds with the capitalist one: for example, the joy it elicits cannot be accumulated like money or commodities.

(v) *Love is worldly.* The feelings between the lovers that arise from the emotional adventures they go through do not separate them from the rest of the world. On the contrary, eros brings them to develop feelings and attachment for their "environment" as well, both for external nature and for other human beings. For example, Lucius declares to his beloved Lucinde: "Everything that we loved before, we love even more warmly now. It's only now that a *feeling for the world* has really dawned on us. You've come to know the infinity of the human spirit through me, and I've come to understand marriage and life, and the *magnificence of all things* through you. For me everything has a soul, speaks to me, and is holy."[22] This assumes a concrete dimension at the end of the (unfinished and fragmentary) novel, when the marriage between Julius und Lucinde stops being dyadic: there is a hint that it is becoming wider, that it is expanding to include other persons and scenarios.

Many of the traits emerging from historical Romantic conceptions seem to have been lost in the cultural, social, everyday legacy of Romanticism. If we think of romantic love today, a much paler, simpler, and politically shallower set of images comes to mind. (Note that I am using the capital letter "R" to refer to the historical Romantic conceptions, and the lower case letter "r" to refer to contemporary ideological conceptions.) To begin with, present-day *romantic ideologies* picture love as an exclusively private affair—and not just in the legitimate sense, mentioned before, that economic or political considerations are not given any right to intervene in love matters. This sense is legitimate, and valuable, because it allows lovers a certain protection—and freedom!—from broader sociopolitical habits, norms, and structures, and from the injustices and forms of domination they might entail. There is a more pernicious tendency, however, to consider romantic love as an "apolitical" or even "antipolitical" human force, as Hannah Arendt famously put it.[23] But if we take lovers as *solely* engrossed in the bliss of their passion, as too abstractly separated from, thus indifferent and uncaring with regard to the larger world to which they belong, we disempower them, making them blind and defenseless in front of the impositions and damages of their societies. The original Romantic view perceives and experiences love as imbued with a more substantial power, a power to rebel against and call into question certain given practices and institutions that regulate our emotions and intimacy. Also, the Romantics considered love as a refined form of knowledge and as a learning process, closely entangled with other types of knowledge and education (aesthetic, artistic, scientific, political, philosophical).

One of the most distinctive and problematic traits of contemporary ideologies of romantic love is the sharp distinction between romantic love and friendship, a distinction that ends up belittling and marginalizing the latter. For instance, Schlegel refers to friendship as "a partial marriage," while "love is friendship from all sides and in all directions."[24] At a first reading, love stands for him for a bodily, passionate, and totalizing experience, whereas friendship is merely an intellectual one. But Schlegel's discourse is actually more layered than this. The "intellectual" experience, for him, is in itself passionate, intense, overwhelming. Friends can merge and form an unity, similarly (albeit not identically) to lovers. In one of the Atheneum fragments, he writes that, when friends assure (recognize) each other in their "mutual worth," "they can sense the presence of their limitations only by the knowledge of *having been made whole through the existence of the other person*."[25] The novel *Lucinde* entails further important reflections on friendship: in particular, it includes a letter from Julius to his friend Antonio, which is also the outline of an essay, in which he chews over the break-up and then recovery of their relationship. There is also a final fragment of a dialogue on "the nature of friendship" staged between Julius and another friend, Lorenzo. These ruminations suggest that friendship, like sexual love, represents a fundamental space for education, a possibility for growth and transformation.

Many post-Romantic authors have diffusely demonstrated crucial similarities and entanglements between sexual love and friendship. Romantic love's main characteristics—its educational, lively, disruptive, worldly character, based upon a recognition of the freedom and equality of everyone involved—can be clearly exhibited by friendships as well. Michel Foucault, for example, speaks about homosexual erotic bonds not as love, but as philia. In particular in the short, much debated interview "Friendship as a Way of Life," he delineates a conception of friendship endowed by a strong self-transformative potential that sounds profoundly Romantic, while at the same time calling decisively into question romantic heteronormative ideologies. With an intuition that reminds of Nietzsche and

Emerson and their idea of the lover as an enemy, Foucault views friendship not as a "safe space," a space of mutual comfort, compatibility and identification, but as an agonistic one. For Foucault, friendship is an experience of "uneasiness," a "desire-in-uneasiness," that provokes unrest, solicits experimentation, opens up a space where to try out and play with our other selves, with others as other selves, with unknown and impersonal selves, with nonidentities.[26] It is especially the possibility of becoming someone else that is cherished and sought after in this type of bond. Self-transformation is not an individual endeavor, though; it requires and implies a change of those habits, expectations, patterns of feeling and behavior that build up given general sexual and gender identities. What comes after present identities and, especially, for Foucault, the masculine identity? It is not clear, but the opaqueness and unpredictability are conditions for imagining and creating new and alternatives forms of life.

A lot of precious material for the conceptualization of eros at the intersection between nonsexual friendship and sexual love is provided by contemporary literature. We have already talked about the proper erotic relationship binding Lila and Lenù in Elena Ferrante's Neapolitan novels. Consider now also *Conversations with Friends,* the celebrated 2017 debut novel by Sally Rooney. The protagonist, Frances, is a talented twenty-one-year-old college student and poet who is still in love with her ex-girlfriend and now alleged best friend, Bobbi. Rather early in the story, Frances gets a serious crush on Nick, an older, depressed, married actor. While she is embarking on a murky yet loving affair with him, her relationship with Bobbi seems to qualify as a "normal" friendship. Sometimes, however, Frances is reluctant to talk to her about her passion for Nick. She dreads Bobbi's judgments; she does not want to lose her esteem and admiration, her recognition. For her part, Bobbi is clearly affected by pangs of jealousy, which seem to have, however, positive transformative effects on her. By reflecting on Frances's own affair with Nick, she brings herself to revise some of her insensible and arrogant behaviors and to address unresolved issues in her life. In a phase in which Nick has fallen out of Frances's favor, she and Bobbi come to be very close again: they were already living together, but now they start to sleep in the same bed, kiss, hold hands, give their friends gifts as a couple, talk all night long, and discuss the widest possible range of topics, from politics to philosophy to their own relationship. A mutual friend, Philip, is convinced that they are now back together.

When Frances denies that Bobbi can be called her girlfriend, he replies: "But she obviously is. I mean, you're doing some radical lesbian thing or whatever, but in basic vocabulary she is your girlfriend." Frances and Bobbi do indeed refuse to let themselves be categorized or to comply with such a "basic vocabulary." Frances is aware that from the outside they might resemble a couple, but when they come to talk about it, which they often do, they develop a joke to avoid clear-cut definitions: "What *is* a friend? we would say humorously. What *is* a conversation?"[27]

Frances and Bobbi's special way of being together hinges upon a sort of philosophical inquiry, led by questions: What is a friend? What is a conversation? These are the questions of a philosophical inquiry into the nature of love. In a Cavellian vein, Rooney's characters identify good intimate relationships with prolonged intellectually and emotionally stimulating and engaging conversations, as the title of the novel already suggests. These exchanges do inevitably imply opacities, misunderstandings, and silences. Nevertheless, they are good conversations, because they keep unfolding, animated by the wish to shed light on the shadowy parts of relationships, to reach new agreements, to break the silences with new, unexpected words. In jointly asking the meaning of "conversation," and thus of friendship and love, and in refusing to formulate answers, Bobbi and Frances establish their own special modality of being together—a proper erotic bond that they strive to set aside from social norms and structures, in which they can be free.

In this example, sexual involvement is not a necessary condition for erotic love, but it is not excluded either. According to Solomon, as discussed in chapter 1, the first essential feature of romantic love is that it is animated by sexual desire. But this looks like just another component of contemporary romantic ideologies. Contrary to Solomon's interpretation, the founding text of the union theory of love, as well as of modern romantic love—namely, Aristophanes's myth in *The Symposium*, does not suggest this link. After having being divided in two, narrates Aristophanes, human beings began desperately and passionately looking for the other half: however, in a first phase, when and if reunited, they did not sense the urgency or the desire to engage in sexual intercourse, since their genitals were still on the back (made for copulate with the ground). Their urgency and desire for closeness and merging did not have sexual connotation, at the beginning. Things changed when Zeus moved their genitals to the front and made them have sex with one another, which was definitely much more fun. Zeus's stratagem has made his creatures *function* more efficaciously: after sexual satisfaction, human beings seem to forget about their loved one for a while and go back to their usual (productive) activities, like work.[28] What is more, reproduction of the species comes more easily and naturally this way. This weird story can, of course, be contested in many respects, but it is significant that, in Aristophanes's speech, the rationale of sex does not belong to the very definition of erotic love, but has more prosaic and pragmatic purposes.

For some, erotic love might be deeply entangled with sexual desires and experiences: sex can be the scene in which human beings can discover, learn about, and experiment with the erotic as I have reconstructed it so far, but it does not have to. In the early 2000s, an *asexual movement* has emerged with the political goal of establishing asexuality as a legitimate sexual identity, and of forming communities and subcultures around this identity. One of its claims is that romantic, intimate, committed, even passionate (erotic, then) relationships can de facto unfold between people who do not feel sexual urges, who are not interested in pursuing sexual activities with anybody. This is connected to the claim that a general lack of sexual desire is not to be viewed as pathological, a manifestation of traumas that must be healed and overcome, caused by depression or other psychological (and social) problems, and cause for frustration and unhappiness.[29] Sexual persons are not to be viewed as "superior" to asexual ones—healthier, and potentially happier and more free. Asexual lovers share many dimensions of their lives, live together, engage in meaningful projects together. Moreover, some of them do share a bodily intimacy that does not lead to sexual intercourse but nevertheless fulfills a need for closeness, mutual caring, trust. Asexual bonds, in other words, can naturally be erotic.

Erotic bonds can also be formed between people who are "just" friends, according to conventional understandings of the term—namely, between people who feel intimately bound together, but are not sexually attracted to each other, although they may sexually desire someone else. In her *Dialogue on Love*, queer theorist Eve Sedgwick talks to her therapist about her passionate, nonsexual attachment to her gay friend and housemate,

Michael Moon. Their relationship has shaped and immensely enriched her, Sedgwick says, giving her access to truths she would have not reached otherwise. It has represented an unrivaled source for joy, but also, naturally, of worries. Similarly to Frances and Bobbi in *Conversations with Friends*, Eve and Michael have a friendship that cannot be grasped by any category. She declares that she is in love with him: "Our bond is very passionate, at least for me; it preoccupies me a lot; it's very physical, though we don't have sex." Their relationship, Sedgwick tells her psychoanalyst, has changed her "in a hundred big and little ways."[30] She feels kind of "addicted" to his "sunshine."[31] At a later stage of her *Dialogue*, Sedgwick makes a more theoretical remark, which reminds closely of the epistemological value attributed to love by the Romantics:

> For me, what falling in love means is different. It's a matter of suddenly, globally "knowing" that another person represents your only access to some vitally
>
> > transmissible truth
> > or radiantly heightened
> > mode of perception
>
> > and that if you lose the thread of this intimacy, both your soul and your whole world might subsist forever in some desert-like state of ontological impoverishment.[32]

In this powerful depiction of friendship, a nonsexual friend occupies a place in Sedgwick's life that, according to a romantic ideology, should be taken by another type of companion. Another trait of the contemporary ideology of romance consists, in fact, in what can be called the "totalization" of the partner. The fantasy is that the person we love romantically ought to fulfill a very wide range of emotional needs and wishes. We expect our romantic partners to be satisfying sexual mates, stimulating intellectual companions, capable of material and spiritual support if needed, sometimes therapists, as well as "partners in crime" for diverse projects (a family, most frequently; sometimes even economic ventures). We assign them all these responsibilities and roles. It follows that romantic love can and should be monogamous: who needs other sexual, spiritual, or intellectual close persons if we have found one ("the One") who can do all these things for us?

Such convictions have been harshly criticized mostly by contemporary theorists of so-called polyamory. Elizabeth Brake has famously coined the term "amatonormativity" to problematize some of the ideological features that I have been mentioned before, and more precisely the assumption that a central, exclusive, romantic relationship is normal for human beings, that it is or must be a universally shared objective, and that such a relationship is preferable to other relationship types. Moreover, the assumption that valuable relationships can only be marital or amorous devalues friendship and other caring relationships.[33] The problem of amatonormative (or mononormative) social and cultural regimes is not that certain individuals or couples form exclusive and totalizing erotic attachments, which become more important than others. The trouble is that alternatives are not taken into serious consideration, or are openly misrecognized, more or less subtly hindered or even punished.[34] The trouble lies with those convictions and practices putting at the top of a relationship hierarchy a kind of dyadic, long-term, exclusive partnership based on sexual satisfaction and preferably legally recognized, putting pressure on individuals to comply with the hierarchy.[35] The effect is an impoverishment of our intimate, interpersonal lives that deprives us of meaningful occasions for experimentation and transformation.

It is important to remark that amatonormative and mononormative regimes are deeply entangled with Western, Christian, state-centered colonialist and imperialist projects. Many Indigenous scholars have pointed out how the sexual, gender, and emotional orders of the settlers are systematically and often violently imposed on the colonized. Scholar and artist Leanne Betasamosake Simposon shows, for example, how Indigenous forms of social kinship, such as those of Michi Saagiig Nishnaabeg nationhood, are at their core relational and diverse and include "practices of nonmonogamy, separation, divorce, and situations where both genders had more than one partner."[36] Such relationships have, however, been put under settler surveillance, destroyed and replaced with the heteronormative nuclear family. With reference to the colonization of North America, Kim TallBear also denounces how both the church and the state have "evangelized marriage, nuclear family, and monogamy," thus breaking up "Indians" collectives and enabling the transfer of surplus land to European and Euro-American settlers. As a result, women's bodies have become regarded and treated as private property.[37]

Philosophers of polyamory have, roughly, two main aims: the first aim
is to show that we *can* romantically, passionately, sexually love more than
one person at the same time, and the second is that in doing so we are not
morally reproachable. One of the powerful effects of polyamory discourse
is the shifting of the definition of love to embrace a diversity of relationships. This means also acknowledging, and being ready to explore, those
relationships that occupy a middle space between friendship and romantic
love, thus ultimately making the conceptual distinction between the two
lose its significance and power to organize social relations and practices in
general.

Bobbi and Frances in *Conversations with Friends* have grasped this, and
so has Simone de Beauvoir. In the first volume of her autobiographical
work *Memoirs of a Dutiful Daughter*, she tells us about her intense, overwhelming friendship with classmate Zaza. At the beginning, Beauvoir
thinks of and categorizes Zaza merely as a "best friend." Friendship occupies a "honorable position" in her personal scale of human affection, but it
is not the most important relationship; it does not have "the mysterious
splendor of love, nor the sacred dignity of filial devotion."[38] But the young
Simone senses that such a categorization cannot match her affects. She
realizes she does not have the right words, emotions, or concepts to explain
(to herself and to others) and to communicate the proper weight of Zaza's
presence in her life. Only her disappearance makes Simone finally see and
feel how her love for her does indeed exceed given rules: "All my happiness, my very existence, lay in her hands . . . I had gone as far as to admit
the extent of the dependence which my attachment to her placed upon me:
I did not dare envisage all its consequences."[39] Simone's relationship to
Zaza is one of deep dependence; it makes her vulnerable, and its "consequences" are unforeseen.[40]

In the literature on polyamory, different kinds of nonmonogamous relationships have been singled out. There are for example, "open relationships"—
relationships that in many aspects resemble traditional romantic ones, be
they legally recognized (marriage) or not. They are mostly dyadic, and
both partners have agreed they can both engage in "secondary" affairs or
relationships with "outside partners."[41] The rules to be followed (e.g.,
whether and how much to tell the other partner) are or should explicitly,
openly, and democratically made up by each couple. In *ethical* open relationships, the decisions around rules cannot be determined by one partner

only, and they need to be negotiated freely. Then there are "group relation-ships": committed, long-term, primary bonds that include three (or four) adults (of any gender), which can be open or closed to outside partners. A group relationship can either revolve around one central person (called a "V") who is primary with all others, or each person may be equally close to every other person involved. The latter constellation can also be called a triad (or quad). Another possibility is to create an "intimate network": a group of persons among which different forms of intense, both sexual and nonsexual relationships occur. Sometimes all members of the group are lovers at the same time; sometimes individuals have only one or two sex-ual lovers within the network, which can then include singles (who have very close friends within the network), couples, moresomes, mixtures. This quite complex type of erotic bond has also been called "relationship anarchy" or an (urban) "tribe." A distinction can be also made between "polyfidelity" and "proper" polyamory. "Polyfidelity" describes relation-ships that are based on the sexual and (or?) emotional exclusivity and fidelity among a group larger than a dyad. For Justin L. Clardy, one of the most precise philosophers of nonmonogamy today, the term "polyamory" should then be reserved for a relationship with very minimal, ongoingly shifting rules and patterns, more open and uncertain, that cannot be defined in advance.[42]

While the philosophy of nonmonogamy and polyamory is a recent development, some Romantics indeed anticipated the polyamorous dis-course. Present-day ideologies would suggest otherwise, but it is wrong to claim that Romantic love has always been conceived of as exclusively dyadic and monogamous.[43] For example, at the end of *Lucinde*, Julius and Lucinde are no longer the only members of the love community they have formed. Julius dreams of a Juliane, and Lucinde of a Guido. Their union has expanded into a far more comprehensive one. Shelley's complex poem "Epipsychidion," moreover, while surely being littered with ideological images, does also sketch out a precious, albeit quite judgmental, image of polyerotic constellation.[44] The poetic "I" declares he does not belong to that "sect" believing that "each one should select / Out of the crowd a mis-tress or a friend," while the rest "commend / To cold oblivion." These per-sons who restrict their passions and loves to one companion only, whom they choose ("select") according to some kind of cold rationality and end up chaining him or her, do comply with "modern morals, and the beaten road," but are in fact just "poor slaves," having their home "among the dead" (149–59). Contrary to an established, bourgeois, monetarized conception (where love has to be taken as "gold" or "clay") "true love" is one that, if "divided," "is not taken away": fed by imagination and fantasy, this love is "like understanding, that grows bright/Gazing on many truths" (161–63). In this passage, Shelley is maybe suggesting that loving more than one person at the same time, far from impoverishing and tiring lovers and loved ones, allows the multiplying of joy and pleasures, while minimizing sorrow (180–81). This is possible, as I read it, as the process of love is thought of in the terms of a learning process (a process of "understanding") that is enriched and refined when engaging with multiple objects of knowledge and inquiry. The poem, which starts with the liberation of a woman (Emily) from a prison, ends up in a utopian natural place inhabited by an erotic *we*, a community of lovers ("Marina, Vanna, Primus, and the rest," line 601).

The account I have developed in chapter 2 is particularly apt, I believe, to conceptually frame polyamory, or "polyeros," as we might more aptly call it within the framework of the present inquiry. This might sound presumptuous, as indeed recognition theorists have mostly depicted love relationships as dyadic. However, one of the advantages of framing eros in terms of recognitive dynamics is that both the giving and attracting of recognition are movements that do not have to make their objects exclusive, cutting off other relationships and subjects. In its desirable form, recognition, we have seen, consists, importantly, (also) *in affirming and fostering the other's freedom*: in perceiving and treating the other not as a (fixed, reified) object but as a free being—free, among other things, to engage in meaningful relationships of loving recognition with others.

Consider the following (fictional) situation. Ariel and Bowie are in a long-term relationship; they love each other. Bowie falls then in love with Cleo, who reciprocates. Bowie has now two parallel erotic bonds, with Ariel and Cleo. Ariel and Bowie reciprocally recognize each other lovingly; Bowie and Cleo too recognize each other with love. Now, what happens or might happen between Ariel and Cleo? One possibility is that Ariel might be "naturally" brought to recognize the object of Bowie's recognition, Cleo. Ariel's recognition for Cleo could amount to respect, sympathy, care, but might also develop into an erotic one. Ariel's attraction to

Cleo might be conditioned, inspired, elicited by Bowie's attraction to Cleo. Cleo, that is, while attracting Bowie's recognition, might be able also to attract the recognition of Ariel, whose recognition is already attracted by Bowie. Something similar can happen, of course, to Cleo too. This "generation" of mutual recognition between Ariel and Cleo, who are both subjects and objects of recognition with regard to Bowie, can be enhanced by the fact that they all start to engage in the same activities together: Ariel, Bowie, and Cleo might start to share dinners, attend concerts and political activities. Shared actions can generate shared emotions, and shared emotions bring them to initiate more actions together, thus reinforcing, deepening, complicating, or jeopardizing recognitive dynamics. It is quite likely, on the one hand, that the bond between Bowie and Cleo would have an impact on the one between Bowie and Ariel: the new erotic connection could strengthen and enrich the "older" one, or it could, sadly, put it to question and weaken it. On the other hand, the bond between Bowie and Ariel cannot but influence the one between Bowie and Cleo. The relationship of recognition, and maybe of erotic recognition, between Cleo and Ariel exerts power on the other two bonds as well. Important to consider is how each dynamic of recognition can have effects on the other dynamics, including the effect to overcome dyadic separated recognitive dynamics and form a new collective erotic entity (a genuine triad in which Ariel, Bowie, and Cleo are all erotically involved with each other.)

If the singularity of each lover does not disappear in the collectivity, but is on the contrary further enhanced by *power with*, polyeros might open up many possibilities for self-experiences and transformations. The freedom of everyone involved, and freedom as collective enterprise, flourish. The highly complex dynamics require a very high level of commitment, involvement, communication, and empathy. It pushes everyone to learn how to better deal with one's own and others' emotions, to listen to and care for others, to endure one's own and the partners' vulnerabilities, to explore dark spots. However, things do not always go as expected; delusions, frustrations, difficulties arise. Power struggles multiply when multiple lovers are in the picture and can become exhausting to navigate. Each lover's power might be increased by multiple lovers and by the multiple erotic *we*, but a great deal of power of resistance is required, both against each partner and against the whole constellation, which might become overwhelming and menacing. Polyeros can become particularly trouble-some in social contexts plagued, as we will analyze in the next chapter, by sexist, racist, and capitalist habits, norms, and structures. Polyerotic bonds are de facto largely hindered (criticized, ostracized, punished) in current social contexts. If they manage to be formed and unfold, they might reenact and reproduce damaging social mechanisms—but they can also manage to powerfully push against them.

Chapter Three

THE MESS WE ARE IN

Toward a Critical Theory of Love

Until now, we have simultaneously followed two paths throughout our map. First, we have tried to grasp something of what erotic love is and could be. We have found out that eros is a form of interdependence, strongly binding human beings while at the same time giving them the chance to (re)gain their independence. By abandoning themselves to and cultivating their dependence on each other, lovers have a chance to discover who they are and who they want to be. Love accommodates power struggles, with transformative consequences. Second, we have tried to determine the desirability of eros—what makes erotic experiences meaningful and valuable for us. In one word: freedom. We should desire to engage in erotic adventures when we can taste freedom and become (more) free, thanks to them. A Romantic heritage, deviating from contemporary romantic ideologies, shines through both paths. The descriptive and the normative dimensions of this inquiry are intertwined: when trying to understand what love is, we inevitably bump into its normative ambivalence. And the urge to face the troubledness that accompanies ambivalence makes us desire a compass to orient ourselves on the map.[1] The idea of erotic freedom that allows us to trace a distinction between free and unfree love should work as this compass.

What is unfree love? It is now time to descend into the gloomier regions of our map, to explore eros's dark sides—*the mess we are in*, to say it with the title of one of PJ Harvey's songs from her album *Stories from the City, Stories from the Sea*. The main thesis presented in this chapter is that erotic love can become a trap, a vehicle of various forms of suffering, oppression, and injustice, of "mortal dangers" (Beauvoir), even. Individuals who are erotically involved might, in the name of love, do terrible things to themselves and to each other. The most widespread assumption nowadays is that eros's badness (its "toxicity," as we would commonly say today) depends on individuals' "pathologies": traumas and wounds in lovers' pasts, for example, might explain fear of attachment and avoidant behaviors, or, conversely, excessive dependence and codependence.[2] Impulses to manipulate and control the other, which lead to destructive and dismantling words and acts, passive and submissive reactions, and dishonesty and lies, are commonly explained on the basis of individual "disorders" (e.g., narcissism, depression, borderline personality). The strategy adopted in this chapter is different. I propose to critically approach erotic phenomena by concentrating on social, objective (dis)orders. Contradicting the overly famous first line of Tolstoy's *Anna Karenina*, every "unhappy" relationship is not "unhappy" in its own way. There are recurrent damaged and damaging patterns, which start to make sense if love stories are not regarded individualistically, but against a background of overarching habits, social norms, and structures. Erotic experiences do not happen in a void. Lovers and friends are workers, owners of properties, carriers of debts, citizens (or noncitizen), wanderers, migrants. They have local, national, transnational identities. Lovers and friends are bodies with certain characteristics and features (e.g., biological sexual attributes, sizes, skin or hair colors and textures, physical or psychological abilities and disabilities) that are more or less favorably apprehended and treated in current sociopolitical orders. Complex intersections of rules and habits shape and direct erotic bonds that include laws (e.g., marriage laws); policies (e.g., those regulating equality of opportunity, or parental leave; also, immigration); organization and valorization of labor (the traditional gendered division of labor, the flexibilization or precarization of labor markets); race-based injustices; structural reminiscences of colonialism and slavery; and many others.

Erotic bonds, the actions and emotions that constitute them, cannot be thought of as a "safe place" per se. Eros is not detached from social, political, economic factors. However, as we have already noticed in chapter 1, it is mostly theorized as if it were. In most philosophical accounts, the phenomenon of love appears as standing alone, and it must be grasped in its distinctiveness. This philosophical tendency, which hinges upon an idea of "worldless" love, can, however, rely on a sociological foundation and explanation. The first section of this chapter tries to look at social theories with the aim of addressing the question: How have love bonds become (viewed as) disentangled from other domains of social life? In other words: how has love become a seemingly autonomous sphere of human interaction? In the following sections, the sociotheoretical thesis of the *modern autonomization of love* will be problematized: first, by showing how other social spheres, and in particular the economic sphere, can have a (blocking) effect on erotic bonds; and, second, by analyzing how constellations of intersecting habitual social norms and structures—those that have, for example, to do with gender and race—can damage eros in various ways. I will more precisely detect three damages of the erotic bond: complicit love, mastery love, and exploitative love.

REASONS? OF LOVE?

Up until now, we have talked about individual friends and lovers finding in love the possibility of (re)discovering, thanks to and within their bonds, how to be individually autonomous. But autonomy in love can be thought of as in yet another way, which has been introduced already in the excursus, in the wake of Frankfurt's idea of "love reasons." According to Frankfurt, love is an autonomous *source* of reasons for action, as well as of values. Love gives us justifications, motives, enticements to regard things in a certain fashion and to act in certain ways instead of others. For example, my love for my partner can constitute a reason for me to move to another country to be with them. These reasons can properly count as reasons for love insofar as they can prove themselves to be sufficiently disentangled from reasons of different orders—universal moral reasons, as well as economic or political ones.

Let's have a look at the TV show *The Americans* (Joe Weisberg, 2013–2018), and at its two protagonists, Philip and Elizabeth. At the beginning of the show, we learn that they are KGB officers who live and work in a suburb of Washington, DC, in the 1980s. Posing as a "normal" married couple with two children and a unspectacular job by day, by night they spy for the Soviet government. Since their arrival in the United States, Philip and Elizabeth are involved in what we can call a committed intimate relationship: as husband and wife, they share large portions of their lives, enjoy sexual intercourses, and make almost all decisions concerning family and work together. They are extremely effective in cooperating and coordinating their actions, and they share strong feelings: for example, a deep devotion and nostalgia for their country, irritation toward their supervisors, and concern for their kids' well-being. Even when given the possibility, they would probably not replace the other as a partner. And yet, presented as instrumental to certain political and moral goals, this relationship cannot properly count as erotic love. Their match is a fiction, part of a KGB plan to infiltrate spies in the United States. Already in the first phase of the show, however, their story takes a (predictable) romantic turn. Interestingly, their falling in love coincides with mounting doubts concerning their commitment to the Soviet Union. Their growing romantic involvement is depicted as dramatically opposed to their political goals. This narrative device mirrors what "true" or proper love (as opposed to other forms of committed, caring relationships) is (or should) be about. Elizabeth and Philip are falling in love with each other *not because of* their outstanding virtues as devoted Communists or because of their high moral principles. These would be just external reasons, not proper reasons of love. They are, in fact, falling in love *even despite* their virtues and principles, knowing that a romantic involvement could probably jeopardize the espionage work.

When we act on the basis of love, according to Frankfurt, we act autonomously, because it is *our own will*, and not an external or alien force, that constrains us.[3] (We have already mentioned—and chapter 4 will develop this further—that sometimes we do sense our own will *as* an estranged force. Pretty often, we are not at one with ourselves.) The emotions of love that we feel and that move us constitute an important part of the kernel of our self; they make us who we truly are. Of course, we are also constituted by other orders of reasons—for example, our political convictions, duties and responsibilities toward our community and ourselves, including those that make us participate in the economic system. Love reasons could be outweighed by these other reasons, could be put aside or ignored, but are never brought about by or dependent on them.

As anticipated in the excursus, love's autonomy, in this sense, does not mean that we can freely choose our love interests. Actually, love is so important for us *because*, and not in spite of the fact that, it generates bonds from which we are unable to withdraw (and if we are, we do it unwillingly and at great cost). In *The Metaphysics of Morals*, Kant formulates this idea in the most precise way: "Love is a matter of *feeling*, not of willing, and I cannot love because I *will* to, still less because I *ought* to (I cannot be constrained to love); so a *duty to love* is an absurdity."[4] Sexual, passionate love arises as a feeling or as an inclination and cannot be constrained by any kind of reason. This is why this type of love, in Kant's view, has to be seen as dwelling outside of the sphere of human moral autonomy and practical reason. Frankfurt's most original contribution consists in accepting the Kantian premise of love's disentanglement from moral considerations by at the same time *regarding it as a proper, autonomous source for ethical rationality*. Not only morality but also the power to love must be seen as defining us as rational and autonomous persons. If, on the one hand, Frankfurt agrees with Kant that love cannot be constrained by reasons that are external, on the other hand he does not conceive of love as a bundle of "transient," "adventitious," "heteronomous" feelings or emotions.[5] On the contrary, the contingent necessities of love express something that belongs to our most intimate and fundamental nature. Unlike the necessities of (Kantian) reason, love reasons are not impersonal, but take into account and deal with the very singularity of human persons.

This view, alas, implies the possibility of developing loving attachments to persons (or to things) who are hurting and harming us. Lovers must be careful. They must try to avoid getting attached to what might be bad for them. As we all know, the attempt is often useless, and Frankfurt does not provide instruments to tackle the problem of reasons of love going astray. As a reaction to this helplessness, S. Matthew Liao has tried to rehabilitate, against Frankfurt *and* Kant, the idea of a duty to love. We have to learn to discern, Liao prompts us, the social pressures, expectations, and mechanisms that have shaped our bodily impulses, our affection and passions. We have to become aware of and reflect upon the mechanisms that make us attracted only, for example, "to people *from a certain social class or certain race*."[6] As a result of such self-reflection, we would then hopefully abandon the pernicious (philosophical and practical) belief in love's uncontrollability and decide to intervene to change problematic reasons of love. Liao believes that moral, critical reasons can bring us to develop a grip on loving attachments, in order to develop appropriate emotions in appropriate circumstances. Emotions, for Liao, can be steered, cultivated, manipulated: we might even develop the power to fall in or out of love. We might become able to prevent ourselves from falling out of love with a certain person and in love with someone else. And if we *can* steer our emotions in this way, we might also *ought* to do that. Liao admits it is difficult to argue that there is a general duty to love someone romantically, but sometimes this duty appears as reasonable and desirable: for example, he thinks, when a marriage risks falling apart.

Liao does not explain why and in what circumstances exactly we should uphold this duty, and which reasons of love are precisely wicked and need to be corrected, tamed, or overpowered by reasons external to love. The interesting part of his proposition consists in his charge against the thesis of the autonomy of love. Liao is right that reasons supporting *bad (unfree) love* must be criticized and dispelled—for that, we need to develop *a critical theory of erotic bonds*, able to reconstruct the structural mechanisms shaping our sentimental lives in detrimental ways, but also able to show how and why these ways are not necessary and could be changed. As I will argue in the next two chapters, however, the question of the possibility of loving differently has little to do with moral duties. Rather, it has to do with the "internal" dynamic of erotic bonds themselves.

Before exploring this path, however, we must acknowledge how Frankfurt's understanding of love autonomy sounds particularly strong, against Liao's criticism, because it is rooted in a series of social theories of modern love. This is usually overlooked by contemporary moral or ethical discussions around love, and by Frankfurt himself. Yet Frankfurt's account seems, as a matter of fact, the obvious result of a specific development of modern society, which produces the separation between different "social spheres" and the becoming-autonomous, or "autonomization," of each of those. The fact that lovers do, think, and feel with a certain degree of autonomy cannot be understood without presupposing a separation or differentiation between (erotic) love and other types of interpersonal relationships that make up our social contexts.

The autonomy of love theorized by Frankfurt can thus be better understood if one reads, in particular, Niklas Luhmann's reconstruction of the historical process of modernization, described as progressive differentiation between social spheres regulated by different "codes," or "media": money, political power, law, art, truth, and love. Luhmann does not regard love as an emotion or as a feeling but as a sort of *technology* generating and making available the language, patterns, and rules that allow individuals to interact in a highly personal, intimate way. In a love relationship, both lovers' perspectives reciprocally become the cornerstone of the partner's world; *both* lovers try, that is, to assume the other's point of view on the world, to perceive, look at, evaluate things as the other does. The reciprocal adoption of the partner's view is described by Luhmann as "interpenetration": both lovers attempt to enter the other's subjectivity.[7] An impossible undertaking, one that becomes, however, somehow possible through the code of love.

The characterization of the individual as an (almost) impenetrable bundle of singular and irreplaceable features, actions, and emotions, and the consequent need for confirmation (recognition!) it elicits, is not an anthropological constant. Rather, for Luhmann, it derives from the specific sociostructural framework of highly complex and differentiated societies.[8] While in traditional, premodern societies individuals were formed on the basis of the general characteristics, values, and structures that also defined their community or class, a complex society makes it necessary for individuals to differentiate themselves from their fellow human beings as well as from their environment. When individuals estranged themselves from the other members of the community, the world started to appear to them as more and more difficult to decipher: it became a "distant world" (*Fernwelt*), in which we struggled to feel at home. The wide range of anonymous, impersonal social relationships, regulated by legal or monetary, political, or scientific principles, allow us to form and unfold our personalities in many diverse and complex ways. At the same time, we develop the need for a narrower, warmer, more friendly, and familiar world—a world of *love*. The support given by the members of the "close world (*Nahwelt*)" has become, according to Luhmann, one crucial condition for entering the distant world and act successfully in it.[9]

The "primary symbol" that has introduced the need for intimacy and mutual confirmation is, on Luhmann's account, so-called *amour passion*.

Passionate love, which has begun to appear from about 1650 onward, is *codified as* an emotion, or a bundle of emotions that defy and do not require any explanation—*autonomous emotions*, that is. According to the semantics of love as passion, lovers lose and alienate themselves in the incontrollable, totalizing whirlwind of their feelings, without being able to justify any of their excesses and emotional outbursts. Passion has thus planted the first seed for the autonomization of love. Life in traditional communities, in "older, locally denser social systems," consisted of networks of relationships that blocked individuals' self-exclusion.[10] The widespread expectation was to share one's life with others within a general given framework. Intimacy restricted to two people was hardly possible. The conditions enabling the emergence of passionate intimacy are to be found, then, outside of the established order. More precisely, these conditions have manifested themselves *in opposition* to it. Passion becomes a motor of social transformation.

The semantics of amour passion has helped to assert and to advance the process of system differentiation, argues Luhmann. As a result of this process, intimate, passionate relationships have also eventually obtained their own separated, legitimate social sphere, and a definite code to regulate them. This is the *romantic* code. Marriage based on passion and intimacy, and not just oriented around procreation or inheritance of property, has become an institution enabling the unfolding of intimate relationship within a socially accepted framework. The principle of passion is incorporated in the romantic conception of intimacy. Passion is proclaimed as "the very principle upon which the *choice* of a spouse should be based."[11] Romanticism marks the beginning of an epoch that grants the individuals the right to enjoy and express their feelings and to find happiness through their emotional life. Specific social and cultural institutions (love-based marriage, the bourgeois family) form the socially legitimate framework for this individual right. Contrary to passionate love, romantic love designates an intimate experience that is supposed to last: only stable, long-term relationships can fulfill the task of successfully recognizing individuality.[12]

The process of differentiation that has brought about the institutionalization of a separated sphere for intimate relationships, Luhmann argues, has had the effect of *normalizing* the subversive, rebellious character of passion. Normalization is required though by the individuals' growing need for confirmation and care. Reversely, the creation of a social sphere in which individuals can get enough confirmation and recognition in their radical uniqueness constitutes one of the enabling condition for the individualization process. Some defining characteristics of amour passion do not disappear, though: romantic love also relies on intense emotions and feelings that cannot be explained by drawing upon reasons of, for example, "wealth, youth, beauty and virtue."[13] In Luhmann's view, to sum up, the *autonomization of the medium of love* has the function to create a social space that provides highly individualized recognition (he employs the term in largely the same sense of chapter 2 of this volume). The autonomy of the sphere of love is characterized, according to Luhmann, by reflexivity, or self-referentiality. All preconditions that do not reside within the medium itself are neutralized. Love is simply *justified by the fact of love itself.*

With *The Transformation of Intimacy*, Anthony Giddens, another sociologist of modernity, picks up where Luhmann leaves us. The book is dedicated to a further development that has invested the sphere of love. This is the passage from "romantic" to "pure relationships." The possibility to conceive of and practice sexual, profound intimacy in a "pure" form is the result, according to Giddens, of a process of *democratization* of personal life, that has peaked with the sexual liberation of the 1960s and 1970s.[14] A pure relationship is an intimate relation that we enter for its own sake, for the different kinds of pleasure and goods that we can enjoy by forming and staying in intimate associations with others. It marks, according to Gidden's social diagnosis, an emancipation from the traditional, patriarchal—in my terms, "ideological"—idea of *romantic* relationships, which mainly end up assuming the institutional form of marriage; it entails strong gender hierarchies and division of tasks and is conceived of as an unbreakable contract. Pure relationships are, on the contrary, not regulated by external norms or traditional customs but, rather, by internal ones—namely, by rules and habits established by lovers themselves within the space opened up by their emotions and loving deeds.

Giddens's pure relationships are animated not by "interpenetrating" (Luhmann) but by *confluent love.* This notion designates lovers' attitude to come close to each other, to come to know each other's wishes and desires, to disclose oneself to the other. While women's dreams of romances have often led to grim domestic subjection to their male partners, confluent love "presumes equality in emotional give and take."[15] Confluent love, moreover, makes the achievement of *reciprocal* sexual pleasure, which presupposes mutual bodily knowledge—a key element. Sexuality is anarchic; there are no strict rules or patterns except those lovers make up for themselves. Heterosexuality is no longer a standard by which every other relationship is judged. Sexuality has become *plastic*, "malleable, open to being shaped in diverse ways,"[16] and "has to be negotiated" within the relationship itself.[17] Giddens does believe, optimistically, in the democratization process. He does mention the enduring imbalance in economic resources available to men and women, especially with regard to responsibilities for care and domestic work. All in all, however, he believes in the moral progress of our modern societies with respect to gender equality, at least in the context of intimate arrangements.

Even if we are not on board with this optimism (and the following sections argue we should not), Luhmann's and Giddens's accounts are precious since they explain how a certain *idea(l)* of love has been gradually established itself in the social reality of modern (Western) societies. The (partial and gradual) realization of the principle of autonomization means that we cannot explain love relationships by referring to institutions exterior to love, to economic and political logics and imperatives—not only. Similarly, Frankfurt does not want to gather love reasons from other kinds of reasons (e.g., impersonal moral ones). If we want to conceive of erotic bonds in terms of freedom, we have to presuppose that a certain differentiation between types of social bonds is possible. But to what extent is this idea de facto *realized* in our societies? Yes, it does, as an idea, orient and guide our self-understandings, practices. We intuitively want to and do differentiate between an economic transaction and an erotic interaction, or between a series of actions or emotions in common that elaborate and realize political goals and an erotic *we* (although there might be, in reality, gray areas between economic reasons and authentic reasons of love, and an erotic *we* can also assume political connotations, as we will see in chapter 6). But maybe the differentiation has happened less clearly and neatly than Luhmann and Giddens have in mind. And what if the process has now been reversed, and other social spheres, especially the economic sphere, come to push against the domain of the erotic, occupying its spaces, weighing on its semantics and logic? What if the growth and the expansion of the realm of economic relations has come to cause the shrinking of the realm of eros?

AGAINST LOVE

The power that a capitalist organization of the market can have on human relationships is considerable, and considerably damaging. The twenty-something Karl Marx realized that already around the middle of the nineteenth century. It might be true that, in modern times, the sphere of economic actions and relations has become disentangled from other domains of social life.[18] However, once the economic sphere has assumed capitalist features, it cannot keep its (invisible and visible) hands off political institutions and practices, or scientific research, or art, or intimate affairs and family life. For the sake of simplicity, we can for now understand capitalism as an ensemble of processes and practices dominated directly or indirectly by imperatives aimed at maximizing individual economic profits. For some categories of economic actors, this means that there is no limit to what we can get with regard to the material and symbolic means for survival and enhancement of life. For other categories of actors, it means that we have to constantly struggle—against nature, against others—to stay alive. Actors in capitalism can never be content with what they already own; they cannot ever rest. Therefore, they cannot have respect for boundaries, including the ones that differentiate between social spheres.

The capitalist logic does rely on the thrust to occupy, make use of, "colonize" every possible resource available, especially those provided by noncapitalist practices. For example, even if we "know" that modern love, as Luhmann put it, "is only to be motivated by love," and grows only "to the extent that it finds love," capitalist money cannot stay out of it.[19] Erotic emotions, sexual desires, erotic pleasures, are rich sources for profits. In capitalism, says Marx in *Economic and Philosophical Manuscripts of 1844*, money is the "supreme god," for it allows to acquire and possess basically everything, including beauty and political power.[20] Money is what mediates between human life and the means to fulfill life (the means necessary to stay alive and to conduct a meaningful life); as a result, it is also the mediator between every human being and other people—it shapes and "distorts" all types of human (and nonhuman) bonds. It cannot but intrude into relationships between friends and lovers as well. Money has the power to transform "fidelity into infidelity, love into hate, hate into love, virtue into vice, vice into virtue, servant into master, master into servant, idiocy into intelligence, and intelligence into idiocy."[21]

This might sound like an exaggeration. But think of all the ways in which, in our society, it is the possession of money that ensures people have good health, access to good education, free time, opportunities to travel: all necessary or helpful conditions to become "open" to meet, spend time with, and engage in meaningful activities with potential friends and lovers. Our "qualities," dispositions, beliefs, identities, are formed through and thanks to the possibilities and experiences opened up by the power of money, and erotic experiences are necessarily affected by them.

Marx has provided just a few hints and sketches of this. It has been especially the effort of the social theorist Eva Illouz, in the last twenty years, to extensively and systematically debunk the assumption of an alleged separation between the private, intimate sphere of love and the economy or the market. One of Illouz's main arguments is that emotions and emotional relationships are mediated not exactly by money, but by the commodities we can (or cannot) buy. Illouz speaks of two tendencies that take place at the same time: the "romanticization" of commodities, as well as the process of "commodification of romance." Commodities enter and steer the erotic sphere in numerous ways. From the beginning of the twentieth century onward—from the beginning of the Fordist and consumerist phase of capitalism—most commodities have been sold with the promise of fostering, revitalizing, increasing intimacy, closeness, and meaningful interpersonal ties. The range of romanticized commodities is quite broad, from cars to cleaning products, from products of the cultural industry (especially movies) to household gadgets.[22] Luxury commodities in particular seem to be endowed with the magic power to establish or reinforce a bond, to crystallize and heighten romantic attraction. As such, they have played a crucial role in the twentieth-century sexual revolution. Middle- and upper-class lovers do heavily rely on these commodities, and not only in the initial phases of a romantic relationship. There are class differences in the possibilities to have access to and enjoy love bonds, especially in the long run, when everyday interactions cannot be eased and interrupted by the romantic escapades enabled by certain purchases, such as travel, fancy dinners, theater, or movie soirees. The time and the care lovers want to dedicate to each other is a function of one's wealth and privileges in the job market. Leisure time and care time are structured and organized according to consumerist logics.

In her latest work, Illouz concentrates on the dynamics of the current "scopic" phase of capitalism that is grounded on the power of visibility and appearances. Scopic capitalism is dominated by individuals' spasmodic yet constant need to craft and present themselves as desirable, sexy, appealing objects, in all domains of their lives. Traditionally women's—but, increasingly, also men's—attractiveness and romantic potential are represented as dependent on the purchase of a large number of beauty, health, and fashion products. "Scopic capitalism" functions according to regimes of "valuation"—namely, series of processes that fabricate and assign value, both economic and symbolic, to persons and things.[23] Mechanisms of valuation shape and organize every social activity, practice and experience. Sexual and intimate encounters, in particular, have become dependent on forms of valuation that start at perception, especially visual: perceiving a potential sexual or love partner consists already in an implicit, prereflexive, and preconscious evaluation, which cognitively and practically orients actors' behaviors, *including their acts of recognition!* By drawing upon researches in cognitive psychology, Illouz speaks of valuating perceptions that happen within a time frame of milliseconds, rely on scarce information, and tend to operate according to binary judgment (e.g., attractive vs. unattractive). What is more, our objects of valuation are not singular, specific, unique: we do not meet someone new and immediately, unreflexively, nonconsciously perceive their irreducible singularity. Quite the contrary: valuating perceptions happen by following widely shared and deeply rooted standards of desirability and sexiness that tend to privilege the characteristics already valued within a certain social order. Illouz mentions those characteristics that define the conventional beauty standards for *white* female bodies—for example, thinness and blondeness. Digital technologies and social networks reproduce and reinforce the evaluative regimes of scopic capitalism, offering mechanisms that allow us to easily select or reject potential sexual and love partners.

In her career, Illouz has critically examined earlier phases of capitalist societies too. In illustrating the emergence of the images, rituals, and representations of contemporary romanticism (and romantic ideologies) at the beginning of the last century, Illouz identifies in particular a specific form of autonomization of love: she calls it the "seclusion of the couple from the rest of the world."[24] The majority of the advertisements of the period she reviews represent the couple in complete isolation. Such seclusion, however, does not correspond exactly to a retreat from the public sphere into the warmth of family life and domesticity. It signifies rather a "withdrawal from the proceedings, rules, and constraints of the urban industrial world and an entry into the euphoric realm of leisure."[25] Leisure is the realm of consumption. Illouz's point is that *the separation of love from other spheres of social life, in particular from the economy, has a precise economic significance.* The couple's separation from the rest of the world, and the happiness this brings about, is achieved by putting a distance between their union and the ordinary things of the world. This requires a whole set of other things, especially luxury ones, that create a festive, celebratory, magical atmosphere. Such promises are permeated by utopian, genderless, and classless "desires for authenticity, freedom and pure emotions"—desires that, however, cannot be pursued without money, a good job and the inclination to engage in consumptive practices.[26]

This argument problematizes—or, at least, downsizes and relativizes—the autonomization thesis because it shows how an alleged autonomy of the sphere of erotic relationships can become functional for the goals of economic rationality.[27] The same argument had already been introduced by Theodor W. Adorno, one of the most important representatives of the Frankfurt school of critical theory. In his collection of philosophical aphorisms or (quite in line with the Romantic tradition) fragments, *Minima Moralia*, we find some scattered but quite piercing notes on love. In the aphorism "Constanze," for example, Adorno critically discusses the typical modern view of erotic love as a natural force, "pure immediacy of feeling," the "voice of the heart."[28] By assuming this view, we postulate love's "supreme independence" from social dynamics—as in radical versions of the autonomization thesis—which prevents us from seeing how love functions, on the contrary, as a tool of (capitalist) society.[29]

Adorno points at the affinity between the market and such "emotional" conception of love especially as follows: there is a short step, he admonishes, between taking the involuntariness of emotions as a justification for any individual inclination or whim and the justification of egoist interests. Fatally, instead of enjoying a life outside of the market, the lover starts rather to act like a perfect *homo economicus.* Adorno is discussing, in this passage, infidelity: those who betray or leave their partners because they do not 'feel' anything for them anymore, or those who seek individual sexual liberty by collecting a number of dates and one-night stands, behave as perfect economic agents. They treat lovers and (potential) partners as commodities to be evaluated, used, maximized, traded off, and eventually thrown away. Illouz sees the apotheosis of this tendency in the current age of digitalized dating spaces. She notices, not unironically, how the designers of internet dating sites seem to have applied, to the letter, "the diagnosis of doom and gloom by critical theorists, such as Adorno or Horkheimer."[30]

Adorno points out, moreover, how fidelity and monogamy mirror capitalist (and patriarchal) logic as well. They reproduce a need for rationalization that induce lovers to invest in one exclusive relationship, foreclosing other options, in order to maximize the benefits.[31] Fidelity cannot but remain a problematic virtue: it serves the most conservative tendencies that present-day capitalism has not yet overcome, such as the will to keep the anarchy of human emotions under control, but also subordination of women.[32] While we might want to draw an analogy between consumerist behavior and infidelity, it is also true that unfaithful or polyerotic women are still more harshly judged and punished than men pursuing multiple passionate affairs. While certain bodies are envisioned as full and proper subjects (of desire, of hedonistic pursuits), others continue to be apprehended, represented, and treated predominantly as objects, and as private property.[33] So, it seems that neither overwhelming passion nor regulated, committed, exclusive relationships can escape the capitalist rationality. Maybe at the beginning of the capitalist (and bourgeois) age, love was able to withstand the "exchange" model of human relationality, but now it is "completely absorbed" by it: love, Adorno holds forth, "is chilled by the value that the ego places on itself."[34]

Until now, we have seen how money and commodities tend to engulf our loves. Marx, Illouz, and Adorno seem to think that this is a mortal embrace. The capitalist logic infiltrating intimate relationships is, in the end, hindering love and our capacity to love. Individuals are irremediably separated from one another: we think of ourselves as fundamentally independent from one another, we do not care for anyone but ourselves, we can relate to each other only at a cold distance.[35] Consider the aphorism "Ne cherchez plus mon coeur," where Adorno introduces the figure of the lover who, far from indulging in passionate affairs, cannot escape "frigid aloofness."[36] By quoting one of Proust's observations in *Time Regained*, Adorno thinks here mainly of those women who chose not to satisfy their lovers' desire, not to concede themselves to men's passion. Their aim—exquisitely economic—corresponds to the attempt to establish and increase their value. And even those who are uninhibited about sex, Adorno insists, elaborate their (economic) strategies to keep an unloving distance, without allowing any real, pleasurable connection.

At this point, we should spell out more clearly the idea of capitalism that underlies Adorno's and Illouz's considerations. There are, of course, oscillations and discrepancies in their views: Adorno does refer mostly to late and state capitalism, while Illouz analyses different phases, from the emergence of consumerist capitalism to present-day neoliberalism and scopic capitalism. However, we can gather from both authors at least one shared thesis: capitalism requires and molds a particular kind of *subjectivity* that orients, shapes, and conditions individuals' attitudes and actions, individuals' relations with one another and their feelings, affects, and emotions. In sum, the capitalist form of subjectivity requires us to rely only on ourselves and to assume almost entirely individual responsibility for our successes and failures. Individual independence is a core value, against both material and emotional dependence. Other people, including beloved ones, are viewed and treated as instrumental for one's survival, or self-realization. In order to survive and be successful, individuals must craft and present themselves, in every domain of social life (from job to sex markets), in desirable ways, which implies the willingness and the abilities to be or perform as adaptable, resilient, flexible, and mobile. Risks and uncertainty are acknowledged as part of life, but they ought to be constantly be calculated, minimized, or exploited as "productive." Every aspect of individual life, including private and emotional life, becomes a source of value: not only we must produce economic value constantly, but we have also to constantly create, maintain, and increase our personal value, in every dimension of existence.

We can say that capitalism, and the subjectivity it produces and requires, affects love in two senses: first, in the sense that a certain economic logic ends up permeating also our sexual, erotic experiences. In this regard, capitalism is not against love per se; capitalist love, however, seems very distant from the picture of free eros sketched in chapter 2 and in the excursus. Capitalist conditions of existence do not constitute a fertile soil for freedom as (collective) self-transformation to properly flourish. The second sense in which the economic system affects love bonds consists in a more direct impediment: human beings who are not strong in performing the capitalist, neoliberal subjectivity, who are not "up to the game" of scopic capitalism, risk being deemed as not worthy of love, as not-desirable objects of erotic recognition. According to this second sense, our societies might be seen as still accommodating (certain forms of) erotic love, but only for certain categories of people. In Illouz's analysis, it is predominantly women's sexual value, and thus their desirability as partners, that is conditioned and even determined by processes of scopic valuation. Regimes controlling the sexual and emotional markets are largely controlled by and organized to favor male desires, wishes, and purposes. Illouz refers critically to the beauty and fitness industry, which sells a massive amount of products, especially to women, who have to constantly learn what kind of work on themselves is needed in order to make themselves into sexy, attractive, and valuable objects, able to affirm their erotic value.

But this is not the only problem. The novelist Sally Rooney, for example, has brilliantly shown how class distinction might intervene in erotic experiences in ways that cannot even be controlled by sheer monetary power. The male protagonist of her bestselling novel *Normal People*, Connell, the son of a cleaning lady, as well as Felix, a warehouse worker, one of the four main characters in her latest novel, *Beautiful World, Where Are You?*, are both entangled in erotic relationships with high-class women, Marianne and Alice. Rooney is very clever in depicting the subtle, ephemeral, and at the same time cumbrous obstacles that come between lovers of different social classes. Neither Connell nor Felix lack the material means to engage in meaningful activities with their girlfriends, for young couples, in Rooney's world, do largely and consciously avoid the lures of consumerist pleasures. Yet both men are intimidated in front of their chic, academically and intellectually self-assured companions; they feel somewhat inferior, although they cannot put a finger on the source of their discomfort and awkwardness. They sense that their most natural and intuitive habits—how they have been socialized and trained to speak, move, dress; their preferences and tastes—do not and cannot match the habits of their crushes. In some passages of the novels, as an evident result of their feelings of inadequacy, they even come to (temporarily) reject Marianne and Alice.

Capitalist norms and structures are not the only problems for lovers. Sexiness and erotic attractiveness and desirability are determined by other factors as well—for instance, race and gender identities and patterns of identification (which capitalism can then incorporate). In *Black Skin, White Masks*, published in 1952, Frantz Fanon had already denounced how *whiteness* is established as the standard for telling desirable from undesirable persons. Two chapters of the book are explicitly dedicated to intimate and romantic relationships between Black women and *white* men, as well as between Black men and *white* women. Black women, he argues, desire to be romantically involved and married to *white* men more than anything else. He chooses as a paradigmatic example the writer and protagonist of the autobiography *Je suis Martiniquaise*, Mayotte Capécia, who is in love with "a white man to whom she submits in everything. He is her lord. She asks nothing, demands nothing, except a bit of whiteness in her life."[37] At the same time, Black men, in the French European context Fanon was referring to, feel that they do not have any chances with *white* women. Fanon analyses here the character of Jean Veneuse in one of René Maran's novels. Only his *white* friends' validation, their assurance that Jean has "nothing in common with real Negroes," gives him the courage to declare his feelings for a *white* woman.[38]

The romantic market of scopic capitalism is harsh for *white* women, but is even harsher for racialized women, women who belong to discriminated and oppressed racial groups. For example, Black women in the North American context[39] are still more prone to being seen and treated as undesirable and unlovable.[40] Undesirability and unlovability result from a bundle of factors—for instance, hegemonic beauty ideals, which privilege *white* skin or features usually characterizing *white* women, or the widespread tendency to reify Black women bodies as hypersexualized objects.[41] Patricia H. Collins thematizes, moreover, the systematic devaluation of Black women within romantic markets due to the seeming shortage of marriageable African American men. She notes how Black women who compete in these markets tend to make themselves more acceptable and desirable by endorsing traditional gender ideologies. In contexts where men are intimidated and repelled by strong women, submission seems to increase their chances of finding a Black male partner.[42] Expanding and revising Fanon's view, Collins detects a gender power differential between Black women and *white* men: the latter have in fact, in general, more power, since they can expand their dating pool to include also *white* or non-Black women, while Black women are sanctioned by their community if they date non-Black men. Explanations for this double standard is rooted in the history of slavery in the United States. Historically, "good Black women" were those who managed to resist *white* men's assaults and advances; on the contrary, Black men's intercourse with *white* women was a proof of their masculinity and even viewed as tactic of resistance against white male power.[43] Since Black men, as also Fanon notices, tend to find *white* women more attractive, Black women's sexual and emotional lives are characterized by constant, painful rejections.

The recent novel *Luster* by Raven Leilani brilliantly shows the struggles of younger generations of Black women to come to term with such norms and structures of racialized desire. The protagonist of the novel falls for an older, *white*, middle-class man in an open marriage. While battling against a crippling insecurity, she strives to reflect upon the blind spots of her lover. He claims that he wants her to be "herself," but, actually, she senses, he wants her to be "like a leopard" in a city zoo, "waiting to be fed," and certainly "not out in the wild."[44] He desires, namely, a tamed version of the stereotyped sexualized Black body, whom he can care for (and hence exercise power over). She complies with his desire, also out of economic neediness (especially after she has lost her job and her apartment). Finally, she is included in his marriage, develops a complicated but genuine bond with her lover's wife, and moves in with them. However, she fears, with pain and shame, that the real and leading reason for this acceptance is that the couple needs her as a caregiver and confidante for their adopted Black daughter. The beauty of the novel consists in the erotic ambivalences that it manages to convey, without resolving or simplifying them. The protagonist is and feels desired and even loved, in some moments. Her erotic involvement has a transformative effect on her: we see her, in the end, regaining her independence (she gets a new job and a new apartment), but also daring to dedicate herself to the activity that is most meaningful to her—painting. At the same time, she feels, and is, objectified and instrumentalized in deeply problematic ways. Racism, capitalism, and sexism have an effect of love relationships, yet the emotions that are felt both by the man and his wife toward her manage to go partially beyond and deviate from racialized, sexist, capitalist norms and structures.[45]

Also, if we consider friendships, social conditions play a role in blocking certain people from forming erotic attachments with certain other people. The difficulties that African American women face in their sexual lives are intimately connected to the difficulties in their female nonsexual friendships. Friendly bonds between Black and *white* women are inhibited because of deep-seated feelings of rivalry, envy, and resentment. Also friendship between (heterosexual) Black women are conditioned by competition over a restricted pool of eligible partners.[46] Nonsexual friendship between men is overly determined by racial norms as well: consider, for example, Vivaldo and Rufus in James Baldwin's *Another Country*, a novel that offers a compelling picture of the ways in which racialized hierarchies affect not only sexual and romantic but also nonsexual relationships. The context of reference is the New York of the early 1960s, but the structural dynamics depicted by Baldwin are not outdated. Vivaldo, a penniless Italian American writer, is doubtlessly attached to the Black jazz musician Rufus. He senses his pain; he intensely desires to reach out and make him understand that he is not alone, and that he can count on him. Yet Vivaldo is struggling with the expression of his feelings, which he cannot even properly articulate to himself: Is he sexually attracted to Rufus, or just strongly attached to him in a nonsexual way? Rufus, for his part, cannot bring himself to trust a *white* man, not as a friend. The two men do not manage to properly connect and recognize each other, in their singular, particular vulnerability, beyond racial barriers.[47]

Persons who defy dichotomous gender identities, persons who are gender nonconforming, persons who cannot and do not want to identify along either the norms of traditional masculinity or traditional femininity face unspeakable difficulties when looking for and entering into erotic experiences. The recent Spanish film *Mi vacío y yo* (*My Emptiness and I*, 2022), directed by Adrian Silvestre, illustrates the adventures and misadventures of a young trans person, Raphi, who is born in a "male body," identifies as a woman, but resists the idea of undergoing sex reassignment surgery. The film can be seen as a powerful and realistic proof of the thesis, outlined in chapter 2, that erotic relationships play a pivotal role in the journey through which we grasp who we want to be, through which we try (and fail) to become this person. Raphi's friends and lovers see or fail to see her, touch or do not want to touch her, are afraid, puzzled, or mesmerized by who she is trying to do, by who she is and cannot be: for example, almost nobody seems to understand why she does not want to undergo surgery. (And, after a while, she seems to make the decision to actually do it.) The film traces a positive trajectory: Raphi is lucky enough to meet a couple of people who accept her unconditionally and push her to further grow and spread her wings. Such optimism, however, cannot hide the fact that a journey of this sort is extremely more troublesome for queer persons; it has to overcome terrible insults, painful rejections, deep incomprehension, and violence.

Because of capitalist structures, and other social norms, like racist and sexist ones, erotic love seems a quite difficult (sometimes impossible?) undertaking—and for certain categories of people more than for others. Now, the way in which social norms and structures can have such impeding effects on erotic bonds can be explained again on the basis of the dynamic of recognition. In chapter 2, erotic recognition was framed as an apprehension and a confirmation of another human being in their irreducible singularity, and in their particular modalities of being needy, vulnerable. Sensing the other erotically leads to a desire to attend to such neediness and vulnerability, as well as to a desire to be similarly apprehended and confirmed. What is more, recognizing the beloved one as they are right now goes together with a (loving) anticipation of how they can be in the future, how they can be different. Erotic recognition is never only the recognition of a fixed, determined, univocal self. However, such a dynamic of *Anerkennung* has preconditions, which can be described by further, neighboring notions. Prior to coming to erotically recognize someone, we need to "identify" and "acknowledge" them somehow. As Heikki Ikäheimo and Arto Laitinen explain, while the term "identification" refers mostly to the determination of the recognizee's qualities (and to the generic determination of its belonging to a certain "species"), "acknowledgment" refers to the appraisal of the recongizee as valuable and reasonable.[48]

Real-life recognitive acts consist always of an amalgam of these three notions of recognition: identification, acknowledgement and recognition qua *Anerkennung*. Erotic recognition as an experience of freedom, on my account, allows precisely for going beyond or challenging preliminary identifications and for confirming and sustaining the beloved's value, acknowledging it, even if we do not know exactly how to identify the beloved, even if, or *especially when*, they reject the available modes of identification. Moments and acts of identification are not problematic per se and might even help individuals find out *who they really are* in the first place, to achieve an identity that feels right to them, that can be valuable and pleasurable. In the example of the movie *Mi vacío y yo*, it is also the identificatory moment of erotic encounters that leads Raphi to construct, refine, and endorse her sexual identity and her identity more generally. The problem, then, arises when norms and structures bind and fix sexual, emotional, romantic, friendly interactions to patterns of identification and acknowledgment that are problematic, and already established, preventing erotic recognition to unfold—or, better said, when certain preconditions of identification and acknowledgment are so predominant that only few people can hope to have access to the proper dimension of *Anerkennung*. The transformative, forward-looking, individualizing force of recognition, as well as the positive, uplifting functions of identification and acknowledgment, can be blocked and suffocated by the constraints imposed by patterns of identification and acknowledgment shaped by given social orders. We can say that in our societies erotic love is a concrete possibility mostly for persons, for example, whose gender and sexuality can be clearly identified, for persons who can be identified as *white*, who belong to the same or similar economic classes, who respond to certain beauty standards—and who, as such, are deemed worthy as objects of desire and love.

THREE DAMAGES

Social norms and structures that filter into our intimate relationships through patterns of identification and acknowledgments can make very hard or hinder the formation of erotic bonds. But social norms and structures can also make erotic love unfold—alas, in damaged ways, and with damaging consequences. In what follows, I identify three damages of love, three ways in which erotic bonds *can* be formed and de facto unfold, but *unfreely*: *complicit love, mastery love,* and *exploitative love*. In complicit love, identifications and evaluative acknowledgments steer individuals' acts of loving recognition in ways that tie them to given, fixed social norms and structures. In mastery love, social norms and structures build up lovers' selves, positioning them vis-à-vis one another with the consequence of suppressing an agonist multilateral process and thus establishing domination or mastery of one over the other. In this case, empowering, transformative erotic recognition is denied to both parties. In exploitative love, finally, such a relation of domination is played out in ways that do indeed advantage the dominant parts, while draining the vital resources of the subordinated ones. You will note that these three damages form a sort of spiral: a certain compliancy is entailed in both mastery and exploitation, while exploitative love consists in a further development of the dominating relationship of mastery love, one in which, however, the dominant parties do not have to rely on explicit violent means, since they do manage to get an advantage. In all the three modalities, a certain instance of recognition is at place, but is skewed—damaged—and contributes to the overall damaging of our societies.

(Caveat: the three damages are not the only situations in which we can feel trapped and suffer because of our erotic entanglements. Our individual histories, past traumas, and wounds, as well as contingent circumstances, can cause unfreedom and unhappiness in many more ways. The task of a critical theory of love, however, can only be that of reconstructing the damages resulting from social, objective, structural conditions.)[49]

Complicit Love

Complicit love occurs when our need or desire to be loved brings us to assume, accept, and conform to a series of problematic standards and norms. The damage is enabled, crucially, by the same dynamic that allows for successful and flourishing erotic bonds.

When erotically in love, we are particularly vulnerable and experience our vulnerability with excruciating intensity. We do not only attract and elicit recognition; we want the recognitive process to continue, and thus we continuously depend on our lovers' recognition. Now, it might happen that in order to (continue to) enjoy it, we comply with the patterns of identifications and acknowledgements that current social orders predispose. We are thus brought to craft our bodies and characters according to given cultural and social standards to endorse and conform to recognizable, easily accessible and acceptable gender, race, and class identities and to engage in convenient, dignified, respectable practices. We perform such "work on ourselves," first and foremost, in order to be accepted and loved by romantic partners.

Consider the traditional model of modern love-based marriage depicted by Jean-Jacques Rousseau in *Emile*, published in 1762. In such a marriage, both man and woman regards and treats the spouse as an autonomous person whose needs must be met. The wife tries to be a good mother, housekeeper, caregiver, by providing emotional support for her husband. Her love and care is crucial to help him face a harsh public world, to engage in strenuous competition for honor, success, and power. The man, in turn, acknowledges the woman as someone with a mind of her own, as someone who *autonomously* chooses to satisfy her husband's needs and desires. The husband must not only appreciate his wife for being an intelligent, educated, caring, sweet, chaste, humble woman; he must also provide for her financially. The man is (has to be) "active and strong," while the woman is (has to be) "passive and weak," and it is precisely this (natural) difference that puts both of them in the position to satisfy each other other's desires and needs.[50] Both husband and wife, for Rousseau, would be able to sense and see the uniqueness of their beloved spouse and attend to the particularity of their wishes and ways of life; the complementarity of their union would provide fulfillment and happiness to both.

This model of spousal love is based on complementarity, but not on equality. While the married woman cannot hope for and really count on the recognition of anyone outside of her marriage, the married man's most valuable and meaningful source of recognition is the public world. The recognition that he receives from his wife has the main function of sustaining and replenishing his ego, so that he can vigorously and successfully face the challenges of work and politics. On the contrary, the recognition the wife receives from him signifies the world to her; it makes up her (almost) whole identity. The model does not only legitimize a certain institutional arrangement of intimate, sexual relationships, but it also justifies and contributes to perpetrate a social gendered division of labor, in which domestic, care or reproductive work is predominantly on women's shoulders.

The picture is less outdated than it might appear at first glance. In *Why Love Hurts*, Illouz provides a rich phenomenology of the ways in which women do still tend to view their romantic relationships as the most valuable source for recognition, which is not the case for men. In analyzing love relationships between African Americans, moreover, Collins presents a picture that structurally resembles Rousseau's. On the one hand, Collins describes men who need to be recognized in their masculinity, basically as able to protect their spouses; on the other hand, women who look for stable relationships agree to forgo their independence and appear as desperately in need of caring protection. Their aim is also to confirm and defend the public image and reputation of their partners, dispelling the social image of Black men as "sexually violent rapists, as brutes, and as irresponsible boys."[51]

My concern here is not so much with the empirical specificities of present-day gender and racialized inequalities and their effect on love relationships, but, rather, with the formal mechanism of such effects. Note that women, in this model, are neither forced nor coerced into marrying someone they do not like or love, nor to perform as caring, chaste, and humble spouses. They do chose an union of this sort, and they try to comply with the norms it requires, because they are convinced that this option does de facto make them feel happy and accomplished. By complying with the role of good wife, housewife, mother, they can secure for themselves the love of their chosen partner and enjoy the type of recognition they are looking for. In Rousseau's model, individual autonomy is, at least to a certain extent, respected. Insofar as there is complaisance with the given roles, the marriage can run smoothly and provide advantages to the two parties.

To complicate things further, let us consider another case, in which recognition through love brings about not only confirmation of a person's value and social status but also an alleged improvement of this person's value and social status. The case is laid out by Fanon, who imagines, in a sarcastic and bitter tone, the "remarkable" event of a *white* man declaring his love "to the mulatto." The "mulatto" is, then, thanks to and through this declaration, *recognized*, hence *incorporated* into the hegemonic group: she is not a slave anymore, but becomes one of the masters: "She was no longer the woman who wanted to be white; she was white."[52] The loving recognition of a *white* man for a nonwhite woman assumes here the seemingly magical power to transform racial identification, turning the discriminated racial identity into the privileged one and bringing forth desired individual change. Woman realizes her deeper wish and becomes *white*. Similarly, if a *white* woman would love a Black man *as a white* man, he would become "worthy of white love" and thus *white* himself.

In elaborating on his recognition theory, Honneth does notice the intertwinement between *Anerkennung* and those standards, conventions, and

rules constituting and steering intersubjective practices of recognition—
the intertwinement, in other words, of *Anerkennung* and patterns of identification and acknowledgment. He speaks of "internalized," "culturally
specific norms of recognition" that regulate behaviors and actions (and
emotions) toward each other, as well as expectations and duties.[53] He critically mentions patterns of recognition that are "normalizing" insofar as
they maintain and reproduce "restrictive, evaluatively anachronistic
ascription of identity in an unjustified manner."[54] Rousseau's and Fanon's
cases illustrate ascriptions of identities that do not necessarily feel restrictive, anachronistic, or unjustified, though. To be recognized as a good
mother and housewife or as *white* might genuinely feel as life-enhancing,
compensating, uplifting, as the result of one's own efforts of behaving and
performing in the correct manner. Where is the damage to be located,
then, exactly? Can we speak of damage at all, if the love relationship
unfolds without trouble, and if lovers are content, sensing that the partner's love and recognition have de facto improved their life?

The damage consists in the fact, I submit, that a recognitive dynamic of
the sort encourages individuals to comply with certain roles, norms, and
identities that are socially accepted and cherished, *whereas such complicity
ends up blocking both individual deviations, or further developments, and a
critical confrontation with accepted roles, norms, and identities.* Loving
recognition that is premised upon a compliance with the traditional gender binary grants a serene, happy bond insofar as both partners do not
contravene the expectations and requirements of their gender. An interracial relationship that follows Fanon's scenario would work, moreover,
only if the brutal racial hierarchy and devaluation of nonwhite bodies and
persons continues to be accepted. But what happens to the woman who
feels that she is not and does not want to be good enough—as wife, housewife, and mother? Or to the woman who decides to actively disrupt these
roles? What happens when a conflict arises between the new racialized
identity conferred through loving recognition and the old identity? What
happens if the Black person recognized as *white* cannot and does not want
to give up her Blackness?

A comparison with the Cavellian comedy of remarriage *The Philadelphia Story* might help at this point. As Cavell's reading suggests, Tracy is
encouraged by her (former) husband to revise and improve her patterns of
behavior, to turn from a marmoreal, untouchable statue of perfection and

(apparent) moral superiority into a vulnerable, imperfect, sensuous human being. This case differs from the Fanon's examples of Black women and men desiring to improve their "essence," defined by their racial belonging: in Cukor's movie, Tracy's personal change and "improvement" can certainly be envisaged as motivated by the loving and recognitive dynamic, which, however, does not push her to embrace particular given social norms and identities, but, rather, *to find out what works for her individually.* This allows her to break free from the quasi-aristocratic class constraints on her gender (e.g., the imperative to look and act like an unattainable goodness), without surrendering to the power of the raising bourgeoisie (represented by her fiancé, George) or to a bohemians' cliché (represented by Mike, the penniless poet). Tracy's erotic choices gesture toward the possibility of a wider social transformation, while Fanon's examples of Black and *white* women exemplify the function of love in maintaining unjust and oppressive racial structures.

The need to be recognized by our lovers in ways that promote compliance with norms and structures is problematic, because it blocks and prevents further personal transformations, and because it represents a means of strengthening, reproducing, and legitimizing the unjust and oppressive norms and structures predisposed by this order.[55] Bonds of love, based on recognitive dynamics, might feed wishes to comply with given hierarchies, asymmetries, and inequalities. In this first form of damaged love, the harm does not exactly come from punishments and sanctions (as will be later the case). The damage consists, rather, in a *preventive, precautionary freezing* of the possibility for individuals' self-experience and self-knowledge. Individual lovers prioritize the desire to be loved and involved in a loving bond against the desire to really understand who they are and can become, what they really want to realize. Complicit love, then, suppresses the realization of erotic freedom. As a result, chances of broader social transformation are frozen.

Love as (Violent) Mastery

A second type of damage emerges when the conditions under which the agonist dynamic unfolds are not of mutual empowerment but, rather, of subjection, domination, or mastery. The most evident and pervasive objective condition deforming erotic agonism is represented by traditional heterosexual gender normativity. Attempts to deviate from and violate social norms determining heterosexual erotic bonds are in many cases not accepted and tolerated and give rise to violent responses.

The conventional or traditional binary gender order can be defined as the bundle of cognitive and affective norms according to which human beings can be identified either as men or as women. There are many ways to explain what these identifications as man or woman imply and require. I propose to define "woman" as the person who understands herself, and is understood by others, as devoted mainly to others, as someone whose main activities and responsibilities mainly correspond to taking care of another's needs and desires while putting aside her own. One can also say woman is the person who takes over the management of others' dependencies, thus attaching herself mainly to a position of dependence on others. This makes it more difficult for her to struggle to be recognized as independent and thus to exercise power or to gain a power position. On the contrary, "man" is the person who perceives and understands himself, and is perceived and understood by others, as focused mainly on achieving and exercising his own independence and being recognized as independent. Man is the one who stands in a power position and exercises his power in order to satisfy his needs and desires. These exercises thus make his own dependencies less compelling and binding. This sharp distinction between the two gender constructs has one main consequence: it *splits* the bond of interdependence between lovers. The intertwinement of dependence and independence falls through, thus polarizing the side of dependence onto one party (on the woman) and the side of independence onto the other (on the man). The power dynamic between the lovers is hence blocked and cannot unfold as a reciprocal empowerment process but solely as unilateral exercise. The bond becomes domination or mastery of man in relation to woman.[56]

Let's have a closer look at the turning of agonist relations into violent mastery. In erotic bonds, both man and woman can in principle exercise *power to*. However, man's capacity to differentiate and affirm himself as independent and autonomous and to be recognized as such is stronger and more effective than woman's. Man has more and better chances to exercise it. Furthermore, both man and woman have, in principle, *power over* the partner: they both need the other in order to be confirmed and recognized as autonomous and independent and to realize and express themselves. In the dichotomous and polarized organization of gender, however, man's needs, desires, goals, and projects are recognized and approved not merely by woman but by a number of other agents outside of the erotic realm as well (as in complicit love). Not only woman but also a number of other agents aid man in satisfying his needs and desires and in the pursuit of his goals and projects. Such a multilateral, multilevel recognition enjoyed by man curbs woman's power over him. On the contrary, her needs, desires, goals, and projects are structured in such a way that they mostly need his confirmation and approval in order to be satisfied and pursued, thus preferring man's recognition over the recognition of friends, family members, and colleagues. Today, women could in principle rely on many forms of recognition, but they seem to be still inclined, to a large extent, to think and feel that the recognition provided by their beloved men is the most important of all (as dictated by romantic ideologies.) For the same reason, man can affect the partner's decisions, values, lifestyles, more extensively than woman. He is in the position of exercising a more permeating, shaping, and constituting power than woman. The dynamic of power between him and her cannot be reciprocal, and she is not in the position to fully exercise her counterpower against him.

This form of damage does often include the previous one: complicity. Both man and woman recognize each other, but the kind of recognition at play here works asymmetrically, in ways that reproduce and strengthen the dichotomous gender structure of man versus woman. While she recognizes him essentially as an autonomous and independent agent, he recognizes her in ways that tend to suppress or obstruct her autonomy and independence. Man might appreciate, like, support, and adore woman, but his modes of recognition do not lead to her empowerment. Rather, he reinforces her privileging dependence over independence, her attitude to care for others while neglecting herself, her tendencies to self-sacrifice. On the contrary, woman's different recognition activities boost his autonomy and independence, thus reproducing and fostering man's traditional identity. Insofar as erotic bonds that function on the basis of man's mastery over woman are also based on complicity, no violation of and deviation from the traditional gender normativity occur. But what are the consequences if she does not accept but rebels against this situation?

The asymmetry in recognition, grounded in domination, does not and cannot deprive woman of recognition *completely* and therefore does not manage to make her *entirely* heteronomous, subjugated, and dependent. Her margins for power are constituted as the object of ongoing negotiations and more or less open struggle; they can be reduced to a minimum, but not completely drained away. Woman, that is, does always have some chances to exercise counterpower, to find ways to satisfy her needs and desires outside of love relationships (or with other lovers). In Western liberal societies, undoubtedly, these chances have been lately increased. However, the traditional gender order has developed defense mechanisms against deviations and rebellions. These mechanisms can be grouped under the name of *gender violence*: women's attempt to preserve or increase her power, in intimate and love relationships, is curbed and blocked by violent means. Violence perpetrated by men against their partners is exerted in different degrees (insults, various forms of manipulation, epistemic violence, sexual or nonsexual harassment, battering, rape). It is triggered in different circumstances and unleashed and sustained by various psychological motives, and it can be of different types (physical, psychological, or economic). In the context of my critical theory of eros, and with reference to the power-based framework presented in chapter 2, gender violence can be cast as fulfilling a threefold function: first, to contain, repress, and stop woman's *power to*; second, to prevent her from resisting and rebelling against man's *power over*; and, third, to make man's dependence on woman less compelling, thus curbing and neutralizing her *power over*.[57]

In order to grasp the multilayered complexity of violence in intimate bonds, gender and other social categories (e.g., race, class, sexuality) have to be taken into account. The split between dependence and independence, and the degrees and modes of power to cope with dependence and gain or lose independence, might be conditioned, reinforced, and perpetuated by an intersection of different factors.[58] For example, underemployed women of color, or immigrant women who do not speak the institutions' language, are likely to be more dependent on their partners and to have fewer possibilities of rebellion and separation than *white*, middle-class women with paid jobs.

Consider now a complicated case: the stormy love affair between the protagonist Rufus and his girlfriend in the first chapter of James Baldwin's novel *Another Country*. From the first moment they meet, during a vibrant party night in New York, the passion sweeping over the African American jazz musician and Leona, a *white* woman from the South, expresses a clear attempt at domination. From their first brutal sexual intercourse to the following stages in their relationship, Rufus keeps trying to violently establish his mastery over her, notwithstanding—or maybe precisely *because* of—the warm feelings and authentic loving interest growing between them. Rufus's escalating violence toward Leona could be explained as a desperate attempt to affirm his autonomy and independence. In this case, this includes the attempt at dispelling the suspicion that Leona's object of love is not Rufus himself as an unique human being, in his irreplaceable singularity. Rufus seems to unconsciously worry, in fact, that Leona is mainly drawn to him *as* a Black male body.[59] The example highlights an aspect of this type of damage that has been overshadowed so far: trying to secure recognition through dominating and violent means does not simply or always only correspond to the desire to control and influence the partner's life. Man's dominating and violent attitudes and behaviors might be also the expression of a desire for loving apprehension and confirmation of a unique, particular self, beyond certain given identifications, in this case sustained by racialized stereotypes. What the tragic encounter between Rufus and Leona reveals, in my reading, is the *desire* for a type of recognition that allows for a connection between persons that is not reduced to unjust and discriminating racial structures. Alas, the desire cannot be fulfilled, and it turns into disaster. The society in which Rufus and Leona live turns it into devastating mastery. Interestingly, Baldwin draws an explicit parallel between Rufus's violent relation of domination with Leona, and his equally harming relation with his first, male, *white* lover, Eric. Rufus himself acknowledges he had despised Eric "by treating him as a woman," and that he had used against Leona "the very epithets he had used against Eric, and in the very same way, with the same roaring in his head and the same intolerable pressure in his chest."[60] Baldwin depicts Rufus's violence against his *white* lovers as the result and effect of a more generalized racialized violence against Black people, and as the ruinous attempt to cope with it. At the same time, Rufus's acts reveal a fragile masculine identity that feels desperately threatened by others' power and needs to aggressively reaffirm its own power.

The formal and general dynamic of mastery love as a form of damaged eros consists in a split and polarization of the erotic interdependence that obstructs the unfolding of reciprocal, transformative agonism. As a result, the relation of power degenerates into a form of domination that does not tolerate challenges and must be thus defended by violent means. The split is brought about by social structural objective conditions—for instance, the traditional distinction between man and woman, as well as by racialized (or class) structures. It is, however, important to stress that the desire for recognition of one's own special and unique self, and for the joy and empowerment that recognition can bring about, does not always or necessarily vanish in this dynamic. The very core of erotic recognition continues to animate the unfolding of damaged love bonds. A social context can be then criticized not only because it structurally prevents individuals to realize this core, but also because it pushes only particular categories or groups of individuals to pursue such a realization—unsuccessfully, though, and at the devastating expense of everyone involved in the relationship.

Exploitative Love

In mastery love, the dominant lovers prevent their partners from unfolding as independent, autonomous, and powerful, and they achieve that by resorting to violent means. Violence is needed to enforce and reproduce a form of domination that does seem hard (or sometimes even impossible) to maintain. Most of the time, these dominant lovers, by insisting on their mastery, do not achieve recognition, and thus the self-realization, emotional fulfillment, and empowerment they were looking for in the first place, and that they need in order to dispel the fear of their own vulnerability. In the third form of damaged love that I want to take into consideration, dominant lovers become exploiters, thus managing to fulfill their wishes while systematically preventing their partners from doing the same.

Take F. Scott Fitzgerald and his wife, Zelda Sayre, when they are young, beautiful, and crazily in love with each other. (The story I tell about them does not intend to exhaustively and correctly report the real Fitzgeralds; it is just a stylized and simplified example.) She belongs to a respectable and wealthy family and has many suitors. She has a genuine talent for writing, dancing, acting, and enjoying life. Her husband comes from a more modest social and cultural background but indulges in dreams of greatness; he is insecure, latently depressed. Eventually, Scott manages to become a successful novelist by drawing upon, even plagiarizing, Zelda's personal diaries. She initially accepts and is even thrilled by Scott's behavior because she envisages this as a collective success, the public recognition of the Fitzgeralds as a glamorous and influencing couple (an erotic *we*!) Zelda abandons her artistic projects to support and care for her beloved husband, who is very much dependent on her and cannot deal with the prospect of Zelda accepting an offer in Hollywood or somewhere else. She ends up miserable and lonely, while F. Scott Fitzgerald becomes a very famous author. How can something like this happen? How has Zelda become so vulnerable and subordinate to her husband's power, although her gifts, social position, romantic options, and intelligence could have lent her a much brighter destiny?

In the type of damage that I call "exploitative," the dominant lovers instrumentalize the partners' vulnerability to them and, in so doing, take advantage of their power over them. As result of this instrumentalization, the dominant parties manage to enjoy, at least partially, the "benefits" of eroticism (e.g., self-assurance, self-confidence, material advantages) while their partners, as Beauvoir would put it, lose themselves in the "reality" of their exploiters.[61] The whole dynamic, as in previous forms of damaged love, is often not consciously pursued.

The idea of exploitation in sexual, erotic love has been most notably explored by Anna G. Jónasdóttir as a key to understanding the general oppression of women.[62] Jónasdóttir maintains that the domination of woman is precisely the result of a certain structuring of social and sexual relational practices. The bundle of these practices, which Jónasdóttir calls a "sociosexual system," consists of a field of social and political power relations in which sexuality and love are formed and performed, thus creating and transforming human beings. Jónasdóttir argues that, nowadays, neither woman's economic dependence on man nor the unequal gender-based division of labor constitutes the pivotal point in man's persisting capacity to maintain and regenerate their dominance over woman. The crux of the problem lies, rather, on the level of existential sexual needs, which are materially and socially formed and not reducible to economic interests. The focal point of sexual struggles is not work, then, but "human love," and the products of this love—namely, "we ourselves, living women and men with all our needs and all our potentials."[63]

In order to explain the domination of women, Jónasdóttir draws a parallel between the Marxian critique of the labor-capital relation and the relation between love and male power. The parallel puts forward an original concept of exploitation, which constitutes the key to understanding the sociosexual system on its own terms, without reducing it to the gender-based division of labor, or to the logic of capital. Jónasdóttir argues that in heterosexual couples in which both parties are equal professionally and share domestic tasks relatively equally, it is nevertheless quite likely that man manages to appropriate a disproportionally large amount of woman's care and love. Think of Zelda and F. Scott Fitzgerald: she is, at least at the beginning of their relationship, better off than he is; moreover, neither of them engages in any reproductive work.[64] And yet Scott" manages to appropriate Zelda's care and love, to exploit her "love power." Jónasdóttir defines "love power" as the "unique human practice that mediates between the social and the natural" in the social transformative process, as "a sensuous capacity and a specific creative force expressed in relational practices."[65] Love power is the activity that makes (and remakes) human beings, individuates and personifies them, thus creating human agency and bringing about transformation both on the level of the self and of the collectivity.

Exploitation in love, according to Jónasdóttir, amounts to the asymmetrical appropriation or extraction of love power. Man exploits love power when he appropriates the caring and loving powers of woman without properly reciprocating. This leaves her "unable to build up emotional reserves and authoritative social forces" that could in principle be used freely and foster her own self-defined interests, as well as the good of all.[66] As a result, man is put in the position of deciding the conditions of the relationship: in my terms, he is put in a fixed and strong *power over* position.

How, exactly, does man appropriate love power, though? Jónasdóttir argues that our contemporary Western social context has its own specific way of structuring love bonds. In our society, love encompasses two different aspects: "loving care" and "erotic ecstasy." The distinction of these two forms of love is precisely a product of the present system, and it is gender-based. In heterosexual relationships, woman is somehow forced to commit herself to loving care so that man can be able to experience ecstasy.[67] Woman, on the contrary, does not feel entitled to man's care and, consequently, to practice ecstasy on her own terms as a self-directed and self-assured human being. Gender norms bring woman and man to love differently. Woman learns to care for her partners in intense, prodigal, enthusiastic ways, aiming at the satisfaction of the highest possible number of their needs and wishes. As a result, man's self-assurance, life force, and agency are fostered and increased. Man's empowerment, which depends, among other things, on woman's loving attitude, allows him to enjoy erotic ecstasy in ways that do not weaken, mislead, or distract but further enhance his individual capacities, self-esteem, and well-being. Scott is intensely attracted to and fascinated by Zelda, but this admiration does not enable her to thrive. Instead, his love perpetrates Zelda's inclination to neglect her own needs and wishes, to give up her freedom, and to not fully express agency, while exacerbating her dependence on and, hence, vulnerability to Scott. Moreover, as her capacities and agency are impaired, Zelda accepts, and sustains, Scott's *power over*, which allows him to influence and control her, to determine the conditions of their common activities and the rules of their relationship.

Jónasdóttir's view is important, for it introduces and thematizes an important form of damage, overlooked in many other critical studies on gender and love, but it is not exempt from criticisms. To begin with, the parallel that she draws between relations of production, which amount to ownership of material resources, and sociosexual norms is problematic. The economic-materialist vocabulary of extraction, appropriation, and transference in relation to love power does not seem entirely appropriate. Love power, as Jónasdóttir defines it, is a nurturing and caring relation that brings about and fosters each other's agency, that empowers the partners and make them flourish. It is a relational, processual activity, constitutive for social life, and not something material that can be grabbed, seized, and moved around. The same objection does not equally apply to Marx's conception of labor power. In Marx's theory, the appropriation of labor is made possible through the medium of money. Money is in fact the universal equivalent that enables the transformation of labor power into capital, thus exploiting laborers and enriching capitalists. There is nothing such as money, in Jónasdóttir's theory, that can fulfill a similar mediating function. Love power, moreover, does not transform nature and produce things, but transforms and empowers other human beings. From this it follows that if someone, as a result of romantic exploitation, were really in possession of love power, he (or she) would also be brought to exercise it and thus benefit others. But exercising love power means, according to the definition, to nurture and to empower the partner's agency, and not to merely enhance the ego.

It is, then, misleading and confusing to state that someone extracts and appropriates love power from their partners. Rather, exploitation occurs, I suggest, when one lover instrumentalizes the other's vulnerability. In so doing, the exploiter (man) takes advantage of his power over woman—namely, of his capacity to influence her in a certain way. Man's way of loving woman is supported and enabled by woman's attitudes to love not only in caring but also in altruistic, selfless terms, and thus to giving up her own expectations and desire for ecstasy. As a result of such asymmetrical, unequal, impairing love practices, *love power is suffocated, blocked, suppressed*; it cannot unfold as an empowering, transforming, free activity that could enhance and enrich both lovers.

Interestingly, a similar form of damaged love has been picked up by Cavell as well, in the context of his reflections on the genre that he calls the "melodrama of the unknown woman." These films, specular to the comedies of remarriage, depict those relationships between men and women that fail to realize a mutual recognition fostering individual autonomy and empowerment. While Cavell's comedies of remarriage are "struggles for acknowledgment" (his "acknowledgment" and my recognition as *Anerkennung* are very similar), in the melodramas, there is "a struggle against recognition. The woman's struggle is to understand why recognition by the man has not happened or has been denied or has become irrelevant."[68] In the pages dedicated to the movie directed in 1944 by George Cukor, *Gaslight*, Cavell introduces the notion of *vampirism*, which comes very close to exploitative love. In vampirism, says Cavell, the exploiter—a man, in most cases—is "living off the spirit" of the exploited.[69] As a result, woman's energy and life resources are drawn off by the man's need for them, and by his power to demand and acquire them.

What are the structural, objective conditions that allow exploitation to happen? Cavell does not give a systematic answer to the question, referring solely to a generic gender asymmetry. For Jónasdóttir, these conditions correspond, as we have seen, to the "sociosexual relations" that structure and organize both gender identities and gender-differentiated conceptions and practices of love. As in the case of mastery love, however, the damage of exploitation depends on complex constellations of intersecting factors.

The damage of complicity can be viewed as reproducing and strengthening such constellations.

So far, I have formulated the basic contours of three forms of love damage by focusing on the relationship between lovers. But what, then, is the role of erotic *collectivities* in giving rise to and reproducing such damages? In complicit and exploitative love, but not in mastery love, the *we* that the lovers form and that surpasses the mere sum of their individualities does play a relevant role.

In complicit love, the erotic collectivity does endow the lovers with a sort of comforting, protective, soothing cloak that cushions the feelings of unease and discontents they might individually develop, therefore discouraging any attempt to step out of certain roles or even question given problematic patterns and norms. The erotic *we* that fulfills this damaging function is a static and fixed one, one that repels adjustments or variations. In nondamaged cases, the relative stability of the collective—for instance, the shared commitment to certain values and ideals, rituals, routines, narrations—have a positive function. It minimizes uncertainties and doubts, thus relieving anxieties and allowing pleasure and joy; it facilitates the organization of everyday life so that time can be devoted to meaningful shared activities. The damage arises, however, when serene habits become repetitive and mechanic patterns that prevent any transformation or even the thought thereof.

In exploitative love, the collectivity represents as well a powerful construct. The erotic *we* has a crucial role in managing and steering the effects of love power. In the exploitative scenario, some participant in the collectivity—traditionally, the monogamous woman—gives up her interest in being lifted up and "expanded" by the erotic bond and dedicates herself to the partner instead, who does profit from the circumstances. These circumstances are brought about by the identification that the exploited one feel with the whole *we*. As Beauvoir writes, critically: "The supreme happiness of the woman in love is to be recognized by the beloved as part of him; when he says 'we,' she is associated and identified with him, . . . she does not tire of saying—even if it is excessive—this delicious 'we.'"[70] Zelda did not raise objections to her husband appropriating her writings because she was genuinely convinced, for a while, that these were *their* writings as a couple, property and expression of the "Fitzgeralds," conceived as an unitary entity. It did not matter if she, as an individual, was not recognized and celebrated, because the celebration of her husband, or of their couple, was the sole recognition she cherished and (she thought was) needed.

In this case, the existence of a strong, rewarding erotic *we* is a key factor in the reproduction of the damage. Rebelling against such exploitation would mean disrupting the collectivity, a disruption that would be painful *for the exploited* as well. It must be stressed, however, that the *we* enabling and sustaining exploitation is not as powerful as a nondamaged erotic one. By enabling only one lover to flourish, the love power that is released is limited; the potential of the *power with* cannot be fully actualized.

In the case of mastery love, on the contrary, the erotic collectivity is quite weak. Engaging in activities together and sharing emotional states seem difficult and even impossible when one lover tries to subjugate the other and exert violence over them on a regular basis. However, the mere fantasy that a certain kind of *we* might indeed be in place represents a reason for the dominated to stay with her abuser, to not break the abusive bond.

Consider, finally, that the power of the *we* is not only psychological and affective, but also materially, concretely embodied in artifacts, rooms, places—for example, properties collectively owned by lovers; things they create, produce, consume, employ or exchange; dwellings or places they habitually hang out at (favorite movie theaters, restaurants or bars, holiday destinations, hiking routes, parks, beaches, cars, virtual spaces). The spaces inhabited by lovers, and the objects constituting them, entail rituals and habitual practices (e.g., cooking or eating food together, patterns for dates and shared hobbies). Such a material, "external," habitual dimension is a constitutive part of erotic bonds. Spaces and objects that mediate between lovers and friends have a crucial function as glue for the collectivity, as they are impregnated and animated by their emotions, thoughts, memories, narratives. If it happens that lovers and friends are overwhelmed, individually or collectively, by negative emotions, and the temptation to drift apart or even to break the bond arises, bumping into a gift or a souvenir of a happy place, into the written testimony of an important conversation, or just continuing to share the same space, can become powerfully dissuasive. The material objectifications of erotic connections might have the power to transform negative emotions into positive ones, but, if the bond is damaged, this collective, emotional, material power cannot but contribute to the damages.

A brief clarification of the critical-theoretical vocabulary employed in these pages is now due, and especially of the two terms, norms and structures, that I have mainly used to refer to social objective conditions shaping our individual and collective lives. When critically analyzing forms of damaged love, various sets of *norms* should be taken into account. There are *gender* norms—those, for example, that allow to identify human beings as males, females, men, and women, and make it difficult and painful to affirm oneself beyond such established identifications. Gender norms appear usually as tightly interwoven with *sex/sexuality* norms, those that dictate what is "natural," convenient, right or wrong, possible or impossible in terms of sexual desires and activities. Then there are *economic norms*, those that establish the rules of the market(s), distribute or (re)produce wealth, determine definitions and organization of labor. There are, furthermore, *racial norms*, those that divide human beings in groups and determine the relations between them, on the basis of certain bodily characteristics and features (e.g., skin color), history (e.g., the history of slavery in the United States), or place of origin. There are also *body norms*, those that define and establish human beings' health, level of attractiveness and beauty (e.g., "colorism," "fatphobia," "ableism"). Finally (but the list is not exhaustive), there are the norms that properly dictate how to love, those conduce men to seek for and value mostly ecstasy and women loving care (Jónasdóttir), or amatonormativity, mononormativity (Brake), or romantic ideologies.

Norms of the sort are very often bundled together, and entanglements or bundles of norms can be called *social structures*. They can be more or less stable, coherent, and cohesive. For example, *white* women from the middle and upper classes are traditionally expected to have certain sexual desires and to perform in certain ways: they are expected and "forced" to comply with standards of thinness and elegance, to acquire a university education and a paid job, and at the same time to be fully devoted wives and mothers. Yet the privileges that come with such compliance might allow them to challenge, for example, norms that define love relationships as heterosexual and monogamous, with relatively fewer hassles. Non*white*

women—for example, African American women in the United States—
have to face greater penalties if they decide to embark, for instance, on
polyamorous projects.[71] Non*white* women and men need to be moreover
more mindful than *whites* when it comes to body norms, and to norms of
sexuality, in order to be deemed attractive and desirable and to not fall
into subjugating, violent, and exploitative dynamics. At the same time, as
Angela Davis has argued, Black women in the United States are in the
position, in virtue of their history, to powerfully call into questions traditional norms and structures of both class and femininity.[72] These are just
a few scattered and superficial examples: we would certainly need more
detailed, concrete empirical analyses of the exact norms and structures
impeding and affecting, with damaging consequences, our erotic bonds.

A further relevant philosophical point is that social structures form
thick and chaotic entanglements: they can be formally or informally institutionalized, or ratified by political central organs (e.g., the state), but they
can also retain the more flexible, mutable character of social practices.
Norms and structures have, moreover, become, to a large extent, *habitual*.
They work as automatisms that often bypass our conscious and rational
appraisal. We come to identify someone as x, y, z and to acknowledge them
by taking into account what x, y, z mean for us and how we feel about them
in rapid, intuitive, spontaneous, prereflexive, and precritical ways (as
Illouz's analysis of scopic capitalism has shown). Not despite, but precisely
in virtue of, this habits-based character of social norms and structures,
erotic recognition cannot do without them. Habitual norms and structures, moreover, are associated with, fostered, sustained by, and bring
forth certain affects and emotions, which we will analyze in the next chapter. Even when we become aware of them, critical reflection *alone* is not
sufficiently efficacious in putting into question, dismantling, or overcoming problematic habitual structures and norms. The power to criticize and
change pernicious social habits of love cannot be solely the power of rational argumentation and reason.

When illustrating erotic bonds gone bad, I have mostly picked up examples of conventional romantic relationships. Monogamous hetero(sexual)
relationships seem to be the most affected by structural damages. But
complicity with certain norms and structures, mastery, and exploitation

might also be in place in polyerotic constellations. Let's consider again our fictional characters Ariel, Bowie, and Cleo. Bowie, who is erotically strongly bound to both Ariel and Cleo, could manage to extract love power both from Ariel and Cleo, leaving them drained and impoverished, deprived of *power to*.[73] Bowie could also desperately try to affirm their *power over* both Ariel and Cleo, thus curbing the counterpowers of both. For example, Bowie could pressure Ariel and Cleo to accept rules and situations they do not quite like. Ariel, Cleo, and Bowie, could arrive at complying with a series of damaging norms and structures in order to get the recognition they need. In this case, Bowie and Ariel were together for a long time and then decided to open up their bond to include Cleo. Bowie and Ariel might form a "proper" couple, thus enjoying a "couple's privilege," while Cleo counts as a "secondary partner." This hierarchy within the polybond might bring the couple to exert *power over* the person who occupies a weaker and inferior position, with effects of exploitation or mastery.[74] Poly lovers are expected and usually try to engage in intense communicative exercise and "work" on themselves and on their relationships: they have to develop a deep awareness of their wishes and desires, foster the companions' awareness and be sensitive to it, try to put themselves in the others' perspectives, to regularly check with each other to inquiry if they are still on board, to reassess the rules and patterns of their bonds. These commitments are constitutive of their relationship format and choices, which should prevent the risks of slipping into complicity, mastery, or exploitation. Alas, the risks cannot be completely avoided; guarantees for avoiding abuses are given *only to a certain extent*.

In the excursus, I have argued that some distinctions between passionate, sexual, romantic love and friendship—for example, the number of lovers or friends one should have, the role that friendship or romance should have in influencing other aspects of our lives—depend on love norms, or romantic ideologies. It is interesting to notice, however, how social norms and structures shaping and regulating sexual passion and romance are more clearly defined, perversive, and demanding than those of friendship. Friendships seem less formally structured and institutionalized than romantic, sexual love. In an article on Hannah Arendt's conception of friendship, Brian C. J. Singer observes that friends do not have to "relate to each other in terms of their social roles," that they can avoid social rituals; they "appear to dwell in a realm apart, emancipated from all the larger (domestic, economic or political) exigencies, a realm of disencumbered sociability."[75] On the contrary, a complex ensemble of rituals, codes, and rules regulate romantic lovers' feelings and practices, for romantic love, according to current ideologies, is still largely considered as the private pillar of public life.

A dazzling illustration of this has been conveyed by the controversial novel *A Little Life* published in 2015 by Hanya Yanagihara. The novel's four protagonists are best friends and have different sexualities and racial origins and come from very different social classes: Jude is an orphan of ambiguous ethnicity, with heavy baggage of unspeakable childhood abuse. Willem is *white*, also an orphan, from a working-class background, who has managed to become a very popular actor. Malcom is a wealthy biracial architect. JB is a painter of Haitian origins who reaches a level of discreet success and then falls prey to a crystal meth addiction. Their friendship is depicted as a complex and agitated (agonist!) social space. As a result of reciprocal influence and persuasion, and the sharing of conspicuous portions of their lives, as well as of the distances that inevitably open up between them, the four men undergo significant transformations. It is interesting, for our purposes, that the complex relationships between the characters are neither profoundly nor essentially shaped by racial, sexual, or class factors. Structural conditions are continuously thematized, but there is something in these bonds of friendship that decidedly escapes the societal power exerted by norms and structures. In a philosophically striking passage, Willem reflects on the meaning of friendship while calling into question the lack of recognition that this form of bond suffers from (in that context, he had just been scolded by Malcom's father for having broken up with his girlfriend and appearing to prefer a "Peter Pan" lifestyle). He remarks that friendship, a relationship that binds people "day after day," not by "sex or physical attraction or money or children or property, but only the *shared agreement* to keep going," is a relationship that "*could never be codified.*" And yet friends are able to witness each other's most significant phases (miseries, long bouts of boredom, occasional triumph), and "feeling honored" by such privilege.[76]

The lack of codification, "normalization," and institutionalization is ambivalent. On the one hand, friendship, in our societies, is not properly recognized. As we will see in chapter 5, not only individual human beings, but also collectivities and types of collectivity, can be or fail to be identified, acknowledged, and recognized. Friends cannot rely on laws and official rules to protect them, nor on scripts and patterns of behavior and emotionality that would considerably help in moments of uncertainty, pain, and loss. The COVID-19 pandemic has dramatically and concretely revealed how these erotic bonds do not count as meaningful, valuable relationships: in many countries, lockdowns, closed borders, and quarantine measures could officially prevent one from visiting a friend, but not a spouse, romantic partner, or family member. As Sophie K. Rosa has written in her book *Radical Intimacy*, "The idea that a monogamous marriage or romantic partnership is more valuable than other kinds of relationships ... was reinforced during the Covid pandemic and successive lockdowns. . . . If you were not in this kind of relationship—whether 'single' or in another kind of committed relationship—government policy signalled that your intimate life was immaterial."[77]

On the other hand, these relationships seem to grant individuals more erotic freedom and to spare them the damages described in previous sections. It seems that the pure and democratic character of modern intimacy, advocated by Giddens, is better realized in relationships that elude the grip of institutionalization and legalization. Social pressures, attempts at disciplining interpersonal and private spaces, and normalization mechanisms seem to weigh heavier on those persons who choose forms of eroticism that are recognized as the central pillar of public life. I do not want to say that lovers in "traditional" ménages (e.g., monogamous, dyadic, legally recognized) cannot experience true eroticism. These erotic bonds are however more vulnerable to damages. What is more, as shown earlier, norms and structures can impede bonds between friends. Finally, I do not want to say that friends cannot hurt each other, or exercise power in ill-fated ways—they do, all the time. Gender, class, race norms could, in principle, bring people to become violent or exploitative toward the most vulnerable of their friends. It appears, however, that the detection of complicity, violent mastery, and exploitation is more difficult and more rare when looking at friendship.

Chapter Four

AVALANCHE

Erotic Emotions and Affects

Being in love and making love can bring us to experience and realize freedom. Love is desirable when it is free. Alas, the social conditions that shape and inform erotic bonds can hinder freedom. Our erotic relationships might make us complicit with problematic norms and structures and subject us to the mastery and exploitation of our partners. The same erotic bond can, at one point, open up freedom and, at another, turn itself into a set of damaging chains. Sometimes, it is hard to tell freedom from unfreedom: the same relationship can make us learn something crucial about ourselves and what we want to do and become, and yet it can subject us to exploitative or violent power. How can we enjoy free love in a sexist, racist, capitalist, amatonormative, ableist, fatphobic world? One possible answer is: we cannot. Under oppressive conditions, free love is no more than an ideal, a fantasy, a delusion. First we have to liberate ourselves from larger oppressive, violent, exploitative habits, norms, and structures, and then we can learn how to love better. In order to make better love, we should make a better world first.

In this chapter and in the following one, I explore a more ambitious conceptual possibility. I try to show how erotic bonds can (partially) realize freedom even under damaging social conditions. What is more, eros could also provide some conceptual and practical tools that foster emancipation or liberation from social damages. Under conditions of unfreedom or oppression, eros could emerge as a sort of power that enables us to better see through our damaging situations and to come up with some transformative solutions. To explore this possibility, we need first of all to think of erotic love as not fully determined by the damaging social conditions reconstructed in chapter 3. Staying with the critique of the autonomization thesis, we cannot claim a sphere of love as separated or differentiated from the rest of the world. *From within* our social situation, though, love can operate as a movement or gesture of resistance or opposition, an internal fracture from which critical and transformative energies can be unleashed. Even the gloomy pessimist Theodor Adorno does not view love as *only* the result and the mirror of economic, capitalist structures. Love is not completely reduced to them: "If love in society is to represent a better one, it cannot do so as a peaceful enclave, but only by conscious opposition."[1] The "if" is crucial here. Love, according to Adorno, might entail, exemplify, *introduce us* to resources for imagining and realizing a better, free society—free, at least partially and in some respects, from those damages that affect our love lives, and our lives more generally. If love is to provide a glimpse into alternative modalities of human interconnectedness, it cannot do so as an autonomous sphere, but only if we grasp its rootedness in society's troubles while at the same time conceptualizing the *nonidentity*, to use Adorno's favorite expression, between love and social conditions.

The present chapter explores eros's exceedance, or its *extravagancy*—from the Latin verb *extravagari*, its capacity to wander (*vagari*) outside (*extra*), to diverge form, trespass, transgress given orders of habits, norms, and structures. To this purpose, I propose we look more closely at the emotions and affects involved in erotic experiences, and, more precisely, at the experiences of being overwhelmed by emotions and affects. An erotic *avalanche*, to quote Leonard Cohen's song from his album *Songs of Love and Hate*, can become a crucial step in the unfolding of erotic freedom—or at least this is the hypothesis to work with in the following pages. An investigation of the *emotionality and affectivity of reasons of love* should help us understand a certain disentanglement of erotic love from damaging conditions (even though we cannot claim that love relationships have become autonomous from them).

Until now, eros has been cast as a social relationship or bond, not as a specific emotion or affect, or as a bundle of emotions or affects. But what lovers and friends do—recognizing, seducing, caring for each other, resisting power, separating from and getting close, becoming one collective entity—elicits complex and interrelated emotions and affects, both positive and negative, both individual and collective. How should we conceptualize them, in order to understand how they contribute to the nonidentity between love and society? Martha Nussbaum's famous account of emotions is a promising starting point, as it is centered on the value of vulnerability and dependence, and introduces us to the positive social and political importance of love. Nussbaum's theory presents, however, three shortcomings, quite widespread in contemporary theories of emotions, that should be corrected: cognitivism, social constructionism, and individualism. First, I jointly discuss and problematize social constructionism and cognitivism by drawing attention to the epistemic and practical value inherent in phases of confusion or nonknowing. Second, I introduce what I would like to call a "critical naturalist" approach to erotic love. Lastly, I expand Nussbaum's individual-based account by sketching out a view of collective or shared erotic affectivity that displays noncognitivist as well as critical naturalist features.

EMOTIONS THAT (ARE NOT) MATTER

Emotions occupy a central place in our lives because they make us realize how finite, limited, unmistakably vulnerable we are—in other words, they make us painfully or joyfully aware of our dependence on other human beings, and on our material and external circumstances. If received, taken up, and interrogated in the right ways, emotions hold a crucial educational role. Far from being irrational, or expressive of the irrational parts of our natures, emotions can constitute valuable tools for better understanding who we are and want to be, both in our individual, private existences and as members of social and political communities.[2] In her important volume *Upheavals of Thought,* Nussbaum outlines the epistemological and educational value of emotions, casting them as "forms of evaluative judgment that ascribe to certain things and persons outside a person's own control great importance for the person's own flourishing."[3] Emotions, in her view, are "eudaemonistic": they have fundamentally to do with eudaemonia, happiness, with the possibility and reality of our self-realization and self-empowerment. Emotions allow us to see things in their import and significance for us. Therefore, there is no need to put them under our rational control, or, even worse, to dominate, repress, or remove them. We should learn to receive emotions in our existences as indications of or even as sources of knowledge with regard to our deepest weaknesses as well as our most cherished goods. It is not our emotional side that makes us vulnerable. We are vulnerable simply because we are human, and emotions can help us to better understand and cope with the specific determinations and potentialities opened up by our vulnerability.

Erotic love seems to constitute the eudaemonistic emotion par excellence. Nussbaum views love as an emotion that, like grief or compassion, can "expand the boundaries of the self, picturing the self as constituted in part by strong attachments to independent things and persons."[4] Lovers see their object of love as "radiant"; they tend to enhance its value, stretching themselves toward it. Thanks to and through their emotion, the value and "radiance" of lovers themselves are also augmented. Love's expansiveness is, however, risky. Consider the paradigmatic, negative example of Marcel, the protagonist of Marcel Proust's *La Recherche* (*In Search of Lost Time*): his love for Albertine, an unknown and ungoverned other, brings him to give in to defenselessness, dependence, and passivity; love, for him, turns into misery, pain, anger, and a desire for revenge. Nussbaum depicts Marcel's possessive, jealous love for Albertine, in which he rebids and reproduces his infantile obsession for his mother, in ways reminiscent of the damage of violent mastery love presented in chapter 3: "The only way Marcel can prevent unbearable pain to himself is to inflict pain on Albertine."[5] But we can do better, admonishes Nussbaum; we should learn how to make better love. A higher and more truly fulfilling love accepts separateness and distance, renounces control and manipulation. It teaches us that we human beings are needy, passive, not self-sufficient, not self-sovereign. By accepting this human condition in ourselves, in those we love, and in our fellow human beings more generally, we can gain a "powerful guidance toward social justice, the basis for a politics that addresses the needs of other groups and nations."[6] In the wake of a series of authors (especially Walt Whitman and James Joyce), Nussbaum thinks of eros as a sensual, even sexual force, conveyed by art (poetry, novels, music) that pushes us to imagine and realize a democratic society, one in which all bodies are cherished and respected, visualized, and treated as equal, able to flourish and to be free. This is not a perfect society, but one in which (ongoing) failures to realize such ideals are welcome with tolerance, irony, and as chances to further learning. The right lovers' "discourses" would educate us, not only with respect to our individual private sentimental lives but also to our public lives.

Nussbaum is aware that the desirability of a democratic form of life, revealed to us through erotic experiences, requires a deep transformation of society's moral and sexual norms. But how do we transform these norms? From Nussbaum's discussion of Whitman, we get a sense of how passionate erotic desire would entail this power. In Whitman, it is the *force of the body* that somehow imposes itself on us and makes us realize that the forms in which we have organized our intimate lives, and our lives more generally, are deeply flawed and need to be revised, precisely in order to let this desire freely flow. Nussbaum seems to regard this thesis positively, although she does not expound on it. She prefers, in *Upheavals of Thought* and in other texts, to defend a *cognitivist* view about emotions, a view whose critical and political force does not hinge on the body but on the intellect. Emotions' intelligence cannot but be embodied, and yet, according to Nussbaum, it is not the bodily component that does the evaluative and, hence, the critical and transformative work. Such a cognitivist account is paired with another view, according to which emotions are *socially constructed*. Both views do clash, I believe, with the Whitmanian sociocritical endorsement of erotic passion and can be proven as not entirely satisfying if we want to further pursue the interests of a critical theory of love (and of a critical theory of society mediated through an inquiry into love). In what follows, I first introduce social constructionism and the critical-theoretical question it leaves open, and then cognitivism as a response to it. After having criticized cognitivism in the next section, I propose an alternative to social constructionism.

Social constructionism about emotions is a metaphysical position according to which emotional states and processes are constituted and shaped not only by individual history but also by social norms and practices. Emotions vary from culture to culture and from society to society, according to "rules for emotional expression and behaviour," "normative judgments," and various taxonomies.[7] One powerful conceptual device to cast and explain socially constructed emotions is Arlie R. Hochschild's account of "feeling rule" in her classic book, *The Managed Heart*. Feeling rules are orders of norms and structures (and habits) that govern emotional exchanges in all domains of social life, both private and public. They set criteria for the proper duration, strength, time, and placement of emotions in particular social situations and roles, such as between spouses, friends, parents and children, superiors and subordinates, or customers and salespersons. Feeling rules guide and govern emotions by establishing senses of entitlement and of obligation, as well as standards to assess and judge their appropriateness in determinate circumstances and contexts or to sanction their inappropriateness. In trying to comply with feeling rules, to cope with but also, in some cases, to rewrite and adjust them, social agents need to do "emotion work." This type of work is unavoidable also in those emotional bonds that appear as the most disentangled and separated from any work-related (instrumental, economic-like) logic, especially in bonds between "parents and children, husbands and wives, lovers and best friends."[8] The stronger and the more deep seated is the conviction that bonds of love were free from emotion work, the trickier and more troublesome this work becomes: when hidden and not acknowledged, emotion work can in fact contribute to tie individuals even more deeply to problematic habits, norms, and rules.

Hochschild brings up the example of sexual jealousy, an emotion that, according to a powerful feeling rule, is taken as an important sign of true, authentic love. Such rule can evidently become problematic: for instance, in the context of the damage of mastery love, as I have illustrated it, jealousy does often count as a justification for dominating, even violent acts. A man's jealousy is interpreted as necessarily deriving from his strong passion for his woman, a passion that she, in turn, is convinced to desire for herself and to reciprocate. Such acceptance of jealousy presupposes and strengthens the problematic conviction according to which the woman is (to be treated as) a sort of private property. The relationship of mastery acquires legitimation, in the eyes both of the woman and of others, as an inevitable manifestation of intense passionate love. Cleverly, Hochschild notes that the foreclosure of jealousy can become part of a feeling rule too. Sexual openness, the refusal of feeling jealous or hurt when sharing a partner, can also come to dictate one's personal emotional experiences in certain countercultures. In polyamorous communities, for example, lovers who feel jealous can be mocked, harshly judged as weak or possessive, and even punished: as a result, they might arrive at repressing such emotion. In the case of sexual jealousy as well as in the case of repression of jealousy, the origin of conflicts and pains is "profoundly social, for it is through social institutions that a basic view of sexual access is elaborated and a moral code promoted."[9]

If we recall the other two forms of damaged love that I presented in chapter 3, further examples of feeling rules contributing to the establishment and reinforcement of unfree love bonds come to mind. Alignment with predominant feeling rules is a central mechanism in the maintenance of complicit love. For instance, women who do actually not assign great importance to certain forms of romantic love might experience intense and debilitating pangs of guilt, with the effect of curbing their independence. Moreover, in exploitative love, feeling rules might induce the exploited lovers to rejoice in the successes and positive experiences of the exploiters, cultivating the conviction that these joys, who de facto favor only their partners, are collectively shared.

For Nussbaum, the possibility of changing problematic social conditions, and thus to realize democratic ideals, is explainable precisely on the basis of the social constructionist position. The ways in which we have learned how to love, the socially constructed rules and norms that shape and orient what we feel and do when involved in intimate relationships, are not completely under our control, but are nevertheless the result of human activities. Since *we* have *made* these rules, we can also change them, by mobilizing "more intelligent human activity."[10] But how does such mobilization occur? What does inspire and move it? Hochschild maintains that tensions and conflicts between different rules, equally influential and normative in a determinate context, can and do indeed occur. Sometimes, a feeling rule is perceived as ambivalent and unclear in itself; it can be misunderstood, especially by "outsiders" or newcomers. Moments of vagueness and uncertainty, when the grip of established feeling rules weakens, can open up spaces for transformations. However, Hochschild does not articulate this point very clearly, while Nussbaum decides to follow another path.

THE POWER OF AFFECTIVE CONFUSION

Emotions can contribute to shape an ethical, social and political context, insofar as they contribute to answer important questions like: How should I live? What is worth caring about? These and similar questions have both individual and collective, political import. Love makes us vulnerable, and when we apprehend our vulnerability we are pushed to reflect about what kind of love, if any, we want to pursue, as well as about our ethical and political values and goals. Nussbaum seems to believe that emotions (of love), even if constructed in problematic, damaged, and damaging ways, do constitutively entail a rational, cognitive kernel that can always be activated and reactivated. This fundamental kernel can give rise to processes of self-reflection, self-criticism, and change: "If we recognize the element of evaluation in the emotions, we also see that they can themselves be evaluated—and in some ways altered, if they fail to survive criticism."[11]

Nussbaum justifies this hope on the basis of a cognitivist view about emotions. Emotions can become self-reflective and self-critical, and maybe even lead us to revise and change harmful feeling rules, insofar as they are, fundamentally, judgments, which involve beliefs and signal values on the basis of reasons. Every component in an emotion contributes to the evaluative process and constitutes an evaluative act. Indeed, Nussbaum calls emotions "upheavals of thought": they are *thoughts*, cognitive processes that *might* then also involve arousals, bodily sensations and feelings, and experiences of "being shaken up or in ferment."[12] The bodily component, however, is in itself not revealing of the emotion's meaning and relevance. For instance, a mere feeling of agitation, accompanied by an accelerated heart rate and high blood pressure, does not tell anything about the emotion and what the emotion is about: it might be anger, or anxiety, or grief. Causes might be various. Moreover, I can experience the same emotion (say, anger), with or without the same sensations (accelerated heart rate). A particular bodily state can be associated with different emotions, and the same emotions can come with different bodily states in different persons. Thus, we need to discriminate, and only a cognitive process can achieve that: for Nussbaum, the emotion corresponds exactly to the cognitive process.

Cognitivism has been criticized on many fronts. To begin with, reducing emotions to evaluations or judgments—namely, to an assent to states of affaires—does both excessively stretch the meaning of cognition and thin out its the emotional complexity. An emotion (e.g., fear) can be triggered by stimuli that "emoters" (persons feeling certain emotions) are unaware of: we can become perfectly aware that we are scared and afraid, without knowing the reasons that have brought it forth—without, that is, being able to formulate a proper evaluation of the situation.[13] In other words, there occur emotions that do not presuppose any of the neocortical capacities associated with a more restricted but more precise notion of judgment (e.g., language mastery, consciousness, concept possession, practical reasoning).[14] This does not mean that emotions are irrational; they do entail a form of knowledge, which is, however, different from an intellectualist, rational one, and, as such, precious.

Another objection against cognitivism takes issue with the disregard for the body that cognitivism cannot hide. As theorists of the "extended mind hypothesis" have argued, "cognition is structurally embodied in the sense that it is subsumed by neural, bodily, and environmental processes (including other embodied agents). . . . Environmental resources play a necessary, constitutive role in cognition."[15] Emotions are simultaneously bodily and cognitive-evaluative, not in the sense of being made up of separate but coexisting bodily and cognitive-evaluative constituents, but, rather, in the sense that they convey meaning and personal significance *as* bodily meaning and significance. For Nussbaum, emotions are embodied and embedded in a larger material and social context; the cognitive element, however, "dominates" the noncognitive elements (that are anyway not considered as part of the emotion). In other words, she sees the bodily components as random. Critics of cognitivism, on the contrary, see them as necessary to understand what an emotion is and how it works. To put it simply: our accelerated heart rate and higher blood pressure should be taken more seriously, as in themselves revealing and as constitutive of meanings, in order to properly understand our emotional situation.

Theorists of "affect studies" have introduced a distinction that might be quite useful in this context: the distinction between *affects* and *emotions*. Affects are not singular instances located in one body; they arise in the encounter between bodies that exercise power over one another, that are simultaneously both active and passive in such exercises. Affects remain largely obscure to us and cannot be controlled. Emotions, by contrast, arise when agents become aware of and concretize affective relations. Christian von Scheve and Jan Slaby define emotions as "affective *upheavals* in experience that are directed at events or objects in the world and that often prompt us to act in specific ways vis-à-vis these events or objects."[16] Emotions signify "consolidated and categorically circumscribed sequences of affective world-relatedness," whereas affects refer to non- or preintentional, non- or prereflexive, and non- or precognitive dynamics.[17] Emotions are always about something (objects, situations) and sorted into culturally established and linguistically labeled categories or prototypes (e.g., fear, anger, happiness, grief, envy, pride, shame, guilt). They realize and conceptualize affects; they clarify, order, and define the messy, chaotic, indistinct, non- or preintentional, non- or presubjective or transindividual, non- or preconscious, non- or pre-discursive affective dimension. Helpfully, Scheve and Slaby note that the term "emotion" stems from the Latin *emovere*, "to move out" or "agitate." Emotions move to action, but such power stems more precisely from the magma of the affective dimension. (On the contrary, Nussbaum argues that emotions are helpful only to understand something in the world, not necessarily to push us to do something about it.) Sometimes, these are actions with transformative effects, on ourselves and our surroundings, coming to the fore when affects manage to take up enough space. The power to break with normatively prescribed and learned ways of relating to the world, to transgress and to overcome them, is in fact the power of "wild and ecstatic" and extravagant affects that wander beyond, escape, and exceed hegemonic, established codes, discourses, and apparatuses.[18]

Deborah Gould, a renowned theorist of social movements who has worked predominantly on AIDS activism, delivers one of the most insightful accounts of affects in this sense. She argues that social and political transformations brought forward by social movements cannot be fully understood if one does not take seriously into consideration the affective side of emotions—namely, their non- or precognitive, non- or preconscious, non- or prelinguistic, bodily, visceral aspects. Affects are somehow registered, but lie outside individuals' conscious awareness; they are inchoate, not coherent; they do not have a fixed object or aim and cannot be articulated as such. Emotions, for their part, manage to seize, circumscribe, and express *something* of the affective energy that freely floats. Emotions capture and make sense of affects according to the norms and structures of the social order. Affects remain always, however, somewhat uncontainable, *extravagant*. Affects and emotions belong together; very often they cannot be analytically separated. Yet the fact that they cannot be reduced to one another, that they are non*identical* with each other, accounts for their unbridled potential, which might lead into numerous directions, including an emancipative unsettling of the conventionalized, fixed emotional orders and feeling rules. Sometimes affects can signal that "something is awry, that things could be and perhaps should be different"; they can "inspire challenges to the social order."[19] Affects are nonrational, but they are not necessarily against reason. They can even contribute to a better reasoning, one conducive to desirable social and political outcomes.

In the context of erotic love, *sexual impulses* could be interpreted precisely as such somatic, indefinite, non- or preconscious affects, which nevertheless (might) have a critical and liberating potential. This has been suggested, for example, by Jonathan Lear in his philosophical interpretation of Sigmund Freud's psychoanalytical theory and work. Lear, in the wake of Freud, thinks that sexual desires are revealing of what we are as human beings, and that they entail the potential for a happier, *less oppressive*, more free organization of the individual psychic life and of social life more generally. Social emancipation or liberation succeeds if we were able to discover, acknowledge, and embrace our desires, even the darkest and most uncanny. Quite in line with the cognitivist view, Lear claims that affects become conscious and intelligible, and that we can acquire the concept with which an affect can be understood, inside of the affective process: "The conceptualization of an emotion is a development within the emotion itself."[20] Eros, for Lear, can be conceived of as this development: the psychological cognitive process by which we become conscious of and take responsibility for our instinctual wishes and drives. Contrary to Nussbaum, however, this is not just a matter of judgment, not an intellectual and cognitive operation, but a broader existential and practical activity in which our instinctual life becomes part of what we are: "It is through love that the boundaries of the soul are redrawn so that what were once taken to be *forces of nature* I now recognize as my own active mind."[21] Eros corresponds to a process through which we recognize how the mind is active in the body, stepping from "a position in which one's life is lived by meanings over which one has little understanding or control to a position in which one actively lives according to meanings one has helped to shape."[22] We will see, though, that "nature" is not simply something we can leave behind and overcome.

Erotic affects are not just sexual. Nonsexual friendships can display similar dynamics, as, for instance, Simone de Beauvoir's account of her relationship with classmate Zaza demonstrates. Curiously, Beauvoir's account of friendship is less cognitivist and activity-based than Lear's account of sex. As we have seen in the excursus, the young Simone was not able to conceive of her connection to her favorite classmate as something more important and excruciating than a "simple" friendship. According to the feeling rules of her social and cultural context, Zaza was just a "best friend," and a best friend is someone one is expected, according to romantic ideologies, to love less than a romantic lover, a parent, or a child. One day, however, she suddenly and unexpectedly feels that she is actually experiencing things differently, and that other categories have to be formulated:

> One afternoon I was taking my things off in the cloakroom at school when Zaza came up to me. . . . radiant with happiness, I told myself: "That's what was wrong; I needed Zaza!" So total had been my ignorance of the workings of the heart that I hadn't thought of telling myself: "I miss her." I needed her presence to realize how much I needed her. This was a *blinding revelation. All at once, conventions, routines, and the careful categorizing of emotions were swept away* and I was *overwhelmed by a flood of feeling* that *had no place in any code.* I allowed myself to be uplifted by that wave of joy which went on mounting inside me, as violent and fresh as a waterfalling cataract, as naked, beautiful, and bare as a granite cliff.[23]

This encounter with Zaza shows, in a sort of irrational manner (it is a revelation that *blinds*!) that theirs is a relationship that does not comply with given "conventions, routines," that breaks with established categorizations of "emotions" and does not find "place in any code." The overwhelming affects of joy and happiness allow Simone to come to a new understanding of herself—in particular, to grasp that the melancholy that she had been feeling was not caused by school boredom, but by the absence of her friend.

When receptive to affects, we are exposed to and feel some "things" we cannot exactly identify, that we cannot immediately translate conceptually, into precise and determinate emotions. This could be our personal cognitive flaw, as we do not know ourselves well enough, as we are largely unaware of our desires, of their meaning and intentionality. But phases of conceptual and rational failure could also be revealing of a friction, tension, or conflict between the usual emotional order and what might promise to develop into alternative modalities of interpersonal relationships and social norms and structures that we *do not know yet*. In the example from *Memoirs of a Dutiful Daughter*, the absent friend is not immediately identified as the "cause" of Simone's intense affects, affects which in turn are not conceptualized as love, because of the prevailing amatonormative feeling rules. Remember also the two male characters of James Baldwin's *Another Country* we encountered in chapter 3: Vivaldo cannot know what his emotions for Rufus or for Eric exactly amount to or might develop into: his interiorized, nonconscious aversion to homosexuality blocks this knowledge. At the same time, he senses the negative emotions his Black girlfriend Ida addresses to him (frustration, sadness, hopelessness), but he does not know where they come from, and he cannot explain them. Baldwin does masterfully show that this is not simply Vivaldo's cognitive fault: Vivaldo is not a racist, and yet he is not able to go into the depth of the damages inflicted by racism, since racial structures and norms are so ingrained in the social fabric that they become invisible, escaping individuals' capacities for critical assessment.

The incapacity or impossibility of articulating our emotions is not to be taken as the final word, though, and emotional cognitive performances, as Nussbaum teaches us, are key. We must, however, recognize that evaluations and judgments, including and maybe especially critical and transformative ones, can be set in motion and boosted *precisely by non- or precognitive dynamics*. Fumbling around in the dark, "getting lost" in our emotional experiences, not being able to appraise them, could work as a drive to revise the coordinates according to which we are used to experience and make sense of our emotions.

Note that an argument of the sort is exquisitely Romantic. The Romantics do not set reason aside, as commonsensical and trivial (ideological!) takes would have it, but see reason as nourished by intuitions and imaginative processes that cannot be entirely explained. According to Wordsworth's declaration of poetics in the 1800 preface to his *Lyrical Ballads*, the foundational text in the British Romantic tradition, creative and learning processes are animated by an affective state, a "state of excitement," that brings to combine and associate "feelings and ideas."[24] Schlegel, moreover, cherishes what he calls "Romantic confusion," which explicitly arises in the sexual bliss of unconventional love as well as in poetic production and bears the potential for changing given values and creating new ones.[25] Another British Romantic poet, John Keats, praises the ability that he calls "Negative Capability," to linger on moments of "uncertainties,

Mysteries, doubts, without any irritable reaching after fact and reason."[26] Keats's passage can be read as an invitation to give up on the desire and ambition to understand what is happening to us immediately and fully, which would only bring us to rely on and thus to confirm and strengthen given conceptual, rational cultural and social coordinates. Accepting a cognitive weakness could open up the possibility of grasping things differently and thus of questioning and changing such coordinates. But disruptive, rebellious, nonaligned affective experiences do not have to and cannot be completely absorbed into consciousness, made completely intelligible, and expressed verbally in order to effectively contribute to processes of practical problematization and social change.[27]

The praise of confusion could furthermore represent a corrective for what Katherine Angel, in *Tomorrow Sex Will Be Good Again*, regards as the imperative of self-knowledge in sexual matters: it is especially women, she observes critically, who are pressured to know exactly what they want and pursue. Women must clarify their desires in order to protect themselves from the risks of becoming targets of sexual violence (or other forms of violence against women): this kind of knowledge is their responsibility— or so the ideology goes. At the same time, women who are sexually and emotionally self-aware and empowered are still largely viewed as unruly, dangerous, and thus in need of being put "in their place." They must be punished because too knowledgeable. In the view proposed here, erotic (self-)knowledge and education are not a moral or pragmatic imperative, a kind of (emotional or hermeneutic) labor that women ought to do, but, rather, a desirable collective possibility.[28] What is more, confusion and ignorance are deemed as acceptable and have to be respected—also, but not only, because they can lead to proper critical and transformative inquiries into our practices of love and sex.

CRITICAL NATURALIST AFFECTS

The "negative" capacity to stay with the trouble—for a while!—requires another capacity (or virtue), which has to do with passivity and receptivity.[29] While lingering on uncertainties and confusion we do not (have to) act: in these moments, we rather wait to see what the affects are going to do with us and disclose. A certain kind of passivity had been already introduced as a central part of the dynamic of recognition. We can recognize our lovers and friends in loving ways only by accepting to be exposed to their powers, as well as by accepting that they are exposed to our power. Being outside ourselves, letting ourselves being passively led, can be scary, and highly problematic, especially from the perspective of a critical theory of love. We can find ourselves led by the damaging conditions presented in the previous chapter; we can be passive toward such habits, norms and structures. But passivity (and confusion) might have another function. As the critical theorist Herbert Marcuse emphatically but poignantly put it, "The faculty to be 'receptive,' 'passive,' is a precondition of freedom: it is the ability to see things in their own right, to experience the joy enclosed in them, the erotic energy of nature."[30] How? And what has nature to do with it? What nature are we talking about?

We have already seen the argument that our passivity in the face of exercises of power can be not only compatible with but also conducive to freedom, provided that counterpower exercises and resistance are intersubjectively allowed and fostered. Let's now further develop this argument on a more metaphysical terrain, one that offers an alternative to the social constructionist position (and to Jenkins's functionalism mentioned in chapter 1). Another author who has cherished the critical value of (some sort of) negative capability—namely, Theodor W. Adorno, can help us in this respect. Particularly fruitful is his critique of Kant's notion of freedom as autonomy.[31] What allows us to be free, on Kant's account, is, for Adorno, at the same time what oppresses us, what makes us obedient to and complaisant with given norms and social imperatives.[32] Acting freely corresponds to a form of action that must rely on the subject's identity with themselves. The subject affirms such self-identity when acting in ways that conform to the norms they have given to themselves: "The subjects are free, after the Kantian model, in so far as they are aware of and identical with themselves." And yet, at the same time, "they are unfree in such identity in so far as they are subjected to, and will perpetuate, its compulsion."[33] Actions of this sort, moreover, must be self-conscious: the subject must be aware of what they are doing and why. But what happens when the subject does not want to, or does not feel they can, follow their own norms anymore? What happens with more or less intentional deviations from the self-identity model? Would discrepancy, nonidentity, simply amount to unfreedom, or would it gesture towards a "larger" form of freedom?

Self-identity, in Adorno's critique, requires separation from the materi-
ality, the body, inclinations—hence, from nature and subjective natural
features. But a disembodied, abstract, artificial subjectivity, in its striving
for freedom, cannot but end up in a sort of inwardly turned Weberian iron
cage, forcing us to compulsively repeat the same moral and social patterns
over and over again. If not embodied, the freedom of self-identity reverts
to unfreedom. There is then a possibility of liberation from unfree Kantian autonomy, which lies in and is triggered and pushed precisely by what
Adorno calls an "addendum," *a somatic, impulsive moment*. The emergence and manifestation of the addendum signifies that the subject is not
and cannot be, after all, identical with themselves. A subject that tries to
be free, and that simultaneously tries not to fall prey to its dialectics, is a
subject that acts in unpredictable ways, does not know exactly what to do,
loses and abandons themselves. The addendum is not the other of reason
and agency, is not completely irrational. It is neither what simply unifies
the two sides: activity and passivity, reason and nonreason, impulses and
drives on the one hand and cognition or deliberation on the other. The
two poles remain deeply connected, yet there is a *dramatic tension* between
them, one is never reducible to the other. Action, including and especially
emancipatory and transformative praxis, needs "*something physical which
consciousness does not exhaust*, something conveyed to reason and quali-
tatively different from it."[34]

Hegel knew that, in order to be free together with others, we cannot just
suppress, forget, dominate nature, or cultivate the illusion we can separate
ourselves from it. We have to find and realize ourselves in nature, in a
world we have not made up by ourselves. We have to find and build up our
homes both with other human beings and within nature. Freedom is not
only about respecting duties, but also about the enjoyment and well-being
that can be found in our ethical and natural life. Impulses, affections, natural elements are not to be repressed or expelled, but incorporated: they
can work as motivation for ethical action and even allow it.

Adorno's idea of the addendum, however, is not satisfied with that and
troubles things further. The Adornian perspective does not limit itself to
reconciling normativity, rationality, or nature. The reconciliation remains
one goal that is striven after, a desirable state, always threatened by the
possibility of disruption. Without tensions and disruptions, moreover,

conciliation cannot occur (on this, Hegel would have agreed). The dramatic friction, or even conflict, between what is given, the impulses and affects we undergo, and what we as free subjects endorse and decide to do, cannot be definitely and completely eliminated. Human subjects, as Adorno writes, "are unfree as diffuse, nonidentical nature; and yet, as that nature they are free because their *overpowering impulse*—the subject's nonidentity with itself is nothing else—will also rid them of identity's coercive character."[35] Impulses, affects, according to the Adornian perspective that I am suggesting, cannot just be completely molded into habits, accommodated and tamed into rational and normative moral and social orders. Impulses continue to signal and express that the subject, even a collective one, is more than it is, that it is and can be(come) different from what it is: "The basis of the aporia is that truth beyond compulsory identity would not be the downright otherness of that compulsion; rather, it would be *conveyed by the* compulsion."[36] I take "compulsion" here to mean being subjected to, passive toward, the force that certain affects, impulses, and bodily imperatives have on us.

Passivity and naturalness, then, make us unfree, but are not the opposite of freedom. Freedom does entail those moments in which we let go of ourselves and our usual, solidified, unsatisfactory complicities with given norms and rules, forget and lose ourselves in ways that reveal the nonidentity with what we are and with the ways the social context wants us to be and to feel. The power or force of our affects can become a factor in the process of freedom. Of course, there is no guarantee that the somatic element will be effective in producing long-lasting, desirable changes. It represents, however, a crucial possibility. We become free (also) by letting ourselves be driven by certain chemical, neuronal, physiological processes, by listening to the pleasures and displeasures of the senses, by passively receiving others' attention, recognition, touch, impulses, and inspirations, by being affected by others' power.[37]

In the previous quote, Simone de Beauvoir makes the experience of grasping that her friendship for Zaza is in fact a form of love and has to be cast as love. The metaphors she deploys to convey such a moment of learning have intense naturalist connotations: the joy comes in a "wave," like a "waterfalling cataract," "a granite cliff." This *naturalist* understanding of eros and of erotic freedom, modeled in the wake of Adorno's idea of the somatic moment as one with a critical and transformative potential, contrasts with a widespread position in the contemporary panorama of emotion theory—namely, what I have already referred to as "social constructionism." For example, in a flaming critique of the self-help psychology literature ("pop therapy") and praxis, Hochschild takes issue with the advice or imperative to get in touch with one own's true, spontaneous, "natural" feelings.[38] In the deluded attempt to recover our authentic, irregulated, "unmanaged" emotions, to gain access to "a *natural preserve* of feeling," a place imagined as "forever wild," we submit, in fact, even more deeply to the management operated by certain feeling rules (e.g., those that attach value to spontaneity, "wildness," irrational upheavals).[39] Adorno, actually, shares exactly the same suspicion: in a passage of his *Notes to Literature* dedicated to Proust, he notes that bourgeois and capitalist (and romantic, in my terms) ideologies have made love into something completely natural, allegedly irrelated and exterior to the immanent economic logics of our society, into something that cannot in any way intervene in these logics with critical and transformative purpose. A critique of this naturalist *ideology* requires that we consciously and actively take up the emotional situation in which we have found ourselves in, and make something with and out of it, including, possibly, "insubordination to society's command."[40] To this aim, receiving, and interrogating, the natural determinations of our bodies, relations, and collectivities are key.

A *critical naturalist view* of eros, animated by the interests of a critical and transformative view of society, does deny the dualism that sharply separates constructed emotions from alleged pure and "untouched" ones.[41] Such dualism presupposes, in fact, a rather poor and reductive set of conceptions of nature. Social constructionists, like Nussbaum, think of nature as "innate equipment" deprived of transformative force; as a bundle of fixed, immutable habits; or as things that "cannot be otherwise" or should not be otherwise.[42] To be sure, Nussbaum does not uphold a strong version of constructionism.[43] For her, not everything that happens with regard to (erotic) love is socially constructed, and she admits that there are some inevitable constraints that biology imposes on individuals and groups of individuals. However, she fears that arguing for some naturalness of sex, love, and desire would end up reproducing and immunizing social norms and cultural formations against critique and change: what we take as "natural," in these domains, is actually "often best explained not by biology but by the depth of social conditioning in the life of every human being."[44]

The critical naturalist position I am developing here refutes to view nature, and our natural determinations, only as duress and limitation. Natural processes can also unfold as enabling forces.[45] The nature of love is not an ontological realm cut off from social practices, but rather a kind of open-ended, troubling process that cannot be reduced to and completely tamed by rules, norms, and structures. The reference to nature does not want to pick out raw physiological, neurological, biological facts "untouched" by social, historical, and cultural interventions. Even the most immediate and spontaneous physiological reactions (heartbeat, giddiness, sweating, or the chemical brain reactions that mobilize serotonin, dopamine, adrenaline, oxytocin) cannot be grasped as isolate phenomena, but must be framed within a bigger and more complex picture. This picture entails bundles of constraints, as well as transactions between different elements in our psyches, bodies, lives. Nature is not only made by laws, but also by the processes through which these laws come to the fore and mutate. Nature is both stable and unstable, repetitive of the same and emergent of newness. Rejecting the social constructionist position with regard to love means to account for the perturbations, disturbances, frictions, and ruptures that arise in the liminal passage between norms, structures, and rules of love and what exceeds them.

Freud's conception of the sexual drive can be described as such a liminal figure. In an often quoted passage, Freud defines the drive as "the psychic representative of an endosomatic, continuously flowing source of stimulation. . . . The concept of drive is thus one of those *lying on the frontier between the mental and the physical*."[46] On this frontier, dualisms such as those between society and nature, or reason and irrationality, are called into question, thus opening up a space of disruption and transformation—or, better, citing Teresa de Lauretis, "a dis-place . . . a nonhomogeneous, heterotopic space of passage, of transit and transformation 'between the mental and the somatic.' "[47]

In his work on Freud, Marcuse frames eros as a positive and powerful force in processes of sociopolitical critique and transformation, and he does it in naturalist terms. To begin with, Marcuse's critical naturalism presents a version of the "naturalization as normalization" argument, also shared by Nussbaum: the argument discloses how the historical processes of human civilization have come to appear as "natural," biological ones.[48] For example, he criticizes the image of the "woman as mother" (i.e., the idea that the highest accomplishment and self-realization for a woman is becoming a mother, and that it is the woman who can function as a "naturally" better caregiver) as repressive, as it "transforms a biological fact into an ethical and cultural value."[49] For Marcuse, there is not direct, immediate access to sexual instincts, nor to instinctual, purely natural pleasures. Some mediatization is always required; pleasure can only be experienced as socially and historically framed and given meaning to. More harshly than Freud, Marcuse deems the processes of civilizations as processes of repression and domination: of men over other men and women, of human beings over their internal and external nature. But oppressive forms of mediation that Marcuse calls "surplus-repression," operating on the basis of a "performance principle"—for instance the "monogamous-patriarchal family," or the capitalist "hierarchical division of labour"—are not necessary.[50]

The relation between eros and society is twofold: first, the organization of sexuality is *functional to* the organization of a society based on the performance principle, especially in the sphere of (waged) work, but also more generally. For instance, only a small amount of time per day can be dedicated to (sexual) pleasures. Most hours are employed in nonerotic activities. If not serving any economic purpose, sexual explorations and experiments must be reduced to a minimum. Second, there is an *analogy* between the two spheres: the same regimentation and alienation that is characteristic of capitalist labor spreads into free time as well. In the realm of sexuality, the performance principle operates especially by suppressing particular senses (like taste and smell) and by excluding and condemning all those acts and behaviors that do not aim at procreation. Also, principles of "centralization" and "unification" dominate erotic practices. The Freudian original "polymorphously perverse" sexuality has to be repressed or channeled, the various objects of the partial instincts have to converge into one sole libidinal object: the genitals of a person of the opposite sex. Similarly to the activities in the work sphere, that must be aimed at the production of commodities, all sexual activities must be aimed at the goals of stability, security, and reproduction. What is more, the principle of monogamy dictates that all pleasures and desires must have one single partner as addressee. If some of the repressions Marcuse criticizes have faded away or disappeared in the post–sexual revolution era, some still persist. In general, in a phrase that does significantly anticipate one of

Illouz's main theses, Marcuse remarks that "sexual relations themselves have become much more closely assimilated with social relations" in general, especially economic ones, and "sexual liberty is harmonized with profitable conformity."[51]

Although Marcuse does not want to point to instincts that are not molded and shaped by historical development, he still seems to presuppose a sort of unrepressed, diffuse *libidinal energy*. This is a force that appears as free from the reality principle of performance and, as such, can work as the motor behind society's "progress to a higher stage of freedom."[52] Marcuse depicts eros as one of the most powerful critical resources against a capitalist and patriarchal society based on the monogamous couple and bourgeois family and led by the performance principle. When such a libidinal energy rebels against the surplus-repression, the conflict assumes a sometimes violent, dangerous connotation. As a result, eros is experienced by individuals, and by society, as a threat to civilization, is perceived as a destructive force. But, Marcuse argues, a "threat" is registered only against the background of a repressive form of civilization, of capitalist and patriarchal domination. The emancipation enabled by eros would amount to harmonic conciliation between nature and society: in a free society, nature would be taken "not as an object of domination and exploitation but as a 'garden' which can grow while making human beings grow."[53] The "life-enhancing, sensuous, aesthetic qualities inherent in nature" would enable men's fulfilment in association with others—and thus the creation of a different, emancipated society.[54]

In a society that is not yet free, eros can work to have a specific social and political impact. The libidinal energy can spread to invest all bodily parts, nonsexual social relations, and all spheres of social life, including (and especially) work. The performance principle, and the related imperative of productivity, would then be replaced by the principle of enjoyment, by the idea of a free development of everyone's needs and faculties: "The erotic aim of sustaining the entire body as a subject-object of pleasure calls for the continual refinement of the organism, the intensification of its receptivity, the growth of its sensuousness."[55] In order to realize this aim, a modification of the socionatural environment and of political institutions is required: objective, social, and political habits and norms that would put *everyone* in the condition to deeply enjoy their sexual, intimate, family, and work lives must be established. Certainly, pleasure and enjoyment do not signify immediate satisfaction of every individual's wish; some constraints and limitations would be necessary. These, however, should be collectively and freely chosen and put into place.[56]

A cautionary note to conclude the section: Marcuse's view does appear as somehow too sanguine and unilateral with regard to the nature of eros and of the freedom of love. Love bonds have, remember, an ambivalent, troubling character. Even when damage-free, love experiences cannot guarantee positive outcomes on the individual level: self-realization might not happen in the end, and pain and suffering might not lead to meaningful transformation. A similar hesitation is advisable on a social and political level too: not every manifestation of erotic power can always be considered as an emancipatory force. Sometimes, certain erotic affects bring to dissolution, disruption, and chaos that cannot be redeemed in light of progress toward social freedom. The critical naturalist approach shows how erotic love has the potential for sensing damages of various sorts, also in societies that should have realized (to a certain degree) Marcuse's conception of freedom. But the potential does not always come to fruition. Note that this caution signifies as well a relativization of Nussbaum's central thesis about the eudaemonic character of emotions in general and of erotic love in particular: sometimes, love bonds put us in the condition to better understand what matters for us, and even how the world should change in order to allow our flourishing. But the journey to achieve such understanding is long and troublesome, and it often does not lead anywhere.

SHARED AFFECTIVITY

Nussbaum's influential theory has been discussed because her social constructionist position and her cognitivism, which are correlated, fall short of the goals of a critical theory. But there is a third shortcoming. For Nussbaum, the individual is the only subject capable of evaluations through emotional involvement. In her work more explicitly dedicated to political emotions, Nussbaum reconstructs in detail how individuals belonging to the same sociopolitical context (e.g., citizens) can feel similar emotions (e.g., pride) toward the same object (e.g., one own's country).[57] The "subject" of the emotion remains, however, individual. She does not explain how exactly supra- or transindividual entities come to share emotions or to jointly feel a similar or the "same" emotion. She talks approvingly of Whitman's connection between a *"perception of common bodily* humanity and vulnerability" with "the genesis of a highly critical and morally aggressive sympathy."[58] She does not explain, however, how to think of the "bodily," sensuous emotions felt by that exceptionally extended collective subject that is humanity in general. Sharing emotions, especially on affective and bodily terms, on this level of abstraction and generality, does indeed seem unthinkable.

But what about the much smaller erotic *we*? We have already seen in previous chapters how lovers and friends can enter and linger in certain emotional, affective states that transcend individualistic and particular ones. But how do bodies and the natural components of affects come to inhabit and traverse such a collective dimension? Krebs claims that in shared emotions of love the cognitivist (or intentional) part must be thought together with nonintentional and bodily parts, like feelings and sensations.[59] It is not clear, however, what role, exactly, is played by the body in her own dialogical collective account.

In chapter 2, I argued that mutual recognition represents one central condition for giving rise to forms of joint or shared action and emotions. In that context, I predominantly relied upon Gilbert's perspective. Her account, however, puts an excessive emphasis on disembodied normativity and disregards the affective side of emotional experiences that, I contend, is paramount in conceiving of their critical and transformative potential. Gilbert suggests that specific feeling or sensations—for example, an anxious or excited heartbeat, pangs of remorse, or stings of jealousy—are not essential aspects of emotions but only their frequent concomitants.[60] On this, she is perfectly in line with Nussbaum. For Gilbert, what characterizes a genuine collective emotion is a joint commitment. The general form of her account is the following: the members of a group have a certain emotion only if they are jointly committed to have this emotion as a body. As many have noticed, however, joint commitment cannot account for how genuine emotions with physiological and behavioral changes can arise, how actions are generated, and what its proper affective phenomenology looks like.[61] Moreover, the normative idea of an emotional joint commitment risks conflating collective emotions with feeling rules: it remains unclear whether collective emotions in the sense proposed by Gilbert can truly emerge against the background of emotional orders that shape individuals and groups in what they are allowed and ought to feel, or display as a feeling. How to distinguish a commitment that autonomously and genuinely emerge in the group and from the group, and what the group (and each of its members) is pressured to feel as a result of given emotional rules?

A strongly articulated position that seems more helpful as a basis for conceiving of collective erotic emotions is provided, I believe, by Mikko Salmela and Michiru Nagatsu: for them, shared emotions, viewed as motivations and even justifications for joint actions, must be understood by simultaneously taking into account a normative-cognitive *and* an affective perspective. Human beings share an emotion, in their view, if they "experience an emotion of the same type" that has a similar evaluative content and a similar affective experience and are aware of that.[62] When a group of people experience a collective emotion, it means they have some shared concern that brings them to appraise some object similarly. The concern refers to desires, goals, norms, or values. It does not always involve a commitment; when it does, the shared emotion has the potential to become politically relevant.

Salmela and Nagatsu more precisely distinguish between three different modes of collective "sharedness," which depend on different levels of intensity: weak, moderate, and strong. In the weakest modality, people share a concern if they have overlapping private concerns. Concerns can then be shared in a somewhat stronger sense when individuals are privately committed to some concern and believe that the others in the group have the same concern. Each member of the group comes to have concerns because they believe that the others have them; this belief is either a reason or a cause, or both, for adopting the same concern. Finally, the strongest mode of collectivity is grounded in the collective commitment of the group members, and in their mutual belief that they share the concern to which they have collectively committed themselves. Collective commitments provide reasons to think, want, feel, and act accordingly. Collective emotions, and the underlying shared concerns, push and motivate individuals to join their forces in planning joint actions; joint intentions are formed in the process.

The account of Salmela and Nagatsu indeed seems useful with regard to the aim of explaining critical and transformative effects of emotions. We can easily imagine concerns with social and political content. A group of people can develop concerns about the forms of oppressions affecting the social context in which they live: for example, concerns for some sexist, racist, and/or neoliberal practices that are affecting their community. Collective emotions stimulated by concerns are capable of initiating collectively intentional joint action spontaneously, without prior deliberation. Conversely, joint actions generate further concerns for the group, or enable further articulation, specification, or revision of the previous concerns.

The normative dimension (commitment) is central here, but Salmela and Nagatsu insist that their approach does not exclude but, rather, aims at including bodily affectivity. Group members are able to feel similar bodily sensations and to affect and stimulate one another so that a sort of affective synchronization arises. The group does not share the emotion, and act accordingly, *as if* it were a collective body (Gilbert); the collectivity of the body is not a fiction. But how to conceive of shared affectivity more precisely? Somatic sensations and impulses seem to amount to highly individualized experiences, rooted in the singular body more profoundly than normative and "mental" or cognitive entities like concerns, commitments, or desires. Paradigmatically: the pain I feel in my body cannot be shared by anyone else. To employ Leonard Cohen's powerful (and maybe brutal) image in his song "Avalanche," I cannot "wear" my lover's "flesh." The categories we employ for describing collective actions fall short of experiences in which groups are collectively affected and overwhelmed on a bodily level. And yet the uncontrollable, unpredictable, perturbing, even ecstatic dimension of affects seems to come out even more intensively and distinctively when shared among multiple bodies. Is it possible to conceptualize collective affectivity?

Some resources can be found, as Salmela also acknowledges, in Émile Durkheim's *The Elementary Forms of Religious Life*, especially in its (few) passages on collective rituals that have recently been widely discussed in the literature on shared emotions and their role in social movements.[63] Durkheim describes the rituals that put society members "far outside the ordinary conditions of life," and "above and beyond ordinary morality" as paramount for society's livelihood and "health."[64] Collective rituals—like dances and feasts—unleash emotional and affective energies that often have the effect of disrupting and questioning old, encrusted normative patterns, those responsible for the degeneration or damaging of social life, and at the same time generating new ones. When individuals gather together, writes Durkheim,

> a sort of electricity is generated from their closeness and quickly launches them to an extraordinary height of exaltation. Every emotion expressed resonates without interference in consciousnesses that are wide open to external impressions, each one echoing to others. The initial impulse is thereby amplified each time it is echoed, like an *avalanche* that grows as it goes along. . . . The effervescence often becomes so intense that it leads to outlandish behavior; the passions unleashed are so torrential that nothing can hold them.[65]

Durkheim's idea of a "collective effervescence" captures something important about affective collective dimension that brings and holds bodies together *in exceptional moments*. As a result of such shared affects, we happen to feel "possessed and led on by some sort of external power" that make us think and act differently than we normally do. By expressing our feelings in "shouts, movements, and bearing," we have become new beings, "transported into a special world" entirely different from the usual one. We are transformed. Events of this sort intensify and transmute the emotions originally felt individually and collectively and sometimes bring new emotions to the fore. Explicitly, Durkheim maintains that the transformations undergone by individuals during these moments of exhilarations and effervescence have as a consequence the transformation also of their "surroundings."[66] A society, argues Durkheim, cannot create and re-create itself without these moments, in which and through which new ideals (ideas about how a society should be organized) emerge immanently, from within the social (and natural) body itself. Social norms and structures are, according to Durkheim, created not only but also, importantly, on the basis of emotional and affective upheavals. The continuation and reproduction requires, for Durkheim, transformation: if a society does not from time to time change its normative orders, it is not social *life* anymore. It freezes, becomes mechanized and repetitive, and ultimately unable to continue to reproduce itself.

Randall Collins has developed this part of Durkheim's work with the aim of grasping the role of political and social events or other nonreligious gatherings for transformative social reproduction in our contemporary societies. He insists especially on the "emotional energy" developed by and within the "interaction rituals" of social movements. A social movement becomes a proper force of change, in his view, insofar as it creates a "focus of attention" and makes its participants feel stronger, more capable, and hopeful. Sometimes, the transformations taking place within the collectivity of social movements "spill over and become outwardly directed," thus constituting and changing the focus of attention of the whole society.[67] In interaction rituals, "human bodies assemble closely enough so that they can perceive the micro-signals they are giving off in their voices, bodily gestures, and facial expressions."[68] Moreover, they focus their attention upon the same object, become mutually aware of it, and thus share an emotion. If these conditions occur to a sufficient degree, they build up a Durkheimian collective effervescence, "the rhythmic entrainment of all participants into a mood that *feels stronger than any of them individually*, and carries them along as if under a force from outside."[69] As a result, there emerge solidarity, the creation of common identities and symbols expressing them, and emotional energy, defined as a longer-lasting feeling that individuals sense on group level and that gives them confidence, enthusiasm, and initiative.

In Collin's view, the sexual encounter does count as paradigmatic example of interaction rituals.[70] As result of sexual rituals, claims Collins, solidarity arises in the form of love: the participants in the ritual come to be bound by love. A certain body or certain bodily standards come to be regarded as sexually desirable, and emotional energy appears as long-term sexual drive. In Western modern societies, sexual interaction rituals—and not just heterosexual ones—have become more and more important in the lives of an increasing number of people, and thus an object of public interest and discussion: as a result, they have had societal impact. Society has become, says Collins, more eroticized, as, for instance, the emergence and progressive legitimization of gay and queer scenes demonstrate. But how and to which extent is this transformative? And transformative of what? The possibility to share affectivity in bodily, preintentional, prenormative terms, according to the critical naturalist perspective sketched out earlier in this previous chapter, has been suggested by Durkheim and Collins. However, one might raise the suspicion that Durkheim's and Collins's perspectives fail to fully capture the effective working of shared affectivity for social and political change. As Salmela points out, some of the functions that collective effervescence are supposed to perform are in fact *preconditions* for the collective rituals to occur.[71] Preconditions include concerns, intentions, and goals that group members or participants in ritual practices already share and must share in order to give in to experiences of collective effervescence. In other words: certain values and norms must be already there and are not created anew as results of the rituals. Therefore, it is unclear how these collective affects can de facto give rise to new values and norms and not just reinforce the participants' commitment to already given ones.

Things get even trickier when it comes to the critical and transformative potential of eros. In a short essay, the Romantic poet Percy Bysshe Shelley depicts love as a "powerful attraction" that connects human bodies, awakening the same mental and emotional processes in different human beings belonging to a (small) community. When we are in love and feel together, suggests Shelley, we sense that the others' "nerves" vibrate to our own, that their eyes' beams "kindle at once and mix and melt into our own," and that lips can talk to each other only if "quivering and burning with the heart's best blood."[72] Lovers remain different, "dissimilar"; they do not really "melt" in a simple union, but give rise to an erotic *we* that cannot be solely framed in terms of commitments or concerns.[73] Nerves and eyes that vibrate together, lips speaking to each other only when feeling similarly sensations, are evocative of a naturalist shared affectivity. Importantly, Shelley remarks here that the community of love does not separate the lovers from the world, but connects them to natural and cosmic entities as well.

How? And to which consequences? Isn't the erotic collectivity way too small and private for really soliciting and initiating a proper social and political upheaval? We can imagine, although a proper philosophical explanation is still lacking, that large groups of people—like those taking the streets and gathering at rallies, demonstrations, and assemblies, as part of more or less spontaneous and organized social movements—can share emotions and generate ecstatic episodes of affectivity that have the consequence to produce some disruption in the normative fabric of our social reality, and even some lasting change.[74] But what about groups of two, three, four, who come together without any aim, besides the pleasure and delight of enjoying each other's presence, or the urgency "dictated" by pure erotic motives?

I try to elaborate an answer to this question in the next chapter, but for the moment let me recap the arguments laid out so far. First of all, to be clear, the fact that erotic emotions/affects have to be thought of beyond the individual-based conception does not mean, contrary to Krebs's view, that love is *in itself solely* a shared emotion or affect, and that one cannot "love" alone.[75] Erotic bonds, as we have seen, consist of a complex bundle of dynamics and processes, that can be accounted for from four different and interrelated perspectives or levels:

(i) The perspective of the individual lovers, and their individual affects and emotions; it is from this point of view, by the way, that one can account for unrequited love (I might desire to form an erotic bond with another person, who, however, does not really desire the same);

(ii) The level of intersubjective relationships between lovers, which are power relationships, grounded in the intertwinement between dependence and independence that can degenerate into damages (relations of mastery, violence, or exploitation);

(iii) The perspective of the collective, of the erotic *we*, that comprehends the following levels: (a) what lovers *do* together (more or less intentionally) that brings them to jointly feel certain things, to enter and be part of emotional states that overcome individual ones. What lovers "feel" together might be then of the following two types: (b) affective experiences that overwhelm them, that they cannot grasp, control, or name, and that sometimes can manifest themselves in antagonism with given feeling rules (intertwined with norms and structures), creating dramas and opening up possibilities. Think, for instance, of two lovers who, after sexual intercourse, sense that they have strangely reached a peculiar blissful state, nothing they have ever known before, not simply pleasure or happiness, but a more profound kind of joy, whose nature they cannot however exactly grasp. Similarly, think of two friends who, after a whole night together, do confusedly feel an unusual exhilaration and sense of empowerment, as if they had made a discovery; they have the impression they are going to see things radically differently, even though they do not know yet exactly why (I will concretize these scenes on the basis of examples from novels and films in the next chapter);

(c) collective emotions, which concretize and articulate in propositional and even conceptual form the affective dimensions, and that might even consist in evaluation of how things are now, *as well as how things could be or become.*
(iv) The level of the objective social conditions (habits, norms, structures, feeling rules) that shape and mold, albeit not completely, what lovers feel and do (a), how they relate to each other (b), and what they do and feel together in their bonds (c). At the same time, this level is moved, influenced, and shaped by (a), (b) and (c).

In the circularities between activities, affects and emotions, the collective power of the erotic *we* is built up. Such *power with* is a central component of erotic freedom. In the collective dimension, freedom does correspond to the practical, emotional understanding of one own's true wishes and desires, and to their (at least partial) realization. But erotic freedom does also require and imply the liberation from (portions) of encrusted habits, given norms, structures, and rules. What is more, it means that the persons forming the erotic *we* come to act together in novel ways, which would have not been possible outside of the eroticism moving them, of the affects and emotions generated by and generating the erotic bond. Crucially, the erotic *power with*, and erotic freedom more generally, are not *directly* transformative at the social and political level. For sure, every erotic *we* is numerically insignificant and not visible enough in the public sphere to move the general opinion, make concrete and material pressure and demands, incisively demonstrate large-scale discontent, or have a bearing on the habitual developing of social life. Persons bound by eros do not always come to act in ways that have relevance for objective norms and structures—and they do not have to in order to qualify as erotic lovers. However, the erotic bond can come to occupy, by virtue of its power and the freedom it releases, a liminal space between the private and the public dimension; in virtue of this in-between, it can have an *indirect* impact beyond the small group it represents.

Chapter Five

JOY AS AN ACT OF RESISTANCE

Erotic Education

In the previous chapters, we have seen how human beings are moved to educate and transform themselves when in love. We do not seek love with the aim of changing our lives or, worse, the lives of our partners and friends. Love is not instrumental, and it does not have clear ends in view: people in erotic bonds do not have any other objective besides being together, participating in common activities, delving into shared affects and emotions. Yet transformation happens, flowing from the (troublesome) experiences of freedom we go through. But eros is not only a private matter. Individual transformation is not the only change made possible by eros. What happens between lovers is extravagant; it may exceed the erotic *we* and spread into other domains of social life. Erotic lovers do experiment, which may have an educational impact on how social actors more generally relate to each other, in both informal and formal contexts. Erotic love, then, could also become *an act of resistance*, as the title of Idle's album says, against social conditions of unfreedom, sparking social and political change.

In the attempt to explain the possible social and political impact of eros, I take lead from some exemplary stories: the film *Weekend*, made by Andrew Haigh (2011); Raoul Peck's biopic about Karl Marx's friendship with Friedrich Engels, *The Young Karl Marx* (2017); and, once again, Elena

Ferrante's Neapolitan Novels. The "strange couples" of these movies and novels make love, converse, act together, and undergo affects they do not entirely grasp; in doing and undergoing all of that, they come to figure out crucial things about themselves, and about the world in which they live. Their actions and passions do not concern them privately and individually, but, rather, bring them to appraise their social environments anew and push them to make some kind of intervention in it. Remember the protagonists of Cavell's comedies of remarriage: their "political" intervention consisted of a public display of what should count as proper marriage— namely, an intimate relationship based on equality, on the reciprocal recognition of the partner as a valuable educator, on the courage to face the concrete possibility of separation as proof of independence and autonomy. The stories that I am going to tell exhibit a similar exemplarity, which has a even clearer social and political charge than the ones told by Cavell. These new examples should allow us to concretely illustrate central motives discussed in previous chapters as well as to introduce two new sets of arguments. The first argument demonstrates how certain erotic bonds, and the experiments they consist of, can be seen as part of movements of struggling for and attracting "public recognition" on a larger social and political scale. The second argument shows how erotic love can create spaces for building, educating, and cultivating critical and transformative subjectivities. I conclude by recapping, at the end of this book, the relation between love and freedom: how eros can disclose for us a journey of freedom toward freedom.

EXEMPLARY BONDS

In the interview "Friendship as a Way of Life," quoted in the excursus, Foucault makes an interesting observation to explain which kind of interpersonal relationships can function as rebellious and disruptive with regard to the social reality in which they take place:

> To imagine a sexual act that doesn't conform to law or nature is not what disturbs people. But that individuals are beginning to love one another— there's the problem. The institution is caught in a contradiction; affective intensities traverse it which at one and the same time keep it going and

shake it up. . . . Institutional codes can't validate these relations with multiple intensities, variable colors, imperceptible movements and changing
forms. These relations short-circuit it and introduce love where there's supposed to be only law, rule, or habit.[1]

It is not homosexual or queer sex per se that represents a threat to the social
fabric of Foucault's (and our) social context; it is the fact that sexual experiences of the sort, and their "sexual intensities," give rise to love bonds that
cannot conform to given habits, laws, and rules. The "institution" mentioned in the second line is, first and foremost, the institution of marriage,
which stands for an entire set of morally, culturally, and socially accepted
relationship forms.[2] The proper transgressive gesture, here, is represented
by eros emerging where it should not and could not, by making its way
through impediments. *Weekend*, the low-budget 2011 British independent
film directed by Andrew Haigh and starring Tom Cullen (as Russell) and
Chris New (as Glen), stages this erotic gesture in its first moments.

Russell and Glen do not have (much) trouble accepting their mutual
sexual attraction. It is the erotic—that is, the properly transformative—
part of their encounter that comes as an unsettling surprise. One of the
most theoretically intense dialogues of the movie occurs at the beginning,
after their first hookup. They had met at a club some hours before. In the
pale and uncertain morning light, they talk about what happens in the
very initial phase of a sexual encounter like theirs:

GLEN: Well, you know what it's like when you first sleep with someone you don't
know . . .
RUSSELL: Yes . . .?
GLEN: It's . . . you, like, become this blank canvas and it gives you an opportunity
to project onto that canvas what you want to be. It's interesting because everyone does it.
RUSSELL: So, do you think I did?
GLEN: Of course you did . . . well, and what happens is, while you are projecting
who you want to be, this gap opens up between what you want to be and what
you really are, and in that gap it shows you what's stopping you becoming who
you want to be.
RUSSELL: And all of this . . . from talking about sex?
GLEN: All of that from talking about sex.

Touching, getting close to, being driven by the other's power, being seduced and seducing: these moves are not thought of by Glen just in terms of pleasure or other positive (and negative) emotions and affects. They have to do with a "gap," a nonidentity, a tension, a liminal space between one's present self and the self one wants to be(come). This is the space of the erotic. Once we (reflexively) dwell in it, we might even become aware of the blockages that either prevent self-transformation, or cloud its desirability.

In the last line of the exchange, Russell refers to the fact that Glen has come to understand "all of this" by making, and listening to, his recordings: Glen records, with the help of a small device, what his numerous lovers decide to tell him the morning after a hookup. This is part of an art project aimed at exposing the intimacy of male gay sex, beyond clichés and simplifications: Glen's lovers speak about their expectations, fears, hopes, and disappointments, the pleasurable and nonpleasurable moments before, during, and after the sexual act, conveying a range of complex nuances. The main conceptual core of the recordings, of all of this "talking about sex," consists in revealing the erotic gap, the perfectionist tension, which he wants to make politically incendiary. And, without knowing it, this is probably the intention of Russell's posthookup writing too: Russell himself, in fact, writes down impressions of his lovers. Although his form is more intimist and diaristic, his urge is, similarly, to understand who he is and who he aspires to become.

Such a motive is, I maintain, perfectionist in the Cavellian sense, and it is not to be interpreted solely as introspection, or self-examination, in search of one's true (sexual) self. Foucault suggests that, instead of asking oneself, "What is the secret of my desire?," it would be more fruitful to look at how relationships "can be established, invented, multiplied, and modulated."[3] Glen and Russell show how an erotic relationship can have an impact, exert a power on broader social bonds, by opening up a space between who one is and who one might (want to) become in the future. The self-transformation entails the promise of a transformation of our form of life more broadly conceived. For this to happen, erotic experiences must *be made public through language*: Glen's recorded "interviews" represent precisely the bridge between intimate experiments and the world beyond them. Note, moreover, that Russell's erotic diary acquires and reveals its meaning as soon as he reads some pages aloud, probably for the first time, to his new friend.

The movie's setting is only partially and ambivalently romantic, according to present-day romantic ideologies. At least one of the two protagonists does not believe in or does not want to engage in long-term, committed relationships: "I don't do boyfriends," Glen declares. In another central dialogue, Glen manifests skepticism toward love-based marriage for gay couples. But, at the end of the movie, although he is leaving for another country, as planned (as he had told Russell on a Saturday afternoon, he was bound to fly to Oregon, in the United States, for a two-years art course), his antiromantic convictions have clearly begun to totter. An erotic bond has formed between the two, and the viewers are left with the impression that they are going to meet again. For sure, Russell's self-transformation has already begun: in the penultimate scene of the movie, in a railway station, he kisses Glen passionately, contravening his former declaration that he does not do public kisses. His habitual insecurity and shyness in showing affection in public—an effect of the shaming gaze of a homophobic society—have begun to thin out.

There is a possibility that opens up at the end of the movie: not only the possibility of a (romantic) reunion, but also that of a different society, in which homosexuality stops being a motive of shame and embarrassment, in need of secrecy or loud, militant declarations, and turn into a creative endeavor, a source of joy and good troubles. The discussion around gay marriage, which is not concluded by a winning argument, is a felicitous and conceptually meaningful representation of the uncertainty and productivity of erotic bonds. If Russell defends the institution of marriage—for, in his view homosexual love is still in need of institutionalized recognition—Glen refutes making himself and queer love dependent upon it. The debate between the two lucidly reveals the eroticism of their connection—that it is the indecision around the form that a relationship might assume, the in-between (in this case, between institutionalization and anarchy), that gestures toward the possibility of social and political alternatives. This point resembles the description of the relationship between Frances and Bobbi in *Conversations with Friends* that I discussed in the excursus: their erotic bond is also expressed through a refusal to define their relationship according to conventional categories ("lesbian couple"; "best friends"), a refusal that becomes the central theme of their long and numerous conversations.

The agonist moment is a crucial element in *Weekend*, although it is not cast as a relation of opposition between the private dyadic couple and the rest of society, but as a constellation of power games within a network of relations. What happens between Glen and Russell during the course of the weekend—their passion, debates, "confessions"—is, crucially, mediated by other relationships and by the words and communications through which they unfold and acquire sense. These are mostly the conversations between Glen and his previous lovers-interviewees, but a crucial role is also played by the provocative, aggressive exchanges that Glen has with heterosexual men: we learn of this habit during his last Saturday night out, when he gathers with friends in what he calls a "heterosexual" bar and demonstratively starts to narrate very loudly his sexual escapades so that everyone can hear. A fight with the bar owner ensues. Sexuality, for Glen, is obviously not a private matter, but a political act and a weapon. However, as Glen's friend Jill tells Russell, and as we see in the film's very last scene, when he is holding in his hands the recording device that had registered their first morning-after talk, Glen is reluctant in making public this particular encounter. The transformative power of eros does not mean to eliminate the boundaries between the private and the public, or to regard sexual or otherwise intimate experiences as immediately and directly political. The real sociopolitical impact of erotic love is to be gathered in a sort of liminal, fragile space between the private and the public: when something private, already shaped by social and political conditions, tries to withdraw, to escape the public grip; when something that was meant to stay hidden, according to established feeling rules, cannot but exceed and trespass such rules; or when we try to speak about and explain some affective experiences we have no words (concepts) for, and that the available emotional public language struggles to comprehend (as happened, you recall, to young Simone de Beauvoir with her love for Zaza).[4] It is perhaps relevant, in this framework, that a central knot for the erotic transformative process depicted in *Weekend*, or for the possibility thereof, is an imagined, impossible conversation. This is the coming-out talk that Russell imagines having with his unknown father, now personified by Glen, as they are still in bed, in the soft light of the last morning they spend together. In this ideal conversation, the father fully accepts the sexuality of his son and declares his pride for him.

The communicative exercises I have highlighted connect the two lovers in a powerful erotic *we*, which is in turn connected with other lovers and with society more generally. The powerful erotic affects and emotions shared in a bond, and the words expressing them, affect and "infect" other lovers as well, inspiring and moving them to pursue similar experiments and experiences—of joy, but also of "uneasiness, a desire-in-uneasiness."[5] Erotic bonds might represent and make visible alternative social practices and "reopen affective and relational virtualities"—for example, those manifesting that queer eros is not just a specific form of desire, but something desirable in itself, as it opens up new venues for desire, as it makes us desire to transform ourselves.[6]

Weekend exemplifies the power of eros with a strong sexual component, but such power can be unleashed in nonsexual erotic bonds as well. Exemplary, in this sense, is the rather intense and passionate friendship that connects the young Karl Marx (August Diehl) and the young Friedrich Engels (Stefan Konarske) in Raoul Peck's *The Young Karl Marx* (*Le jeune Karl Marx*, 2017). The film's subject matter is indeed social and political transformation, which is presented both historically and conceptually. The movie depicts a turning point in the history of European and global working class struggles, in the years prior to the European democratic and liberal revolutions in 1848. Among other events during this troubled time, the League of the Just is turned by Engels and Marx's scheming into the Communist League, and the two of them (with the help of their partners) put together *The Communist Manifesto*. Social and political transformation appears in the movie as the fruit of cooperation between intellectuals, working people and political activists. In Peck's vision, change results from the interaction of praxis and theory, whereby theory is in itself the product of a cooperation, a mix of different forms of knowledge (the practical knowledge of working people, of social sciences like economics and sociology, and of the conceptual elaboration of philosophy). The point of the movie, on which I will focus, consists, more narrowly, in the role of friendship in transformative processes of the sort.

The encounter that marks the beginning of Karl's and Friedrich's bond seems to follow a classic romantic script. They meet in Arnold Ruge's apartment—actually, for the second time—and at the outset are both cautious and wary, hesitant, displaying a seeming scorn. The gazes they exchange are inflamed, as if they were caught in a sort of seduction game. Who is going to resist longer in giving the first token of recognition? It is Engels who surrenders first, declaring his amazement for Marx's *Critique of Hegel's Philosophy of Right* and calling him the biggest materialist thinker of their time and a genius. Karl grins and immediately proceeds to sing the praises of the "colossal" *The Condition of the Working Class in England*, written by Engels between 1842 and 1844 in Manchester, where his father owns textile factories. A long and intense drinking night ensues in which they exchange points of view, critical notes on each other's writings, and intimate confessions. In the end, they relocate to his apartment and scribble down the first draft of what will become later known as *The Holy Family*. The sequence is able to brightly convey the true passion that has swamped them: they do not only appreciate and esteem each other on the basis of intellectual achievements and shared political convictions and goals, but are also drawn to each other in ways that are partially unexplainable: they come from very different social and cultural backgrounds and could have been rivals instead of allies. The energy they unleash together, at least in the way Peck represents it, is difficult to explain on the basis of rationality alone.

The power dynamic that I have reconstructed in chapter 2 is brilliantly summed up in this scene as well, and in the development of their friendship in the next years. Individual empowerment, and *power to*, appear here clearly as the result of the other exercising *power over*, while at the same time requiring a continuous, not necessarily intentional, exercise of counterpower. The collective power reached by this friendship is prodigious. Engels supports Marx in different ways: he sustains him financially while pushing him when he feels tired, desperate, and hopeless. I take the point of the movie to be that Marx would have not been able to sharpen or even formulate his ideas if not for his friend's knowledge and input. The focus, however, is not on one single man: although the title, and some scenes, risk putting the individual Karl at center stage, the film does manage to portray the truly collective nature of transformative action. Marx's and Engel's interventions, their writings, speeches, and actions, are depicted as proper collective endeavors. Their specific individual contributions are visible and identifiable, and yet, taken as such and put one beside the other, they could not explain the final, impressive results. It is their duo, their *we*, and not the sum of their individual undertakings and talents, that has to be taken into account to understand the events at the center of Peck's film. Even the writings that Marx signs alone appear here as having been written by the two of them together.

Interestingly, the erotic collective is depicted as expanding to include their partners, Jenny Marx and Mary Burns. Note that this erotic "quartet" is rendered in rather experimental fashion: Jenny is an aristocratic who has challenged class barriers in order to be with the man she loves (at that point, at least) and to join the struggle. Mary Burns seems to be wanting to organize her life in polyerotic terms, as we learn toward the end of the movie. Shaking her rather bourgeois prudishness, she tells Jenny during a walk on the beach that she is going to give up on motherhood, as she prefers to concentrate instead on her political activity and does not want to profit from her boyfriend's "dirty" wealth. Nevertheless, she is contemplating the possibility of letting her sister have a relationship with Friedrich and become the mother of his children when she grows up.

Marx and Engels would have not become such a "power couple" had they not developed their friendship and extended their erotic bond to their partners. Their bond is not merely an example of collective agency and collective emotion and affectivity; it also shows what this kind of friendship *might do to people* in relation with their social context. Its power is not unlimited, for sure (Marx and Engels were already highly politicized, after all), and not every erotic bond can obviously produce the astonishing consequences of the founders of Communism. The central motive of Peck's biopic is certainly to show the exceptionality of Marx and Engels as historical figures and thinkers whose work is still central today and to reconstruct some of the early phases of their education, as in a classic Bildungsroman. But, in the film, the subject to be educated and built up is a collective one—or, better said, a series of collective subjects: the duo Friedrich–Karl, as well as the various political collective agents that have participated (and still have to participate) in past and future revolution(s), as we see in a final array of images, including Che Guevara, the fall of the Berlin Wall, Nelson Mandela, and the Occupy Wall Street movement. Like the education undergone by Cavell's characters, the *Bildung* of *The Young Karl Marx* leads the individuals to see and try to actually realize their true desires and "nature," but not just. In realizing themselves, individuals educated in this way gain resources to better understand reality, approach it with critical eyes, relate to the world with the aim of changing it for the better, and find the strength to overcome the troubles that every engagement of the sort necessarily implies. Friendship is depicted as a fundamental part of this education.

The last exemplary tale brings us back to Ferrante's Lina and Elena. Especially in the third and fourth volumes of the Neapolitan Novels, which portray the social and political upheavals in Italy and Europe during the 1960s and 1970s, and their dwindling in the 1980s and 1990s, the proper political power of the erotic connection between the two women comes to the fore. As in the previous example, friendship is here depicted as a space of mutual recognition, support, and power exercises, in which people learn who they are, what they want, and how to realize it, as individuals and as public and political figures. These are the years in which Lenù establishes herself as a successful writer and public intellectual: her participation in the students and workers revolts, political articles, and contributions in the feminist debates of the time are inspired by her conversations and (often unspoken) confrontations with Lila. They feed on their shared experiences in the social context in which they have both grown up (and to which Elena returns after many years spent in the bourgeois milieu of Florence), and even more deeply on the urge to make sense of the many differences that keep them apart. These are also the years in which Lila joins, albeit reluctantly, the violent class struggle against the fascist capitalists of her home town. Having sensed at a very early stage that the struggle is doomed to end with the capitulation of the workers and the Communists, she retreats from the public scene and decides to fight a more underground battle in her neighborhood of origin, trying strategically to undermine the power of the local mafiosi. Her intensions are pure, but the compromises that her intelligence and the objective limitations of her position force her to make end up in ambivalences that she is not able to manage and that will eventually destroy her.

In these phases of their lives, the relationship between Lila and Lenù is intimately intertwined with other love and friendship bonds, especially those they cultivate with Nino, the (quite shady) man with whom both women are passionately in love; Enzo, Lila's partner; and Pasquale, a very good friend who turns, in the saga's third volume, into an alleged terrorist. The main erotic bond of the novels is not just a dyadic relationship: it expands to include and is animated by—sometimes through troublesome and painful dynamics—other connections. But let's concentrate, for the sake of simplicity, on the agonist bond between the two brilliant friends. Lila and Lenù both feel deep ressentiment toward the other. Lila resents Lenù's upward class mobility, and her apparent good time with motherhood. Lenù is tormented not only by jealousy (she will never get rid of the suspicion that Nino has always loved and admired Lila more), but also, more excruciatingly, by the criticisms that she imagines Lila would want to raise, if she would dare to have a honest conversation with her. Through Lila's eyes, Elena senses her own self-deception and questions her talent. And yet, thanks (also) to Lila, she gains a political education: she is moved to study the political reality of her present, to develop her standpoints. The self-crippling doubts that besiege her do not prevent her political subjectification process through alternate phases of success and failures. In a specular fashion, Lila delineates and sets boundaries to her political and personal power as well. Similarly to Elena, she becomes who she is by differentiating herself from the model provided by her best friend, without renouncing (until the final scenes, at least) to engage in those shared activities and emotions that provide the material and the possibility to give a sense to her life, but also the life of the community to which, in different ways, they both belong.

The story told by Ferrante is important because it shows that individuals not only become able to cope with their social and political reality, to engage in activities aimed at changing and improving it, but also to feel their limits as agents, thanks to their erotic bonds. It also shows how these bonds do not have to necessarily be harmonious and joyful; they unfold their power, on the individuals and on their broader context, even if the troubles they give rise to are overwhelming and maybe, in the end, even undermining of a friendship. The process of becoming a (political) subject develops as result of joint activities and emotions, through the collective undertaking that gives a meaning to the activities and articulates the affects, but the process includes, and is pushed forward, by individual attempts to gain independence, through exercises of power and counterpower, from the other and from an erotic union that is perceived as too strong and too absorbing. The moments of separation, at least until a certain point, are not to be seen as separation from love, as an interruption or a break of the erotic connection, but what makes it lively, powerful, transformative.

These examples—*Weekend*, *The Young Karl Marx*, and the Neapolitan Novels—have been chosen to introduce the two sets of arguments I discuss in the following two sections. I will try to explain how erotic bonds of sexual love and nonsexual friendship, might have the power to influence broader social norms and structures. Such an impact is twofold: first, as *Weekend* shows, erotic love opens up spaces of experimentation. Erotic experiments might call for public recognition, or they might affirm themselves as independent from it: in both cases, they force society at large to put in question, revise, and change some of its habits, norms, structures, and feeling rules. Second, as *The Young Karl Marx* and the Neapolitan Novels show, erotic love can open up spaces in which critical and transformative capacities are cultivated and put to use.

PUBLIC RECOGNITION: STRUGGLES AND ATTRACTIONS

Lovers and friends are heavily influenced by the contexts in which they happen to fall in love or in friendship, many times with damaging consequences. At the same time, the erotic process might give rise to moments of deviation, critique, disruption *from* and *from within* given orders. Eros shows that this order can be different from what it is; it plays out the inherent mutability of habits, norms, structures and feeling rules. Free erotic love can become a space of *experimentation* in which possible alternatives for social relations are delineated and practiced, in which changes are anticipated and tried out. These experiments have the power to reverberate in the broader social and political fabric as well, even in the case in which a political and public intervention is not consciously and directly intended.

Again, recognition theory can help us shed light on the relation between erotic bonds and the context in which they are embedded. This time it is not the recognition that happens between individual lovers and friends, but recognition between social groups—not only individuals, in fact, but also groups of individuals, smaller and larger *wes*, desire and seek recognition from other social groups, or from a constellation of groups. To employ North American philosopher John Dewey's term: a group seeks *public recognition*.

According to Dewey, a society is lively, "healthy," when it harbors tensions and struggles between groups that can be addressed and overcome in intelligent ways. Social conflicts arise when a dominated or oppressed group, a group that lacks "public" or "social recognition," becomes aware of this lack and the suffering it brings forth, thus starting a series of actions aimed at achieving recognition.[7] A lack of recognition happens when the group's needs, interests, aspirations, and rights remain unseen or are not acknowledged as legitimate, as making a valuable contribution to social life. This implies that there are other social groups who manage to impose their needs, interests, aspirations, and rights, as the only acceptable, justified, and sometimes even visible ones. The dominant groups' hegemony represents a problem for the common well-being because, by misrecognizing, suppressing, or even being unaware of the wishes and claims of the oppressed groups, it reifies, naturalizes, and blocks social life.[8] It prevents the emergence of alternatives and the formulation of solutions to various social problems, and it perpetrates the same order. The only way for avoiding the "petrification" of social life consists in accepting the challenge arising from oppressed groups struggling for visibility, recognition, and legitimation. Note how, from a Deweyan perspective, negativity, conflict, and troubledness are considered as potentially valuable and desirable. Social conflicts, expressions of domination, are also spaces where social problems are nestled and therefore can become visible and urgent, so that they can be addressed.

In the early stages of a conflict, those who initiate the struggle are seen, but they *also see themselves* only as a disorganized and disconnected mass of individuals. After a while, it is the "general public eye" that sees *them* just as a "conglomerate of individuals in opposition to their society": actual participants in the movement itself, on the contrary, "begin more and more to conceive of themselves as a social group."[9] Their needs, wishes, desires, interests, goals, and identities are not given in advance. We struggle because *we* want to be recognized, to be granted certain rights, to obtain certain goods, or to be seen in the ways we wish to be seen by others. But the contents, meanings, and consequences of recognition claims, and the contours of the struggling collectivity itself, come to be shaped within the ongoing struggle. In the end, once the oppressed group is recognized *as a group* by the entire society, advancing determinate requests, things begin to change on a broader scale too. But struggles are ambivalent: on the one hand, the formation, demarcation, solidification of groups' identities and the clarification of their desires and claims do often represent a gain for a particular group, and, as such, are fruitful for society at large. On the other hand, the achievement of clarity and certainties might and often do bring forth new forms of oppression, exclusion, discrimination—that is, new troubles.[10]

Can Dewey's argument apply also to smaller, private erotic collectivities? I believe it can. Consider *The Argonauts*, the beautiful genre-bending memoir in which Meggie Nelson narrates her love story with gender nonconforming artist Harry Dodge. Nelson learns, together with Harry, to experience and cast their erotic bond ("nuptial") beyond established dualisms (not only "masculine-feminine," but also "question-answer," and "man-animal"): she describes it as "the outline of a becoming."[11] When, at a dinner party, an acquaintance identifies Harry as a woman ("So, have you been with other women, before Harry?") and Nelson herself as a "straight lady," she is taken aback. The annoying interlocutor goes on talking and tries to reduce their relationship to a sexual pattern ("Straight ladies have always been hot for Harry"). But recognition, we have seen, can sometimes manage to go beyond established patterns and categories of identification and acknowledgment: Nelson does indeed define her romance as "an individual experience of desire" that manages to "take precedence over a categorical one."[12]

A decisive scene for the idea of public recognition outlined in this chapter happens when a friend mocks a mug she finds in Maggie's kitchen that her mom had given her as a present: "I've never seen anything so heteronormative in all my life," utters the friend.[13] The mug is one of those that can be purchased online and have a photo of one's choice emblazoned on it. The photo on Maggie's mug depicts her family and herself all dressed up to go to *The Nutcracker* at Christmastime—a family tradition. In the photo, she is seven months pregnant; Harry and Harry's son from a previous union look dashing in their matching suits. Evidently annoyed by the friend's remark, Nelson asks herself and her readers, not rhetorically, what it is about this picture that exactly conveys the "essence of heteronorma-tivity." She lists some possible answers: the fact they are all clearly partici-pating in a long tradition of families being photographed at holiday time, the fact that her mother made her a mug as to signalize social acceptance, or the fact of her pregnancy. Alas, none of them seems to convincingly capture what Nelson's "tribe" is and means to her and should be and mean to the people she loves—namely, an intense adventure of individual and collective change. *The Argonauts* tells the story, to be more precise, of two transformative journeys, Harry's gender transition (from "woman" to "man") as well as Maggie's pregnancy and motherhood, as well as her transition from a single woman, somehow cynical and depressed, to a pro-fessionally self-confident and loving woman (not merely a "woman in love," in Beauvoir's sense). The two journeys are interlocked: the one has an impact on the other—it is the same journey and it is not. What is more, the book embeds this erotic bond in its social and political context (they tie the knot hours before Proposition 8 briefly becomes law in California) and, coherently with this political interest, narrates the effects of Harry and Maggie's erotic bond on other people.

The passage with the mug can be read in two ways: either Maggie's friend lacks the figurative, emotional, conceptual instruments for appro-priately recognizing such unconventional collectivity and forces it into a wrong category (not only persons, but also a *we* can be "misgendered"!), or she does not lack them, but refuses to engage in proper recognition activ-ity, maybe annoyed or envious that such an unconventional intimate experiment can also be a source of serenity, simplicity, enjoyment, that it has actually *already* found its place within larger lineages and traditions. Both cases demonstrate how the recognition of a small, private, particular erotic *we* does depend on larger habits, norms, and feeling rules. There-fore, small groups (erotic bonds as well as families or tribes originated in such bonds) do desire to be publicly recognized and struggle for public recognition.

It could be now helpful to illustrate this dynamic with reference to the struggle for legal and nonlegal recognition of same-sex marriage. One could argue, in fact, that this is the way in which erotic bonds can most evidently contribute to overall social and political changes. In our Western liberal democracies, there are still many social contexts in which sexual, romantic, passionate love between persons of the same sex and gender nonconforming people is not respected, understood, and celebrated as true and proper love, or is regarded as inferior and deficient in comparison to heterosexual love. In such contexts, bonds between gay men, lesbians, and gender nonconforming persons constitute crucial erotic experimentations. The right to marry for these people would correspond to a form of recognition, provided by the entire society, that not only promises to have a beneficial impact on queers' material lives and identities but also on other people's lives, and on the institutions regulating them too. One of the central arguments in favor of same-sex marriage is that this powerful form of recognition from above (state recognition) would contribute to changing the institution of marriage itself, making it more egalitarian and less oppressive, as it would decouple it from heteronormative habits and expectations. A change in the institution of marriage would concern social members of all sexual orientations and represent an important step toward the overcoming of heterosexism on the whole social scale. This transformation would affect a branching of other norms and structures as well, from work life to practices of rearing and educating children.[14] Remember how Cavell thought of marriage as "the central social image of human change."[15] Proponents of same-sex marriage have a similar idea(l) of marriage in mind, I believe, when they claim the desire and the right to being recognized by and within the same institution.

However, queer theorists and activists have compellingly criticized struggles for public recognition focused on marriage rights. These critiques reproduce and specify an objection that had been raised against recognition theory more generally. The objection, intimately related to the damage of complicity analyzed in chapter 3, raises the suspicion that the conditions under which recognition can be awarded, in the framework of a given social order, end up reproducing and reinforcing the order itself, thus undermining the progressive claims advanced in the struggles. In order to obtain recognition, that is, one is "forced" to comply with the norms and structures that already allow and provide such recognition to the privileged groups. Critics of same-sex marriage reject the hypothesis according to which the extension of legal recognition to nonheterosexual couples could effectively manage to theoretically and empirically revise the institution of marriage itself. Given the normative weight that this institution already has within our societies, same-sex couples craving for recognition would be rather pushed or nudged into gradually taking up the traditional characteristics of heterosexual ones. They would have to show that they "deserve" recognition by assuming—maybe not always consciously, explicitly, and willingly—traditional rules, like monogamy, gender dichotomies, the asymmetric division of labor within the couple, or the (neoliberal) privatization of social reproduction within the family. In order to bring about a substantial change, same-sex marriage would, then, have to destabilize not only gender and sexuality norms, but also, for example, a neoliberal agenda that privatizes care and restricts it to within the boundaries of the nuclear family. Such challenge is very hard, and probably too much to ask from erotic experimentations.[16] Therefore, public recognition seems to imply mechanisms of disciplination, domestication and normalization, both for individuals and for forms of intimacy and kinship. Struggles for public recognition risk, in the end, to assimilate experimentations within a given, problematic paradigm, legitimizing rather than transgressing and disrupting it.

The discontent with struggles for recognition of queer marriages is backed up by skepticism of legal recognition of multiple partnerships. When intended and practiced in its most radical, anarchic form, polyerotic bonds refuse to comply with normative and prescriptive fixed standards. As argued by Christian Klesse, polyamory (or polyeros) is inherently fluid, processual, and, as such, only able to exert the "transformative" and "transgressive" potential to "trouble" conventional intimate relationships as well as traditional sexual and gender identities.[17] Public recognition would work, according to this line of argument, only by forcing alternative relationship forms to be identified on the basis of "universal models construed around conjugal relationships"—that is, mostly, on the basis of the marriage model.[18] Like same-sex relationships, poly people would then be forced to accept constrictions in order to prove their legitimacy and desirability: "Constraint is the price that polyamorists are expected to pay for inclusion into marriage."[19] The effect would be a dismantling or softening of its rebellious force.[20]

The concessions that the struggling groups would have to make to the given normative order and their defenders are explained by the radical critics on the basis of what they see as an intrinsic requirement of recognition. Demanding recognition within a given society, from those social groups that profit the most from public recognition at a given time, implies and requires a somewhat positive evaluation of those values and practices largely accepted and cherished. One of the basic rules of recognition can be formulated as follows: if A desires to be recognized by B, B must be considered by A as a valuable recognizer. Radical disruptions of given orders of norms, structures, and rules, then, cannot be what people or groups desiring recognition can really aim at. This is also true in the case in which A is a social group and B is another social group or ensemble of groups embodying the values and norms of their social context. If lovers want their erotic bonds to be recognized through the institution of marriage, it means that they at least partially approve of the institution, that they recognize its virtues and advantages.[21]

This problematization of the recognitive paradigm, however, especially with concern to marriage as its legal medium, is not in opposition with the Deweyan account, as I interpret it. Dewey never reduces social changes to legal changes only (although these are obviously important). Social transformation, in his broad view, is transformation of institutional arrangements, which are interwoven with habits that exceed legal and normative frameworks, and with the ways in which persons *impulsively* cope with their social reality.[22] Changes in feeling rules are integral part of the Deweyan picture too.[23] From a Deweyan perspective, struggles for public recognition with regard to erotic love would have the consequence of introducing alternative models of love, sex, and friendship. In recognizing certain experimentations, in acknowledging their existence, their reality and value, more and more people would come to perceive and believe in new possibilities. The proposed Deweyan framework does not aid us to understand the precise institutional and legal form that these alternatives are going to take up. The details of the specific arrangements cannot be known on a philosophical, general level of inquiry, but, rather, are the result of context-specific struggles. On a mere philosophical level it would be impossible to determine once and for all whether marriage (for same-sex or queers, in polyerotic constellations or not) is an important goal, achievement, or provisional step within a broader process of emancipatory transformation. Note that this uncertainty or undecidability is exactly conveyed in dialogue between Russell and Glen on the topic of gay marriage. The uncertainty and open-endedness stand, we can say, for the space of the erotic itself.

Struggling groups or experiments are moved by the desire to bring other groups to see and acknowledge *that they are there* (*that* there are, *actually*, persons of same or nonconforming sex who engage in erotic bonds, or *that* erotic bonds might be formed between more than two persons), that they are *real* (that same-sex or queer lovers *do* love each other; that there *are* erotic bonds that *de facto* connect more than two people) and that they have an intrinsic value (that same-sex, queer, polyerotic relationships can be good and desirable, that they are "worth it"). Public recognition in a Deweyan sense does not necessarily confirm the given order, but it *can* transform it, in more or less pronounced ways. By using James O'Higgins's words in an interview with Foucault, one can say that struggles for public recognition must aim at "asking broader and deeper questions about the strategic roles played by sexual preferences and how they are perceived," "provoking society at large to rethink its own presuppositions regarding sexuality."[24]

At this point, we can even make a step beyond the recognition-theoretical account as it has been defended until now by reflecting on the fact that *getting recognition* (becoming visible and recognizable, and in a positive manner) does not necessarily imply or request to recognize the dominant groups, or their values and practices. Groups and types of erotic bonds that are not yet recognized do not necessarily have to desire recognition and act in ways that display this desire *in order to solicit or provoke recognition from others*. Erotic experimentations do not have to hope to be incorporated into existing norms, structures, and rules; even if they completely refuse to accept defenders or just practitioners of traditional love relationships as proper recognizers they can still *attract* their recognition. This is a variation, or an implication, of *the passive power of recognition* that I have illustrated in chapter 2. This idea is also fruitful, I believe, for making sense of the collective power of erotic bonds.

Let's consider Glen's behavior in *Weekend*: it is very clear that Glen does not seek a proper dialogue with heterosexists; he does not want to convince defenders of heteronormativity that gay sex, and love, is "good"— that is, compliant and compatible with given conceptions and practices of good sexual and intimate relationships, his scorn for which is evident throughout the movie. Coherently, he does not believe in the right to marriage as an achievement for homosexuals. His art project intends to show publicly what gay eroticism is about, but not to compare it with heterosexual eros (which is not represented in *Weekend* either). And yet the power of his recordings, and of the entire movie itself, consists precisely in the fact that it can *move* everyone to *take an interest* in this kind of sex and love, to regard it from novel perspectives, to learn about and from it. Glen's personal struggle for recognition consists in a series of actions aimed at publicly displaying his and his friends'/lovers' affects and emotions. A struggle of this sort wants explicitly to change—enrich, complicate, deepen—other people's perceptions, beliefs, understanding with regard to gay sex and love. More ambitiously, it gestures toward a more diverse and loving society, a society that would allow and foster more frequent and serious intimate conversations about who one really is, wants and wishes.

If we look again at Cavell's exemplary discussion of comedies of remarriage, we find similar dynamics. The couples in his movies couples engage in erotic experiments in the sense that I have illustrated here. Cavell discusses bonds that are exemplary because worthy of attracting public recognition and thus provoking larger reflections on the forms of community and democracy that we want and should want. These are private experimentations (the husbands and wives involved do not have explicit or direct political intentions) that are able to anticipate and represent a different form of communal life: one in which everyone, both man and woman, is willing to rely on others in order to deeply understand what they want and want to be and try to realize it in highly individual fashion—for instance, breaking with class and gender conformism, or announcing the possibility of a society without classes and not based on gender power differentials. Cavell addresses the interrelation between the private and the public more explicitly when discussing Cukor's *Adam's Rib*. The two protagonists, Adam and Amanda, have an exemplary egalitarian marriage. Such a model cannot remain a private exception, but needs to be, especially from Amanda's perspective, publicly recognized. Husband and wife are both successful lawyers and are peers at home; he recognizes her as his equal both at work and in life. Alas, his defense of Tom Ewell, the unfaithful husband whose wife tried to kill him after discovering his cheating, puts in doubt his own feminist convictions. Therefore, Amanda, by taking up the defense of Ewell's (guilty) wife, must become her husband's opponent, challenge him in public, in the courtroom. By letting their agonist erotic dynamic unfold publicly, Amanda aims precisely *at being recognized* as her husband's equal by the entire public sphere.[25] Such recognition would then

come to correspond to the public recognition of the model of an equal
marriage as a worthy and desirable model (worthy and desirable, I would
say, still more than seventy years after the release of the movie).

What is the role of affects and emotions for attracting public recognition? Two main functions can be identified: first, emotions and affects can
work against the established feeling rules ordering the emotional life of
dominant groups who already enjoy public recognition. Second, oppressive groups can display emotions or affects that *work differently* from what
we are used to see from dominants standpoints.

A paradigmatic example of what we can all an "agonist affect" is the
kind of anger that subordinated groups often feel.[26] In her essay "Hardle-
to-Handle-Anger," the intersectionalist theorist María Lugones speaks of
the anger experienced by women of color, which manifests itself in uncontrollable, exaggerated modalities. I call it an "affect," according to the categories sketched in chapter 4, because it appears as largely unintelligible
from the perspective of the "world of sense" of the dominant groups—that
is, on the basis of established and dominant habits, norms, structures, and
feeling rules. This anger, or rage, does not want to communicate something clear and determinate; it does not demand respect and recognition
from the present-day world, but from a world that is yet to come. It "con-
tains a recognition that there is more than one world of sense" and points
toward new and alternative ones.[27] "It announces an emerging self toward
whom the 'one' tied to the official world of sense feels ill at ease"—a self
that is both individual and collective. Glen embodies Lugones' anger in
exemplar fashion.[28] He is clearly angry, and his rage is not softened, miti-
gated, or forgotten during and by his sexual encounters. On the contrary,
his intimate relationships feed the rage, push him to express it in ways
that, as I have already said, do not imply the recognition of others and do
not seek others' recognition. It can produce an "echo," it can "reverberate,"
however, as Lugones puts it: it can induce others to interrogate this affect,
try to make sense of it, to look for novel modalities to cope with and overcome it.

As for an emotion that may unfold differently, thus opening up new
possibilities of interaction and of norms of love, let's consider the example
of jealousy as it is discussed within polyerotic circles. In particular, it is the
processual nature of the emotional experience that jealousy gives rise to
that sounds theoretically appealing. Persons who accept and cherish the

possibility to be passionately, sexually in love with more than one person at the same time and organize their lives accordingly are not necessarily and usually exempt from jealousy. Their commitment to the polyerotic experiment, however, encourages and pushes them not to take this emotion as an inevitable, univocal, and simple given fact, but to collectively explore and articulate it. When assumed as object of loving communication and reflection, this emotion does in fact often undergo mutations. Jealousy might come to appear as a sort of "mask" concealing something else: other emotions or affects (e.g., fear of losing the beloved one, lack of self-confidence, psychological or existential fragility due to other causes), or certain beliefs or emotional habitual patterns ingrained in conventional social norms that persist in spite of an explicit but superficial endorsement of alternative poly norms (e.g., the belief that "true love" can only be exclusive, the urge to "possess" and control the other). By identifying the cause of jealousy, or what jealousy can alternatively be, in other emotions or emotional rules, lovers' focus of attention changes; their view angles open up, and other aspects of their selves and their lives begin to be subjected to critical scrutiny. In special fortunate cases, jealousy can be dispelled or overcome. At its place, another emotion, "compersion," might arise. "Compersion" is defined as the happiness, or even joy, felt by one lover when their partner experiences happiness and joy thanks to their relationships with other persons.[29] Such an emotional process is, currently in our social contexts, more common (but not obvious) between nonsexual friends, but it has been reclaimed especially by polyerotic experimenters.

What does the process of dealing with jealousy, which might or might not flow into compersion, show? What is the educational potential of polyerotic experimentations, and how can it attract public recognition? First, the process offers a practical and convincing example of how some negative emotions can be better addressed and elaborated when openly and honestly thematized by everyone involved in the process, and that emotional transformation is most commonly the result of an intersubjective, collective work. For sure, openness and honesty have limits. The elaboration of jealousy and the emergence of compersion do not require or entail a claim or commitment to full transparency. Shadows, opaqueness and difficulties in communication and emotional articulation must be viewed as constitutive and unavoidable parts and phases of (*ambivalent!*) erotic bonds. They should be tolerated, even embraced and cherished: they in fact express respect for the beloved's independence and distance, which is key, as argued in chapter 2, for a lively process of mutual recognition.

The example of compersion, moreover, does show how erotic emotions are not simply "transmitted" between two lovers, shared in the dyad alone. Erotic emotions are inclusive rather than exclusive. Compersion is paradigmatic of the expansiveness of erotic emotions. To come back to the bond connecting Ariel, Bowie, and Cleo (in the case that it is not a damaged one): the joy experienced by Cleo together with Bowie might arouse joy in Ariel as well, and it can even contribute to and increase the joy experienced by Ariel with other partners. Compersion can thus help better illustrate what already sketched out in the excursus: dynamics of recognition and experiences of empowerment and flourishing can be extended from one couple to another, or properly shared between more than two persons. If Bowie feels empowered in their relationship with Cleo, because of the recognition they get, and thanks to Cleo's particular ways to exercise power over them, through the emotion of compersion Bowie's power can turn out to be beneficial, empowering, in the relationship with Ariel as well, in ways that favor Ariel. Compersion can also work as a motor driving Ariel to recognize Cleo in erotic ways. If Ariel, Bowie, and Cleo are altogether connected in an erotic bond on the basis (also) of this emotion, the three of them are in the position to experiment and increase their powers.

Note that compersion is an affective and emotion *possibility*: it cannot be assumed as a new feeling rule or as the basis of a new normative order. As already noted, polyerotic bonds are not per se damage-free or a guarantee of freedom. Sometimes, they are just a matter of individual, private choice and preference; they do not have to involve or point toward larger political engagement. They *might*, however, become experimental in ways that have moving effects on society at large, and this in virtue of the collective emotional dynamics they exhibit. As my examples suggest, these include the process, intersubjectively shared, that transforms negative into positive emotions. They encourage human beings to find new and creative ways to embrace and address negative emotions, instead of suppressing or "removing" them. Such dynamics, moreover, show how positive emotions (might) have an expansive and positively "contagious" nature, tending toward inclusion instead of exclusion. One might even argue that polyeros is best suited for representing the possibility of erotic bonds' power spreading beyond the private sphere: the emotional processes that characterize erotic love in polyerotic constellation do paradigmatically exemplify, in fact, how affects and emotions that are experienced and shared between lovers and friends cannot stop at the border, so to say, of a singular subject of emotions or affects. Erotic emotions and affects are expansive and extravagant: they exceed enclosed subjectivities and relationships, connecting more subjects and more relationships.

Some theorists have even tried to defend the anti-capitalist potential of polyerotic love.[30] Do polyerotic experimentations bear resources for contesting what in chapter 3 I have called the neoliberal form of subjectivity? These resources might be conceptually explained, I tentatively argue, precisely on the basis of the emotional/affective "performances" I have described. On the one hand, one must admit that class (and other) privileges allow or facilitate the success of polyerotic constellations: material security and comfort give us the freedom to fully dedicate ourselves to our loved ones.[31] But, on the other hand, the argument can be formulated in reverse fashion: neoliberal capitalism is a factor impeding polyerotic bonds to develop in widespread and democratic ways. Hence, "successful" or just good-enough polyerotic bonds display, in exemplary fashion, some practices of resistance.

Polyerotic experimentations might generate the power to call into question a certain subjectivity that is required today in neoliberal societies, and that can be defined by the following traits:

(a) this is a subjectivity that requires individuals to rely only on themselves and to assume almost entirely individual responsibility for their successes and failures. Individual independence thus becomes a core value against both material and emotional dependence;

(b) other people, including loved ones, are viewed and treated as instrumental for one's well-being and self-realization. In order to survive and be successful—that is, in order to achieve self-realization—individuals must craft and present themselves, in every domain of social life (from job to sex markets) in desirable ways, which implies the willingness and the abilities to be or perform as adaptable, resilient, flexible, and mobile;

(c) every aspect of individual life, including private and emotional life, becomes a source of value. Individuals must not just constantly produce economic value; they have to constantly create, maintain, and increase their personal value, in every dimension of their existence.

Now, *polyerotic experiments may attract public recognition* insofar as:

(a) they are able to show how individual independence is unsustainable and undesirable. For sure, the risks that come together with emotional and material dependence on lovers multiply. However, free, nondamaged polyerotic bonds exhibit practices for navigating such multiple risks, and they show the generative nature of intersubjective dependence. Moreover, polyeros often does embody practical modalities for organizing mutual dependence that break with institutionalized given forms: for instance, the model of the nuclear and bourgeois family is replaced by diverse types of communities of care; social reproduction work is performed in nonprivatized forms; there is an incentive for inventing new housing solutions and social spaces for care and social reproduction.

(b) Polyerotic experiments reveal individual vulnerabilities and push to find ways to creatively and positively deal with them. In polyeros, negative affects and emotions are particularly difficult to conceal; they must be addressed, talked through, and constantly articulated and negotiated. If, on the one hand, such communication offers a possibility for better "seeing," or recognizing, our partners, it does reveal, on the other hand, the impossibility of full transparency. The more extensive and deeper the communication becomes, more zones of incommunicability, reciprocal opaqueness, and incomprehension emerge. The uncertainties, doubts, and troubles necessarily implicated in the process have two effects: first, they reveal the impossibility or difficulty to instrumentalize other human beings and their affects and emotions. Second, they disturb and block the neoliberal imperative of self-optimization, making the person less fit for the challenges of the market(s). One might object that the polyerotic lifestyle is one that celebrates and romanticizes mobility and precariousness. I would argue that this is not the case: while it is true that polyeros does not deny and does consciously assume the constitutive ambivalence and processuality of human relationships, uncertainty does not become a justification for economic or emotional exploitation; it does not lead to it. On the contrary, polyerotic experiments foster recognition of human vulnerability, rooted in interdependence, and thus encourage finding material, collective, sustainable, democratic, inclusive modalities to take care of it.

(c) Polyerotic experiments "succeed" in bringing lovers and friends to engage in long, sometimes strenuous emotional discussions. As said, these discussions are continuously opening up new venues for struggles. As such, they appear as utterly unproductive: the time spent in reflecting upon and collectively transforming affects and emotions, as well as in negotiating all over again life arrangements that refuse to follow conventional patterns, does seem to effectively escape any economic, capitalist valorisation.

LEARNING TO CRITICIZE AND TRANSFORM

In previous chapters, I have argued that eros is a space for individuals to experience freedom. Individual freedom is not a static condition, but a process in which human beings gradually learn what they are and want, and where they try to realize their wishes, desires, and projects *with a little help* from their friends and lovers. Freedom is thus not solely an individual process: lovers and friends can come to understand and to realize what they are collectively, insofar as they try to realize their shared wishes, desires, and projects together, as collective endeavors. The concept of erotic freedom is, moreover, intimately connected with a multiple account of power. To be free means to acquire various forms of *power to*, be able to exercise *power over* and counterpower, to be and *feel* empowered, both individually and collectively. In the previous section, I have argued that the power of erotic bonds might become relevant beyond the private level, for the persons in love. By acquiring a certain publicity, erotic bonds can attract a recognition that has an impact on social contexts in broader terms.

The power of erotic love might now come to acquire social and political relevance in another sense as well. Eros can become a space of education in which friends and lovers develop and refine virtues, capacities, and knowledge that apply not only to themselves but also to the world they inhabit together. Through their erotic bonds, individuals can come to feel dissatisfied and impatient with their social contexts, learn to articulate such affects and emotions, and translate them into cognitive and practical tools for critical scrutiny and desires to resist and change. Such understanding of eros as a critical and transformative learning process might be viewed as a reformulation of some thoughts that Plato presents in the *Symposium*. In the exchange between Diotima and Socrates, the woman from Mantinea famously casts love as a processual activity of "physical and mental procreation in an attractive medium."[32] Making love means doing certain things with generative, creative consequences: as result of love-making, new human beings, artifacts, laws, processes of reasoning, and parcels of wisdom come to light. As creatures who love, we are always in the process of becoming immortal, even though we will never be immortal: eros, Diotima is telling her disciple, occupies a middle ground between mortality and immortality, between human and gods. In this chapter, I am suggesting that eros could also work as a sort of precondition for Diotima's vision: prior to generating beautiful things, and the knowledge of them, eros should help to apprehend how things are *not* "beautiful," how they are indeed damaged, and why and how they should and could change in order for human beings to experience (some portion) of goodness and beauty. Eros can foster capacities and power of social critique, the desire and striving toward something that we might envision, confusedly at first, as better than what we have right now. Eros can be the passage from who and where we are and who we will be and where we will arrive—it is the journey toward what "will be." (Alas, we might realize after a while that we have taken a wrong path.)

This motive is concretely illustrated, I believe, in the passage of the *Symposium* that comes right after Socrates's report of his exchange with Diotima, and that should break with it—but, actually, it does not. This is the part of the story where Alcibiades speaks about his love for Socrates, a "desire to explore and be explored by that other as other."[33] In her illuminating essay on this passage of Plato's work, Nussbaum reimagines Alcibiades's words: "I make myself cracked, *put myself into the power* and under the judging, defining eye of the other outside me."[34] In the society depicted by Plato, homosexual lovemaking requires both the figure of *erōmenos*, who is usually a younger, beautiful boy who plays the passive object of loving recognition, who attracts love but is not (and should not be) himself aroused, and the figure of *erastēs*, the older man who explicitly displays his interest and actively and, often unsuccessfully, pursues his object of desire. Alcibiades, in the first stage of his affair with Socrates, behaves as he usually does in his erotic encounters: he performs the *erōmenos* role, acting as a self-sufficient individual who provokes but does not reciprocate desire. The experience of love, however, makes his passive power waver. He realizes he cannot be content with himself anymore; he *is* dependent on Socrates's recognition, he *does* desire to open himself up to his influence and judgment, to be "contaminated.'" The passive power of recognition must become reciprocal. Alcibiades discovers his acute desire to both know the other and to make himself known. Activity and passivity, attracting and giving love, being recognized and recognizing, are deeply interconnected movements. Socrates's words and actions, admits a distraught Alcibiades, overwhelm and put a spell on him, disturb his "mental composure," and make him dissatisfied with the slavishness of his life.[35] Socrates's power over his younger lover pushes Alcibiades to feel shame and, consequently, to question his life, his values, his habits. He feels compelled to try to become a better version of himself.[36] And, to be sure, Socrates as well is not unaffected and untroubled by Alcibiades's presence.[37] Importantly for the purposes of this chapter, the disruption of the conventional sexual roles in Plato's context does not solely interest the individual level. In an exemplary manner, and because of the exemplarity of both Alcibiades and Socrates in their community, their relationship is disruptive with regard to the entire social context. Love reveals itself as the power to shake the pillars of the sexual normativity of the time: the hierarchical division of "sexual labor," so to speak, between passive *erōmenos* and active *erastēs* (and between the youth and the elder).

In an iconic short essay, "The Uses of the Erotic: The Erotic as Power," Audre Lorde develops, I believe, this Platonic inspiration along the path just sketched out. For her, erotic love is a form of deep, passionate connection between persons (but not only: it is also a connection with oneself, and with the world, through various media, artistic in particular), characterized by one central affective experience: joy. Joy implies "the chaos of our strongest feelings,"[38] an uncertainty that gestures towards a critique of given feeling rules, established norms, and new "beginnings of our sense of self."[39] *Joy as an act of resistance*, as the title of Idle's album declares.

Erotic joy is ambivalent. While it corresponds to a strong sensation of wholeness, completeness, it also feels like "never enough." It must be replicated, multiplicated, expanded. In the case of erotic love between persons, Lorde stresses the collective moment, in which the undergoing erotic passions are shared and actively take them up: "The erotic functions for me in several ways, and the first is in providing the power which comes from sharing deeply any pursuit with another person. The sharing of joy, whether physical, emotional, psychic, or intellectual, forms a bridge between the sharers which can be the basis for understanding much of what is not shared between them, and lessens the threat of their difference."[40]

The reference to differences that are threatening does not point to the conception of fusion-love we have seen and criticized in chapter 1. The metaphor of the bridge suggests that individual differences, and the related distances, cannot be fully overcome, even in the most intense moments of joy. Audre Lorde is very probably thinking here also of the passionate, sexual love bringing together individuals, women in particular, divided by racial differences, as Black and *white* women, as well as of relationships of friendship between heterosexual and lesbian women.[41] The power of the erotic, then, is the power to overcome what I have called "impediments of love" (see chapter 3), and, more generally, to intervene in the social context organized around these impediments: "That deep and irreplaceable knowledge of my capacity for joy comes to demand from all of my life that it be lived within the knowledge that such satisfaction is possible. . . . For once we begin to feel deeply all the aspects of our lives, we begin to demand from ourselves and from our life-pursuits that they feel in accordance with that joy which we know ourselves to be capable of."[42] This reminds of Cavell: "The open pursuit of happiness is a standing test, or threat, to every social order."[43] Erotic experiences make us (re)discover some special forms of *power to*, both active and passive—in particular, how to engage in activities, and how to let oneself go, in ways that bring about extremely pleasurable sensations and emotions in oneself and in others. These are experiences that become generative, soliciting us to look for the same or similar affects in other sectors of our existence, in contexts we do not usually regard as erotic. This urge to expand the erotic experience makes us realize that the world in which we are currently living is one that systematically and structurally suffocates and impedes erotic freedom, and freedom more generally. According to Lorde, this is a society that discriminates, oppresses, and harms people on the basis of gender, sexuality, and race, and that is based on the imperative of profit, and that either tends to ignore people's emotions or to instrumentalize them in view of their potential for profit.

The damaged society cannot, however, completely prevent erotic experiences to take place. The critical naturalist approach elaborated in chapter 4 should have given some grounds for how to think of the nonidentity between social habits, norms, structures, and feeling rules on the one side and erotic experiences on the other. When entering into interpersonal bonds of erotic love, or engaging in erotic activities (e.g., artistic ones), we feel that things could be different, and that it is our right to demand the change, and that we are or may become powerful enough, both cognitively and practically, to attempt it: "Our erotic knowledge empowers us, *becomes a lens through which we scrutinize all aspects of our existence*, forcing us to evaluate those aspects honestly in terms of their relative meaning within our lives."[44] The erotic joy is an affect that pushes us to cultivate particular, critical faculties of cognition. These are, furthermore, connected with practical powers, which prevent us from "settl[ing] for the convenient, the shoddy, the conventionally expected, nor the merely safe." When we take on erotic affects of the sort, we start to give up "being satisfied with suffering and self-negation, and with the numbness which so often seems like their only alternative in our society." In touch with the erotic, we "become less willing to accept powerlessness, . . . resignation, despair, self-effacement, depression, self-denial."[45]

In Peck's movie, before the blossoming of his friendship with Friedrich, Karl Marx was rather resigned, desperate, depressed. He could not envisage how to realize his literary and political ideas. His social and cultural context, the intellectual circle in which he was (not) at home, were stifling and disempowering. The encounter with Friedrich Engels, and their close collaboration, changed his situation radically. Lorde herself can vouch for the erotic power of relationships between women: "As a Black lesbian feminist, I have a particular feeling, knowledge, and understanding for those sisters with whom I have danced hard, played, or even fought. This deep participation has often been the forerunner for joint concerted actions not possible before."[46] In another famous paper, "The Master's Tools Will Never Dismantle the Master's House," Lorde starts from the networks between women to problematize and further expand a feminist critique of care: the desire to nurture, experienced by women, should disentangle itself from the heterosexual background, should take as its object not only men and children, but also other women, as friends or lovers. As such, desires to care can have remarkable empowering consequences.[47] Mutual care, support, and inspiration, however, cannot suppress the differences and do not prevent tensions and conflicts. This has emerged glowingly in Ferrante's novels. The years-long erotic bond between Lila and Lenù can be seen as the main drive of both women's education. Not only their union, but also the need to reaffirm and impose their individual independence and singularity have brought them to intensely care for while at the same time exercising power over each other. It is their loving agonism that has made them into autonomous agents, capable of emancipating themselves, in different ways, from their oppressive and violent social context, as well as to gather the strength to struggle to change it, each of them in their own fashion and by relying on different weapons.

Something similar has been envisaged by the Marxist feminist thinker Alexandra Kollontai, theorist of and actor in the Russian Revolution. In "Make Way for Winged Eros: A Letter to Working Youth," dated 1923, she theorizes one form of eros, "winged eros," as the form of love with more revolutionary potential. Winged eros, which rejects, among other things, bourgeois monogamy norms, is a revolutionary force because "the person experiencing love acquires the *inner qualities necessary to the builders of a new culture.*" While bourgeois ideology demands that a person should only display such qualities in their relationship with one partner, the new ideology Kollontai wants to account for wants men and women to "develop these qualities not only in relation to the chosen one but *in relation to all the members of the collective.*"[48] For Kollontai too, free ("winged"!) eros amounts to a type of intersubjective relationship in which special political qualities are cultivated, qualities that promise to transform the given reality. Erotic feelings, multiplier of human happiness, have the power to "emerge from the private into the public sphere."[49] Kollontai had a clear vision of the new social (and moral) order the revolution was striving at: a Communist order, in which private experiences of love between persons have to come second to the love for the collectivity. This is not the only possible direction or conclusion though. Eros has a rebellious core, not completely assimilable to any given social reality, moral doctrine or political organization—it does not (have to) teach us in advance where to go.

Let's recap how we can see the erotic as a special modality, or set of modalities, to relate to each other, which contributes to an erotic education that form critical and transformative subjectivities—that is, free subjectivities, able to experience freedom and to contribute to the realization of a free society. Erotic education consists, to begin with, in the development of critical and transformative *passive, sensuous powers*. These include the capacity to abandon and lose oneself, release control, let oneself be caught up in situations and dynamics beyond one's, and society's, control. They require a certain trust both in oneself and in the other persons involved. One might only hope the experience will bring about both cognitive or intellectual as well as bodily pleasures, but there is no guarantee that pain and suffering can be avoided.

Erotic education, moreover, aims at developing the communicative capacity to "build bridges" (Lorde) among differences experienced as painful and harmful. Differences are painful and harmful because rooted in intersections of damaging objective conditions. Communication, importantly, cannot solely work along rational channels, as exchange of reasons or rational claims. These subjectivities are also endowed by *empathetic powers*, capacities to perceive, imagine, and see the world from and through others' eyes and (partially) feel the affects and emotions they are feeling. For Lorde, empathy is particularly relevant from a critical standpoint insofar as it allows a sharing of affects and emotions connected to the harms of social (racial, gender, sexual, capitalist) oppression. For instance, empathy can allow oppressed subjectivities (persons and groups) to feel other subjectivities' anger, understand its roots, and act accordingly, across the divides of race, class, and sexuality. In order for change to happen, we have to understand and feel that "I am not free while any woman is unfree," and that if we are contributing to other women's oppression, we are at the same time strengthening our own as well.[50] The realization of this concept of freedom is explicitly conceived of by Lorde in terms that recall the recognition-base account of love developed in chapter 2: freedom is realized, according to her, thanks to emphatic communication, which she calls the *recognition* of other women "as other faces of myself." Moreover, cherishing something similar to Schlegel's "romantic confusion," Lorde claims that "within the interdependence of mutual (nondominant) differences lies that security which enables us to descend into the *chaos of knowledge* and return with true visions of our future, along with the concomitant power to effect those changes which can bring the future into being."[51] Erotic bonds are, of course, not the only spaces in which such communication and creative dealing with difference can happen, where we learn how to take up others' perspectives. We can build bridges with different women, and with gender nonconforming people, in ways that do not imply or require erotic love. However, erotic bonds constitute a powerful resource in this respect.

Thanks to an erotic education, we develop the capacity to feel erotic affects and emotions that do not just seek to evaluate a given reality (Nussbaum) and have to be judged as appropriate (and even rational) to the extent to which they fit reality. What is more, these are emotions that *create*, in a certain sense, *another reality*, or, rather, *anticipate the possibility of another reality*, making visible what is not visible yet, how things could be different. They help to create other standards and criteria on the basis of which to evaluate their appropriateness and their (social and political) value. Such emotions manage to, as Martin Hartmann puts it, "constitute the reality that must be taken into account in judging, evaluating or assessing" the same (and other) emotions.[52] Transformative emotions, as Hartmann calls them, emerge and can be clarified in intersubjective (communicative) exchanges, and they have the power to *present and articulate* a world, rather than *representing and fitting to* it. They help to shape a world in the attempt to critically cope and deal with its problems.

Lugones's understanding of anger, which I have discussed in the previous section, might be considered as an example of a transformative emotion, or affect, employed in a sociocritical sense.[53] In a racist context, the anger of a certain racially discriminated minority is misunderstood and hence judged as exaggerated, "unfitting," blindly violent, irrational, counterproductive. The only way to make sense of it is to imagine and anticipate another "world of sense," in which the irrational and indeterminate anger becomes a recognizable and understandable emotion. Such imagination, moreover, should contribute to actions oriented at actualizing a world in which the unspeakable suffering of people of color becomes intelligible, thus helping to clarify responsibility for it, acknowledge it, and outline reparations, solutions, and alternatives to it.

Erotic bonds are traversed by affects and emotions that have this transformative quality as well. Joy is one bright example. As mentioned, erotic joy has two aspects or dimensions: in one respect, it is what lovers and friends feel in the most intense moments of their being together. At the same time, this is an indeterminate, hence more radical, affect. Joy has the power to point toward what we might feel (but we do not know yet) in another world, one in which eroticism would not be relegated to the bedroom alone, or be systematically impeded or damaged. The enthusiasm, exhilaration ,and hope, as well as the anger and anxiety, that, for instance, Karl and Friedrich or Lila and Lenú have experienced together empower them, both as individuals and as a *we*, in ways that refine, strengthen, and nourish their intellectual and political virtues and powers. The consequences of these affects gesture beyond themselves; they do not let the lovers and friends be satisfied with the status quo, with what they are or have, but push them to see what could be different, and make them believe they can contribute to making a difference.

CODA: FREEDOM AND EROTIC JOURNEYS

In this chapter, at the end of the journey that our exploration of eros has been, I have attempted to show how and in which sense erotic bonds are not only dependent on or shaped and influenced by larger social and political norms, structures, and feeling rules: they can have a transformative impact on them too. I have sketched out two modalities of erotic love becoming, in *indirect* fashion, public and political as a critical and transformative *we*-power. Erotic love, when and if able to actualize freedom, can open up a space of experimentation. This can be deemed as compatible with existing liberal and democratic values, as Nussbaum envisioned it, but not only. Eros can be a refuge in which people hurt by various forms of social oppression or domination can rest, find support, comprehension, and care, but, again, not only. Erotic love can, furthermore, become a sort of laboratory for forming, cultivating, and experimenting with certain cognitive and practical capacities and virtues that solicit us to not be content and satisfied with how things are. Such a learning process is animated, *moved*, by a pivotal affective and emotional dimension. The formation of critical and transformative subjectivities requires, in particular, the cultivation of passive, empathetic, imaginative powers. We become critical and able to contribute to larger processes of change *also* when we learn how to let ourself go, get lost, abandon ourselves to situations that we cannot control. When we become able to communicate with others by relying on sensual, bodily thrusts that lead us to recognize, affirm and cherish the others' unique singularity, to see the world through their eyes without the ambition or presumption to come to really know or control them. When we trust our affects and emotions to imagine and anticipate "new worlds of sense."

Exploring the sociopolitical weight and depth of erotic love does not mean building upon an erotic normativity on a general social and political scale. Love, especially its erotic version, cannot become the principle that organizes, steers, and informs the whole society. Social relationships or bonds between persons and groups are and have to remain of a different sort. Erotic relationships are intense, ambitious; they require intimacy, time, and energy. We cannot, should not, and would not want to engage in relationships of this sort with everybody and at any time.[54] However, especially when erotic bonds unfold by rejecting and challenging given habits, norms, structures, and rules, thus by actualizing freedom, they can give rise to dynamics of public recognition. This does not only mean that modalities of love that are not at a certain moment in a given time publicly recognized (e.g., homosexual, queer or polyerotic love, or just a truly equal marriage) start to struggle to achieve such recognition and, hence, end up remodeling the entire social fabric. What is more, and more radically, bonds that are not interested in receiving others' recognition, since they explicitly reject the requirements and conditions that such a concession would inevitably imply, have anyway the power to attract public recognition. They can, that is, move others to take an interest in them, make them observe what they do, learn that, and how things could be different, have an effect by affecting them with unknown emotions or opening up novel ways to deal with them.

Why, ultimately, is erotic education desirable? To which aim do we learn critical and transformative virtues and powers and struggle to receive or attract public recognition? Eros does not open up for us a clear vision of what a good society is and could be; it has very limited utopic powers. It can, however, teach us what it means to be free, how can we realize freedom together with other persons and as collective endeavors. The virtues and capacities we develop and refine, thanks to our lovers and friends, and the effects of public recognition, should be aimed at overcoming some of the damages oppressing us, curbing—that is, our freedom, not only in intimate but also in broader social domains.

In "No Name in the Street," James Baldwin sketches his biographical trajectory by connecting it to the social and political upheavals of the 1950s, 1960s, and 1970s. A singular, private story is always deeply entangled with public events and transformations—this is the main sense of Baldwin's operation. At a certain point in the story (during his Paris period), he feels the compulsion to mention his experience of falling in love, which he introduces as something he has "learned."[55] His story, he admits, would be a very different one if love had not forced him to attempt to deal with himself. Baldwin here suggests that his learning process about social and political matters has been inspired (also) by an erotic (self-)experience. When one falls in love, he writes, "the world changes then, and it changes forever. Because you love one human being, you *see* everyone else very *differently* than you saw them before—perhaps I only mean to say that *you begin to see*—and you are both *stronger* and more *vulnerable*, both *free* and *bound*. Free, *paradoxically*, because, now, you have a *home*—your lover's arms. And bound: to that mystery, precisely, a *bondage which liberates you* into something of the glory and suffering of the world."[56]

In love, we experience ourselves at our most vulnerable, as we shockingly feel and realize our dependence on others. Such bond(age), however, does also make us feel and realize our strength and our power, both individually and as part of collectivities and in relation to them. Baldwin is here relying on a metaphor that is central for Hegel as well, and for Hegelian considerations on love: that of feeling at home, in a new home, together with others, in which we learn who we are and want and could be. In virtue of erotic experiences, our bodily, sensuous and cognitive capacities to sense not only the injustices and wrongs of the world, but also the beauty and the joy it can generate, are awakened and sharpened. Eros can push us to be more involved in this world, to contribute to overcoming its damages and to intensifying its glory—to become, in other words, *more free* (while being also painfully aware of the possibilities and realities of unfreedom).

Instead of being conceived of as a home, an image suggesting closure and stability, freedom can, then, perhaps be better pictured as a journey. Freedom is the path we undertake from one home to another one, a series of adventures taking place on the road, as masterfully exemplified by Cavell's couples. It is a journey unfolding through moments and phases in which we feel uprooted, displaced, lost. Unlike other, solitary journeys, this can be undertaken only together with others, who guide and teach us how to proceed, and who invite us to be their guides and teachers. Contrary to Plato's picture of the *scala amoris*, of love as an ascending learning process that allows us to reach better and more refined forms of beauty and knowledge, we cannot always be sure if we are going up or down, if we are really learning, and if what we are learning is really worth it. Contrary to Dante's fantastic journey in *La Divina Commedia*, accompanied by the two persons he loved the most, Virgilio and Beatrice, we often cannot clearly tell heaven from hell, but we are not persisting in a limbo either. While we travel, we do discover worlds, internal and external, natural and social, old and new, and we might also contribute to (re-)create them and make them into better places—to inhabit *and* to travel through. The hope is that the map we have followed, revised, and enriched in this book could help to provide orientation in dangerous, exciting voyages of and toward freedom.

NOTES

INTRODUCTION: THE TROUBLES WE DESIRE

1. Noreena Hertz, *The Lonely Century: How to Restore Human Connection in a World That's Pulling Apart* (New York: Currency, 2021).
2. Karl Marx, *Economic and Philosophic Manuscripts of 1844*, In *Collected Works, Vol. 3, 1843–1844*, by K. Marx and F. Engels (New York: New York International Publishers, 2005), 229–346, 325.
3. Eva Illouz, *Why Love Hurts? A Sociological Explanation* (Cambridge: Polity, 2012), 6.
4. Eva Illouz, *The End of Love: A Sociology of Negative Relations* (Oxford: Oxford University Press, 2019).
5. The are then perhaps condemned to what Lauren Berlant has called "cruel optimism": Lauren Berlant, *Cruel Optimism* (Durham, N.C.: Duke University Press, 2011).
6. See Kate Julian, "Why Are Young People Having So Little Sex?," *Atlantic*, December 2018, https://www.theatlantic.com/magazine/archive/2018/12/the-sex-recession /573949/ (accessed May 29, 2024); and Zoë Heller, "How Everyone Got So Lonely," *New Yorker*, April 11, 2022, https://www.newyorker.com/magazine/2022/04/11/how -everyone-got-so-lonely-laura-kipnis-noreena-hertz?fbclid=IwAR32rJoarW1FbE8 wCIhVwIYW2Ji6OkrG91KyOdqbUfWNCB_7zI6pyNLRC8E.
7. See, for example, Arlie Russell Hochschild, *The Managed Heart: Commercialization of Human Feeling* (Berkeley: California University Press, [1983] 2012); and Estelle Ferrarese, "Precarity of Work, Precarity of Moral Dispositions: Concern for Others in the Era of 'Emotional' Capitalism," *Women's Studies Quarterly* 45, nos. 3–4 (2017): 176–92.
8. Courtney Blackwell, Jeremy Birnholz, and Charles Abbott, "Seeing and Being Seen: Co-Situation and Impression Formation Using Grindr, a Location-Aware

Gay Dating App," *New Media & Society* 17, no. 7 (2015): 1117–36; Kane Race, "Speculative Pragmatism and Intimate Arrangements: Online Hook-up Devices in Gay Life," *Culture Health & Sexuality* 17, no. 4 (2015): 1–16.

9. Mitchell Hobbs, Stephen Owen, and Livia Gerber, "Liquid Love? Dating Apps, Sex, Relationships, and the Digital Transformation of Intimacy," *Journal of Sociology* 53, no. 2 (2017): 271–84.

10. See, for example, Elyakim Kislev, *Relationships 5.0: How AI, VR, and Robots Will Reshape Our Emotional Lives* (Oxford: Oxford University Press, 2022).

11. Luke Brunning, *Romantic Agency: Loving Well in Modern Life* (Cambridge: Polity 2024).

12. Pamela Haag. *Marriage Confidential: Love in the Post-Romantic Age* (New York: HarperCollins, 2011).

13. Katherine Angel, *Tomorrow Sex Will Be Good Again: Women and Desires in the Age of Consent* (London: Verso, 2021).

14. The essay is in Maggie Nelson, *On Freedom: Four Songs of Care and Constraint* (London: Jonathan Cape, 2021), 78.

15. Nelson's intent, in this essay, is also to challenge the popular view, held especially by liberal feminists, that respect of "consent" is enough as bulwark against sexual violence. For an insightful critique of the consent-paradigma in such discourses, see Daniel Loick, "'. . . as if it were a thing.' A Feminist Critique of Consent," *Constellations* 27, no. 3 (2020): 412–22. For a convincing reformulation and defense of the meaning and role of sexual consent, see Manon Garcia, *The Joy of Consent: A Philosophy of God Sex* (Cambridge, Mass.: Harvard University Press, 2023).

16. Lillian Fishman, *Acts of Service: A Novel* (New York: Hogarth, 2022); my italics.

17. Asa Seresin, "On Heteropessimism," *New Inquiry*, October 9, 2019, https://thenewinquiry.com/on-heteropessimism/.

18. Illouz, *End of Love*, 9.

19. John Dewey, *Lectures in China, 1919–1920* (Honolulu: University of Hawai'i Press, 1973), 72.

20. John Dewey, "Lectures in Social and Political Philosophy (China)," *European Journal of Pragmatism and American Philosophy* 7, no. 2 (2015): 1–39, 8.

21. Dewey, *Lectures in China*, 64.

22. Some of them are: Berit Brogaard, *On Romantic Love: Simple Truths about a Complex Emotion* (Oxford: Oxford University Press, 2015); Paul Kottman, *Love as Human Freedom* (Stanford, Calif.: Stanford University Press, 2017); S. I. Carrie Jenkins, *What Love Is and What It Could Be* (New York: Basic Books, 2017); Patricia Marino, *Philosophy of Sex and Love: An Opinionated Introduction* (New York: Routledge 2019); Simon May, *Love: A New Understanding* (Oxford: Oxford University Press 2019).

23. According to May, *Love*, part 5, the love for children is at the moment the most strong, uncontroversial form of love. This thesis is not uncontroversial, though, as, for example, critical discussion of motherly love shows; see Rachel Cusk, *A Life's Work* (London: Faber and Faber, 2008). One limitation of the present volume is that it does not consider such discussion, and does not analyze, more generally, the troubles to be found in the intergenerational dimension of love. Eros is taken here as love between adult human beings. Erotic bonds between persons who can be defined as "adults" and persons who cannot be defined as such raise a series of

overly complex issues that, unfortunately, cannot be addressed within the framework of this work.

24. In this book, I do not consider love between human beings and unanimated objects, animals, machines (e.g., robots), cities, or collective social entities (football teams, political parties, homeland countries or places of origin). As I argue, erotic love relies on the possibility and desire of reciprocation and symmetry (a possibility that is, of course, not always actualized). The object of love is something that we must take as a subject, that is capable of the same cognitive and affective "performances" we are capable of, and that is in principle able to display the same degree of vulnerability as ours. Erotic freedom is premised on the similarity and reciprocity of the subject and object of love.

25. María Lugones. *Pilgrimages/Peregrinajes: Theorizing Coalition Against Multiple Oppressions* (London: Rowman and Littlefield, 2003).

1. SOME KINDA LOVE: A (PROVISIONAL) MAP

1. Carrie S. I. Jenkins, "What Is Love? An Incomplete Map of the Metaphysics," *Journal of the American Philosophical Association* 1, no. 2 (2015), 349–64, 349.

2. Jenkins, "What Is Love?," 360.

3. Jenkins, 361.

4. Brian Earp and Julian Savulescu, *Love Drugs. The Chemical Future of Relationships* (Stanford, Calif.: Stanford University Press 2020). Earp and Savulescu discuss Jenkins's "dual-nature" theory for examining the possibility, acceptability, and desirability of intervening in love relationships with the help of chemical substances, "love drugs" (e.g., MDMA) with the aim of "enhancing" them. Jenkins, for her part, is convinced that her metaphysical approach is helpful to question and dispel some ideologies that mess up our emotional lives, in particular the ideology of monogamy, see also Carrie S. I. Jenkins, *What Love Is and What It Could Be* (New York: Basic Books, 2017).

5. Paul Kottman, *Love as Human Freedom* (Stanford, Calif.: Stanford University Press 2017).

6. Kottman, *Love as Human Freedom*, 4–5.

7. Plato, *The Symposium* (Cambridge: Cambridge University Press 2008), 210a1–212a10. Jonathan Lear has interpreted Freud's views around erotic love in a similar way in *Love and Its Place in Nature. A Philosophical Interpretation of Freudian Psychoanalysis* (New York: Farrar, Straus, and Giroux, 1990).

8. Plato, *Symposium*, 177a–d. Symposia, in ancient Greece, had the role of forming the elite youth and educating about desire, including sexual desire. They were supported by the institution of *paiderastia*, the socially regulated and appreciated intercourse between an older man, the *erastês*, and a younger, often teenage boy, the *erômenos*: "The symposium was a place where one learnt how to value and desire the right sorts of things and in the appropriate manner. It was a place where virtue was supposedly reinforced and passed on to the young, a place where men were both displayed and made," Frisbee C. C. Sheffield, *Plato's Symposium: The Ethics of Desire* (Oxford: Oxford University Press 2006, 5).

9. Plato, *Symposium*, 189c.

10. Plato, 191d3–5.
11. Plato, 192e6–7.
12. Friedrich Schlegel, "Lucinde, a Novel," in *Lucinde and the Fragments* (Minneapolis: University of Minnesota Press, 1971), 41–140, 48–49.
13. Schlegel, "Lucinde," 46.
14. Schlegel, 48. Anticipating a dynamic that I will illustrate in the next chapter, however, Schlegel/Lucius also says: "Not hate, as the wise men say, but love, *separates* living creatures, and shapes the world; and only in love's light can you find this and observe it." (106, my italics) Love union entails a tendency to separation, leading to lovers' independence and autonomy, which is the condition for the couple's generative relation to the world.
15. John Keats, *Selected Letters of John Keats* (Cambridge, Mass.: Harvard University Press, 2002), 390.
16. Robert C. Solomon, *About Love: Reinventing Romance for Our Times* (New York: Madison, 1988), 11.
17. Solomon, *About Love*, 47.
18. Robert Nozick, "Love's Bond," In *Examined Life. Philosophical Meditations* (New York: Simon and Schuster 1989), 68–86, 70.
19. Nozick, "Love's Bond," 74.
20. Nozick, 73–74.
21. Erich Fromm, *The Art of Loving* (New York: Harper Perennial [1956] 2006), 28.
22. Curiously, according to Immanuel Kant, the reification of the object of love might work as a moral warranty. Per se, sexual love is "pathological"; it does not fall within the realm of morality, because it entails a passivity and submission under (natural) inclinations that cannot be overcome. The only way in which this kind of love can be made tolerable from a moral perspective consists in framing it within the institution of marriage. Kant defines the marriage contract as "the union of two persons of different sexes for lifelong *possession* of each other's sexual attributes." Immanuel Kant, *The Metaphysics of Morals* (Cambridge: Cambridge University Press [1797–1803] 1991), 96; my italics. Possession of a person's sexual attributes is equivalent to making this person "into a thing," reifying them (97). From a moral point of view, this is tolerable only if reification is reciprocal.
23. Fromm, *Art of Loving*, 19.
24. Michael Hardt, "For Love or Money," *Cultural Anthropology* 26, no. 4 (2011): 679–80.
25. Irving Singer, *Meaning in Life, Vol. 2: The Pursuit of Love* (Cambridge, Mass.: MIT Press [1994] 2010), 135.
26. Bennet Helm, *Love, Friendship, and the Self: Intimacy, Identification, and the Social Nature of Persons* (Oxford: Oxford University Press 2009), 18.
27. Keats, *Selected Letters*, 390.
28. Nozick, "Love's Bond," 80.
29. See, e.g., Solomon, *About Love*, 163.
30. Roland Barthes, *A Lover's Discourse: Fragments* (London: Vintage, [1977] 2018), 11.
31. Barthes, *Lover's Discourse*, 32.
32. Simone de Beauvoir, *The Second Sex* (London: Vintage [1949] 2011), 707.
33. Solomon, *About Love*, 273.
34. Solomon, 322.

35. Nozick, "Love's Bond," 82.
36. Michel de Montaigne, "On Friendship," in *Essays* (London: Penguin, 1993), 91–104, 97.
37. Montaigne, "On Friendship," 100.
38. Nancy K. Miller, *My Brilliant Friends: Our Lives in Feminism* (New York: Columbia University Press 2019), 110–11.
39. On this, see the very helpful book by Paul W. Ludwig, *Eros and Polis: Desire and Community in Greek Political Theory* (Cambridge: Cambridge University Press 2002).
40. Aristotle, *The Nicomachean Ethics* (Oxford: Oxford University Press 2009), 1155a1–16.
41. In books 8 and 9, Aristotle spends some time discussing all the different relationships of philia between people who are, for different reasons, not equal—as, for instance, between father and son, or man and woman, but also between nonequal men who engage in the standard form of love affair in ancient Greece: pederasty. Aristotle is interested in all the "complaints" and "incidents" that can arise in friendships of this sort, as when two lovers love each other for different motives—one, for example, for the sake of pleasure and the other for the sake of utility (Aristotle, *Nicomachean Ethics*, 1164a6–8). The core of the problem, in many of these relationships gone astray, lies in the fact that these people "love" their friends not for the persons they are, but for some of their qualities, which can (or cannot) procure them pleasures and advantages. Love that is not unconditional, but, rather, conditioned by the other's qualities, is therefore often unhappy love.
42. Aristotle, 1156b7.
43. Aristotle, 1156a3–6.
44. Fromm's idea of love discussed in 1.1. is partially inspired, I think, by this Aristotelian position.
45. Aristotle, *Nicomachean Ethics*, 1156b7–18.
46. Aristotle, 1157b31.
47. Aristotle, 1170b10–14.
48. Aristotle, 1158a12–13.
49. Aristotle, 1157a6–7.
50. Aristotle, 1157a10–12.
51. Alan Soble puts the care or concern theory of love succinctly as following: "x wishes y well for y's own sake, not for x's, and x acts accordingly to promote specifically y's well-being, not necessarily x's own," Alan Soble, "Union, Autonomy, and Concern," in *Love Analyzed*, ed. R. E. Lamb (Boulder, Colo.: Westview, 1997), 65–92, 78. For other versions of care theories of love, see, e.g., Neera K. Badhwar, "Friends Are Ends in Themselves," *Philosophy and Phenomenological Research* 48 (1987): 1–23; and Hugh LaFollette, *Personal Relationships: Love, Identity, and Morality* (Cambridge: Blackwell, 1996).
52. Harry G. Frankfurt, *The Reasons of Love* (Princeton, N.J.: Princeton University Press 2004), 42; my italics.
53. Harry G. Frankfurt, "Autonomy, Necessity, and Love," In *Necessity, Volition, and Love* (Cambridge: Cambridge University Press 1999), 129–41, 133.
54. Frankfurt, *Reasons of Love*, 61. Isn't this very close to the union theory of love?
55. Aristotle, *Nicomachean Ethics*, 1169a25–33.

56. Aristotle, 1170b10–14.

57. Aristotle, 1166a32, 1170b6.

58. Frankfurt, *Reasons of Love*, 42.

59. Aristotle, as we have seen, considers sexual love that has not reached the stage of perfect friendship a deficient form of philia. However, contrary to Frankfurt, who sees erotic love as too much tied to self-love and to the need of being reciprocated, Aristotle interprets this deficiency *precisely* as lack of reciprocity and equality.

60. Philip Pettit, *The Robust Demands of the Good: Ethics with Attachments, Virtue, and Respect* (Oxford: Oxford University Press 2015), 12.

61. Neera K. Badhwar, "Love," in *The Oxford Handbook of Practical Ethics*, ed. H. La Follette (Oxford: Oxford University Press, 2003), 45–46.

62. For another compelling criticism of Frankfurt's view along these lines, see Niko Kolodny, "Love as Valuing a Relationship," *Philosophical Review* 112, no. 2 (2003): 135–89, 142–46.

63. Angelika Krebs, *Zwischen Ich und Du. Eine dialogische Philosophie der Liebe* (Berlin: Suhrkamp, 2015), 52–53.

64. Care theorists could respond that, even if care is not everything that love is, without care we would not have love.

65. David J. Velleman, "Love as a Moral Emotion," *Ethics* 109, no. 2 (1999): 338–74, 353.

66. Velleman, "Love as a Moral Emotion," 361.

67. For a critique and at the same time development of Velleman's view, see the beautiful article by Vida Yao, "Grace and Alienation," *Philosophers' Imprint* 20, no. 16 (2020): 1–18.

68. Jonathan Lear, "The Authority of Love," in *Contours of Agency. Essays on Themes from Harry Frankfurt*, ed. S. Buss and L. Overton (Cambridge, Mass.: MIT Press 2002), 279–92, 286.

69. Lear, "Authority of Love," 287.

70. Harry G. Frankfurt, "Reply to Jonathan Lear," in *Contours of Agency: Essays on Themes from Harry Frankfurt*, ed. S. Buss and L. Overton (Cambridge, Mass.: MIT Press 2002), 293–98, 294–95.

71. Frankfurt, "Reply to Jonathan Lear," 296.

72. Krebs, *Zwischen Ich und Du*, 52.

73. See, e.g., Friedman, "Romantic Love and Personal Autonomy," 170; Ann Ferguson, "Love Politics: Romance, Care, and Solidarity," in *Love: A Question for Feminism in the Twenty-First Century*, ed. A. Jónasdóttir and A. Ferguson (New York: Routledge, 2014), 150–164; Nicola Barker, *Not the Marrying Kind: A Feminist Critique of Same-Sex Marriage* (New York: Palgrave Macmillan, 2012), chapter 5; and Federica Gregoratto, "Recognizing Care, Caring Recognition: Democratic Love and the Problems of Care Work," *Thesis Eleven* 134, no. 1 (2016): 56–72. The fact that women, as a result of social and historical processes of psychogender development, tend to care more than men, and to excel in care(-related) activities, must however not necessarily become object of criticism from a feminist standpoint. Feminist theories comprise also positive ethics of care; see, for example, Nancy Chodorow, *The Reproduction of Motherhood* (Berkeley: University of California Press 1978); and Carol Gilligan, *In a Different Voice* (Cambridge, Mass.: Harvard University Press 1982). In a way, these feminists embrace a care model of love.

74. Angelika Krebs, "Between I and Thou—On the Dialogical Nature of Love," In *Love and Its Objects: What We Can Care For?*, ed. C. Maurer, T. Milligan, and K. Pacovská (London: Palgrave Macmillan, 2014), 7–24, 22.

75. Neil Delaney, "Romantic Love and Loving Commitment: Articulating a Modern Ideal," *American Philosophical Quarterly* 33, no. 4 (1996): 339–56, 341.

76. Marilyn Friedman, "Romantic Love and Personal Autonomy," *Midwest Studies in Philosophy* 22, no. 1 (1988): 162–81, 165; my italics.

77. Friedman, "Romantic Love and Personal Autonomy," 169.

78. Helm, *Love, Friendship, and the Self*, 34, 213. As Margaret Gilbert puts it, "Anyone wishing to understand the human condition needs to understand not only what it is to act on one's own, but what it is to do something together with another person," Margaret Gilbert, *Joint Commitment: How We Make the Social World*. (Oxford: Oxford University Press 2014), 10.

79. Following Aristotle's strategy, Helm identifies intimate, close friendship (philia) as the paradigmatic and more general form of love. In his view, romantic, sexual love constitutes a particular case of friendship, in which the joint exercise of the lovers' autonomy is bound to a "certain sorts of joint activities—having candlelit dinners, seeing films or plays, having sex, and so on—that they understand to be activities each participates in exclusively with the other as a part of this plural person" (288). Parental love represents, on the contrary, an asymmetrical relationship in which only one agent (parent) takes care of the other's (child) autonomy.

80. Helm, 185.

81. Helm, 39.

82. Helm, 300.

83. Krebs, "Between I and Thou," 7.

84. Krebs, *Zwischen Ich und Du*, 170–74.

85. Also according to Niko Kolodny, people develop relationships of love and friendship when they find themselves participating in certain activities together, like "enjoying your leisure together, sharing a sense of humor, getting to know one another, exchanging confidences, providing assistance, and so on." These patterns of interaction give then rise to "noninstrumental concern" for one another; Kolodny, "Love as Valuing a Relationship," 169. Kolodny defines love as the activity of valuing a particular relationship with a particular person—a relationship that has been already formed and has its own particular history and a relationship that is about to be formed.

86. Krebs, 229.

87. In her praised debut novel, *Conversations with Friends* (2017), Sally Rooney does interestingly contribute to a dialogical account of love. She is able to portrait the intimate entanglements between different kinds of communicative (via email, texts, Facebook posts, face-to-face conversations) and bodily interactions. She shows how the more articulated, dense, direct, "transparent," and generous a message or a conversation is, the more margins for misunderstanding, opacity, puzzlement there emerge. Love and friendship, in the novel, appear as possible precisely in the ephemeral space between agreement and disagreement, understanding and misunderstanding, recognition and misrecognition, self-loss and self-discovery.

88. Alain Badiou, *In Praise of Love* (London: Serpent's Tail, 2012), 22.

89. Helm, *Love, Friendship, and the Self*, 174.
90. Krebs, *Zwischen Ich und Du*, 83.
91. "Therefore while in tyrannies friendship and justice hardly exist, in democracies they exist more fully; for where the citizens are equal they have much in common." Aristotle, *The Nicomachean Ethics*, 1161b8–10.
92. Gilbert, *Joint Commitment*, 267.
93. In fact, Gilbert thinks of the marital collectivity as a form of "fusion" (*Joint Commitment*, 265). To tell the truth, moreover, Krebs does not embrace a fully "static," "habitual" conception of dialogic love (*Zwischen Ich und Du*, 192); she is indeed able to accommodate a certain degree of agonism within romantic love, especially in her interpretation of Henry James's fiction.

2. "HE HAS KISSED HER WITH HIS FREEDOM": BOUND BY AMBIVALENCE

1. As mentioned at the beginning of chapter 1, Carrie Jenkins wanted initially to lay down a purely metaphysical philosophy of love, devoid of ethical connotations. However, her first popular book on this subject matter, *What Love Is and What It Could Be*, is centered around an ethical and political critique of monogamy. A following book, *Sad Love: Romance and the Search for Meaning* (Cambridge: Polity 2022), grapples precisely with the ethical significance of romantic love that, in her view is not to be found in a theory of happiness. Her alternative, however, is vaguely spelled out.
2. For example, bell hooks writes: "Domination cannot exist in any social situation where a love ethic prevails. . . . When love is present the desire to dominate and exercise power cannot rule the day." bell hooks, *All About Love. New Visions* (New York: HarperCollins , 2000), 98.
3. Simone de Beauvoir, *The Second Sex* (London: Vintage, [1949] 2011), 724–25.
4. Simone de Beauvoir, "It's About Time Women Put a New Face on Love," in *Feminist Writings*, ed. M. A. Simons and M. Timmermann (Chicago: University of Illinois Press, 2015), 76–80.
5. Beauvoir, *Second Sex*, 723.
6. Beauvoir, 782. Note, importantly, the active role that relationships between men and women, including intimate and love ones, have for more general political projects, in Beauvoir's view.
7. Simone de Beauvoir, "What Love Is—and Isn't," in *Feminist Writings* (ed. M. A. Simons and M. Timmermann, Chicago: University of Illinois Press, 2015), 99–102.
8. Beauvoir, *Second Sex*, 426.
9. Beauvoir, 781–82.
10. Beauvoir, 270. According to Penelope Deutscher, Beauvoir would regard "the 'highest' human achievement" in terms of generous reciprocal recognition, opposed to "appropriation, narcissism, subjection, and objectification." Deutscher, *The Philosophy of Simone de Beauvoir: Ambiguity, Conversions, Resistance* (Cambridge: Cambridge University Press, 2008), 43–45. Deutscher is doubtful, however, that the ethical ideal of reciprocal recognition could ever be definitely accomplished. She stresses, on the contrary, the necessity to insist on the complexity and even impossibility of this ethical ideal. As I anticipate in this passage on Beauvoir, and develop

223

further in the chapter, however, relationships of recognition, like freedom, are constitutively ambiguous. They do often fail, but moments or phases of failure do not rule out phases of (momentary) realization.

11. This view of freedom is in line with the existentialist philosophical tradition that Beauvoir has massively contributed to develop: see, especially, Simone de Beauvoir, *The Ethics of Ambiguity* (New York: Philosophical Library Open Road, [1948] 2015). Here, however, I read Beauvoir as more in line with the Hegelian tradition of social philosophy.

12. Axel Honneth, *The Struggle for Recognition: The Moral Grammar of Social Conflicts* (Cambridge: Polity, [1992] 1995). On Honneth's work, see, especially, Jean-Philippe Deranty, *Beyond Communication: A Critical Study of Axel Honneth's Social Philosophy* (Leiden: Brill, 2009); and Dagmar Wilhelm, *Axel Honneth: Reconceiving Social Philosophy* (London: Rowmann and Littlefield, 2019).

13. Axel Honneth, *Struggle for Recognition*, 95; my italics. See also Axel Honneth, *Freedom's Right: The Social Foundations of Democratic Life* (Cambridge: Cambridge University Press, [2011] 2014), 141f.

14. G. W. F. Hegel, *Outlines of the Philosophy of Right* (Oxford: Oxford University Press 2008), § 168.

15. Martha Nussbaum, "The Speech of Alcibiades: A Reading of Plato's *Symposium*," *Philosophy and Literature* 3, no. 2 (1979): 131–72, 160.

16. Aristotle, *The Nicomachean Ethics* (Oxford: Oxford University Press 2009), 1155b31–56a5.

17. Italo Testa, "Recognition as Passive Power: Attractors of Recognition, Biopower, and Social Power," *Constellations* 24, no. 2 (2017): 192–205.

18. See also Italo Testa, "How Does Recognition Emerge from Nature? The Genesis of Consciousness in Hegel's Jena Writings," *Critical Horizons* 13, no. 2 (2012): 176–96. On the significance of being an object in erotic experiences, see Caleb Ward and Ellie Anderson, "The Ethical Significance of Being an Erotic Object," in *The Palgrave Handbook of Sexual Ethics*, ed. D. Boonin (Cham: Palgrave Macmillan, 2022), 55–71.

19. Consider, moreover, relationships between adult human beings and newborns, how babies are able, unintentionally and without doing almost anything, to attract attention and care from their caregivers.

20. Hegel, *Outlines of the Philosophy of Right*, § 158A; my italics.

21. G. W. F. Hegel, *On Christianity: Early Theological Writings* (New York: Harper Torchbooks, 1961), 278.

22. Hegel, *Outlines of the Philosophy of Right*, §4A. See Frederick Neuhouser, *Foundations of Hegel's Social Theory: Actualizing Freedom* (Cambridge, Mass.: Harvard University Press 2000), 105–6.

23. G. W. F. Hegel, *Lectures on the Philosophy of Religion* (Oxford: Oxford University Press 2006), 428; my italics.

24. Hegel, *On Christianity*, 278–80.

25. Hegel, 317.

26. Hegel, *Outlines of the Philosophy of Right*, § 158A.

27. Hegel senses that lovers' independence, their alterity, might represent an enriching resource when he writes: "The beloved is not opposed to us, he is one with our own being; we see us only in him, *but then again he is not a we anymore—a riddle, a*

miracle [ein Wunder], one that we cannot grasp." G. W. F. Hegel, "Entwürfe über Religion und Liebe," in *Frühe Schriften, Werke 1* (Frankfurt am Main: Suhrkamp 1986), 244; my italics.

28. In the Jena *Realphilosophie* of 1805–1806, Hegel introduces for the first time the term "recognition" in the marginalia to his discussion of love: lovers, in this passage, are depicted as natural individuals, with uncultivated selves, who are recognized as such, G. W. F. Hegel, "Jena Lectures on the Philosophy of Spirit (1805/06)," in *Hegel and the Human Spirit*, ed. L. Rauch (Detroit, Mich.: Wayne University Press, 1983), 107.

29. Honneth, *Struggle for Recognition*, 100–101.

30. Honneth, *Freedom's Right*, 151; my italics.

31. There is a debate that has been troubling philosophers of love for a while, which can be referred to as the "bestowal vs. appraisal of value" debate. The issue is the following: Do we fall in love with a certain person on the basis of certain features of them that we appraise as valuable, or do we find such features (and our loved one) valuable because we have fallen in love, thus bestowing value upon them? In other words: Is love conditioned by certain traits or characteristics, or is love unconditional (and also inexplicable)? (For a good overview of the debate, see May, *Love*, chapter 2). I believe that a recognition-based account of love can provide a good way to deal with the dilemma: on the one hand, it is the lover's irreducible singularity, which is revealed, grasped, and cherished by loving recognition, that arouses love and keep it going. However, lovers themselves cannot pin down what features exactly have sparked and do sustain their love. If they could, they would end up reifying, precisely through their recognitive acts, their beloved ones, constraining them into a set of fixed, determinate traits. (Jim Reeves's song "I Love You Because" offers, I believe, the better formulation of this solution: "I love you for a hundred thousand reasons / But most of all I you 'cause you're you"). What is more, lovers do not love each other by recognizing who they are at the present moment, but for how they can and will become in their futures. Such an open and transformative character of love is not grasped in the "bestowal vs. appraisal of value" debate.

32. Elena Ferrante, *My Brilliant Friend: Book 1* (New York: Europa Editions, 2012); *The Story of a New Name: Book 2* (New York: Europa Editions 2013); *Those Who Leave and Those Who Stay: Book 3* (New York: Europa Editions 2014); *The Story of the Lost Child: Book 4* (New York: Europa Editions 2015).

33. Lenù's teacher plays an important role in her formation as well, but nobody else's recognition matters to Lenù as much as Lila's recognition.

34. Lila is not able to pursue the same brilliant career because her family, contrary to Lenù's, has actively prevented her to enroll in middle school and sent her to work in a shoe factory instead. This small and at the same time gigantic class distinction between Lenù and Lila is not, however, the only reason for Lila's less evident transformation. Another might be found in Lila's unwillingness to publicly display her vulnerability and neediness and to accept people in her life to guide and influence her—in her parade, that is, of almost invincible independence. In a certain sense, Lila is the embodiment of a Sartrean kind of freedom that, while trying to continuously assert itself above every otherness and overcome every given situation, systematically fails to realize itself. Lenù, on the contrary, is not afraid to show her

weakness and hesitation, letting other people leave their marks on her and thus bringing her away from where and who she was. One must notice, however, that this assessment of Lenù's and Lila's lives is tied to the specific perspective of the narrator, Lenù herself, who, in her old age, once she has already gained a considerable amount of financial, social, and academic recognition, looks back at her life and starts to recollect it. From a less bourgeois point of view, Lila's accomplishments cannot be considered small: in particular, she manages to acquire class consciousness, understanding and rebelling against the fascist and criminal economic structures controlling her district. Lila's and Lenù's different fates present indeed a mirror of the capitalist organization of social life, which allows and rewards individual class mobility but brutally represses structural transformations.

35. The following taxonomy of powers is inspired mostly by and elaborates on Amy Allen, *The Power of Feminist Theory: Domination, Resistance, Solidarity* (Boulder, Colo.: Westview, 1999).

36. Testa, "Recognition as Passive Power," 193.

37. I have been inspired for this sketch of Beauvoir's and Sartre's love and power relationship by Deirdre Bair, *Simone de Beauvoir: A Biography* (New York: Touchstone, 1991).

38. Friedrich Nietzsche, *Thus Spoke Zarathustra: A Book for All and None* (Cambridge: Cambridge University Press 2006), 33.

39. Ralph Waldo Emerson, "Friendship," in *Essays and Lectures* (New York: Penguin 1983), 351.

40. Emerson, "Friendship," 350. On the contrary, the figure of the "neighbor" corresponds to the person who always cuddles us, does not question what we do, cannot (or does not want to) show us what we could and can become to realize our freedom; Nietzsche, *Thus Spoke Zarathustra*, 44–45.

41. Nietzsche, *Thus* 40.

42. My version of recognition theory intends, therefore, to pick up and develop the insights of those who criticize Hegelian recognition theory for conveying an overly optimistic picture of human beings and their associations: see, for example, Jessica Benjamin, *Like Subjects, Love Objects: Essays on Recognition and Sexual Difference* (New Haven, Conn.: Yale University Press 1995); Illouz, *Why Love Hurts?*, chapter 4; Judith Butler, "Taking Another's View: Ambivalent Implications," in A. Honneth, *Reification and Recognition: A Look at an Old Idea*, ed. M. Jay (Oxford: Oxford University Press 2008), 97–119; and Amy Allen, "Recognizing Domination: Recognition and Power in Honneth's Critical Theory," *Journal of Power* 3, no. 1 (2010): 21–32.

43. See, most notably, the collection of essay *Recognition and Social Ontology*, ed. H. Ikäheimo and A. Laitinen (London: Brill, 2011).

44. Margaret Gilbert, "Mutual Recognition and Some Related Phenomena," in *Recognition and Social Ontology*, ed. H. Ikäheimo and A. Laitinen (Boston: Brill, 2011), 271–86, 276.

45. Gilbert, "Mutual Recognition," 277.

46. Sophie Lucido Johnson, *Many Love: A Memoir of Polyamory and Finding Love(s)* (New York: Touchstone, Kindle edition, 2018).

47. Simone de Beauvoir, *A Transatlantic Love Affair: Letters to Nelson Algren* (New York: New Press, 1997), 81.

48. Ronald de Sousa, "Emergence and Empathy," in *Institutions, Emotions, and Group Agents: Contributions to Social Ontology*, ed. A. K. Ziv and H. B. Schmid (New York: Springer, 2013), 141–58, 148.

49. Allen, *Power of Feminist Theory*, 127.

50. Gilbert, "Mutual Recognition," 277.

51. Amélie, O. Rorty, "The Historicity of Psychological Attitudes: Love Is Not Love Which Alters Not When It Alteration Finds," in *Friendship: A Philosophical Reader*, ed. N. K. Badhwar (Ithaca, N.Y.: Cornell University Press, 1993), 73–88, 77.

52. Johnson, *Many Love*.

53. Stanley Cavell, *The Pursuit of Happiness: The Hollywood Comedy of Remarriage* (Cambridge, Mass.: Harvard University Press, 1981).

54. Although the films analyzed by Cavell portrait only persons of opposite sex, there are no reasons for intending his view as constrained by heteronormativity. I discuss queer and nontraditional forms of erotic bonds, in a Cavellian sense, in chapter 5.

55. Stanley Cavell, *Cities of Words: Pedagogical Letters on a Register of the Moral Life* (Cambridge, Mass.: Harvard University Press, 2004), 24, 26.

56. One of the central features of the comedies of remarriage is the absence of the female protagonists' mothers. The only exception, Tracy's mother in *The Philadelphia Story*, does tellingly portrait a woman with a failed marriage.

57. Cavell, *Cities of Words*, 32.

58. Cavell, *Pursuits of Happiness*, 82.

59. Cavell, 103.

60. Cavell, 141.

61. Cavell, 201.

62. Cavell, 216.

63. The metaphor of the shared journey, or trip, seems thus better apt to grasp the nature of love than the Hegelian home metaphor.

64. Honneth, *Freedom's Right*, 146.

65. Emerson, "Friendship," 353.

66. John Dewey, "Philosophies of Freedom," in *The Later Works of John Dewey*, Vol. 3: 1927–1928, ed. J. A. Boydston (Carbondale: Southern Illinois University Press, [1928] 2008), 92–114, 108; my italics.

67. Axel Honneth, "Three, Not Two, Concepts of Liberty: A Proposal to Enlarge Our Moral Self-Understanding," in *Hegel on Philosophy in History*, ed. R. Zuckert and J. Kreines (Cambridge: Cambridge University Press, 2017), 177–92, 182.

68. Honneth, "Three, Not Two, Concepts of Liberty," 185.

69. Luke Brunning's concept of romantic agency, which he elaborates mainly in the framework of the ethical implications and challenges of nonmonogamous relationship, is very useful for further clarifying my erotic freedom as power. Luke Brunning, *Romantic Agency: Loving Well in Modern Life* (Cambridge: Polity 2024).

EXCURSUS: WHY EROTIC LOVE?

1. See, for example, Martha Nussbaum, *Political Emotions: Why Love Matters for Justice* (Cambridge, Mass.: Harvard University Press, 2013).

2. See, for example, Michael Hardt and Antonio Negri, *Commonwealth* (Cambridge, Mass.: Harvard University Press 2009); and Michael Hardt, "For Love or Money." *Cultural Anthropology* 26, no. 4 (2011): 676–82.
3. bell hooks, *All About Love. New Visions* (New York: HarperCollins, 2000); Martin Luther King Jr., *A Gift of Love: Sermons from Strength to Love* (London: Penguin Classics, 2017).
4. I am not talking just of family bonds based on biological, natural ties. Even when people decide to adopt a child, or an adult person, the choice of adoption is not made on the basis of individual emotions, and it follows a deliberative path based on a different affectivity than the erotic one. Once the adoption has gone through, moreover, the possibility of breaking the bond is and should be made more difficult than in erotic love and friendship.
5. Harry G. Frankfurt, *The Reasons of Love* (Princeton, N.J.: Princeton University Press, 2004).
6. Simone May, *Love. A New Understanding* (Oxford: Oxford University Press, 2019), 15.
7. Harry G. Frankfurt, "On Caring," In *Necessity, Volition, and Love* (Cambridge: Cambridge University Press, 1999), 155–80, 170.
8. Anne Carson, *Eros the Bittersweet* (Dublin: Dalkey Archive, 1986), 45.
9. Carson, *Eros the Bittersweet*, 153. Carson is referring here to Plato's dialogue *Lysias* and speaking of the *beginning* of eros, which is the moment that, for her, is especially beyond our control.
10. Unfortunately, May does not discuss Hegel, and possible divergencies between their theories; he mentions him only very briefly, and categorizes him as a union theorist. Andreja Novakovic, in her *Hegel on the Family Form* (Cambridge: Cambridge University Press, forthcoming) offers a striking and original depiction of what it means, for Hegel, to inhabit a loving home, or a family, which comprises relationships of romantic love (between husbands and wives), but also between siblings as well as parents and children. I am grateful to Andreja for the many illuminating conversations related to these topics.
11. May, *Love*, 42.
12. Friedrich Schlegel, "Fragments," in *Lucinde and the Fragments* (Minneapolis: University of Minnesota Press, 1971), 141–256, 248.
13. See, for example, Schlegel, "Fragments," 220.
14. Percy Bhysse Shelley, "A Defence of Poetry," in *Selected Poems and Prose* (London: Penguin Classics, Kindle edition, 2017).
15. Shelley, "Dedication Before Laon and Cynthia," in *Selected Poems and Prose* (London: Penguin Classics, Kindle edition, 2017), lines 55–63.
16. Schlegel, "Lucinde," 97–98, 106.
17. Schlegel, 101.
18. Manfred Frank, *The Philosophical Foundations of Early German Romanticism* (Albany: State University of New York Press, 2003), 122.
19. G. W. F. Hegel, *On Christianity: Early Theological Writings* (New York: Harper Torchbooks, 1961), 304.
20. Schlegel, "Lucinde," 44.
21. Schlegel, 45.
22. Schlegel, 113; my italics. It must be remarked that this quote, like other passages in Schlegel, presupposes a rather problematic gender dualism—the man teaches the

woman human spirit, and the woman teaches the man marriage, life, and beauty. I expound on Schlegel's and his figuration of mutual recognition in Federica Gregoratto, "Sex, Gender, and Extended Recognition: Friedrich Schlegel Revisited," in *The Philosophy of Recognition: Expanded Perspectives on a Fundamental Concept*, ed. M. Congdon and T. Khurana (New York: Routledge, forthcoming).

23. Hannah Arendt, *The Human Condition* (Chicago: University of Chicago Press, 1998), 242.

24. Schlegel, "Fragments," 218.

25. Schlegel, 215.

26. Michel Foucault, "Friendship as a Way of Life," in *The Essential Works of Foucault, Volume 1: Ethics: Subjectivity and Truth*, ed. P. Rabinow (New York: New Work, [1981] 1997), 135–40, 136.

27. Sally Rooney, *Conversations with Friends* (London: Faber and Faber, Kindle edition, 2017), capter 30.

28. Plato, *The Symposium* (Cambridge: Cambridge University Press, 2008), 191b.

29. See, for example, Anthony Bogaert, "Toward a Conceptual Understanding of Asexuality," *Review of General Psychology* 10, no. 3 (2006): 241–50; Luke Brunning and Natasha McKeever, "Asexuality," *Journal of Applied Philosophy* 38, no. 1 (2021): 497–517.

30. Eve Kosofsky Sedgwick, *A Dialogue on Love* (Boston: Beacon, 1999), 24.

31. Sedgwick, *Dialogue on Love*, 25.

32. Sedgwick, 168.

33. Elizabeth Brake, *Minimizing Marriage: Marriage, Morality, and the Law* (Oxford: Oxford University Press, 2012), 88–89.

34. Elizabeth F. Emens, "Monogamy's Law: Compulsory Monogamy and Polyamorous Existence," *NYU Review of Law and Social Change* 29 (2004): 277–376.

35. See Clare Chambers, *Against Marriage: An Egalitarian Defence of the Marriage-Free State* (Oxford: Oxford University Press, Kindle edition, 2017).

36. Leanne Betasamosake Simposon, *As We Have Always Done: Indigenous Freedom Through Radical Resistance* (Minneapolis: University of Minnesota Press, 2017), 110.

37. Kim TallBear, "Making Love and Relations: Beyond Settler Sex and Family," in *Making Kin Not Population*, ed. A. E. Clarke and D. Haraway (Chicago: Prickly Paradigm, 2018), 145–64, 147–48. See Sophie K. Rosa, *Radical Intimacy* (London: Pluto, 2023), 46–49.

38. Simone de Beauvoir, *Memoirs of a Dutiful Daughter* (New York: HarperCollins, [1958] 2005), 158–59.

39. Beauvoir, *Memoirs of a Dutiful Daughter*, 160–61.

40. In her novel published posthumously, in which Beauvoir explores in more (fictional) details this crucial young friendship, dependence is depicted in more reciprocal terms. Zaza/Andrée/Élisabeth Lacoin does lovingly recognize Sylvie/Simone too. Simone de Beauvoir, *The Inseparables* (Dublin: Penguin, 2021).

41. Deborah Anapol, *Polyamory in the 21st Century: Love and Intimacy with Multiple Partners* (New York: Rowman and Littlefield, 2010), 16.

42. Clardy, *Why It Is Ok to Not Be Monogamous* (New York: Routledge 2023), 33.

43. On this bourgeoning debate, see, for example, Carrie S. I. Jenkins, "Modal Monogamy," *Ergo* 2, no. 8 (2015): 175–94; Natasha McKeever, "Is the Requirement of

Sexual Exclusivity Consistent with Romantic Love?," *Journal of Applied Philosophy* 34, no. 3 (2017): 353–69; Luke Brunning, "The Distinctiveness of Polyamory," *Journal of Applied Philosophy* 35, no. 3 (2018): 513–31; Harry Chalmers, "Is Monogamy Morally Permissible?," *Journal of Value Inquiry*, 53 (2019): 225–41; Federica Gregoratto, "Loving Vulnerability: Eleven Negative Theses on Polyamory," *Compàs d'Amalgama* 4 (2021): 56–60; Clardy, *Why It Is Ok to Not Be Monogamous*; and Luke Brunning, *Romantic Agency: Loving Well in Modern Life* (Cambridge: Polity 2024).

44. In particular, the loved woman ("Emily") is presented in a highly idealized, transfigured fashion, as some kind of eternal deity: "An image of some bright Eternity / A shadow of some golden dream" ("Epipsychidion," in *Selected Poems and Prose*, lines 115–16), an ethereal embodiment of love that has the power to equalize "all things," making a "worm beneath the sod" blend with God (127–29). Moreover, the poem presents an idea of love as a force of fusion (see especially lines 52, 551–87).

3. THE MESS WE ARE IN: TOWARD A CRITICAL THEORY OF LOVE

1. I take the metaphors of the map and the compass as basic instruments for social-critical inquiries from John Dewey, *Lectures in China, 1919–1920* (Honolulu: University of Hawai'i Press, 1973,) 64.

2. I do not like the talk of "toxic love" for two reasons: first, in the ways it is usually employed, in mainstream psychological discourses, the adjective assumes a overly moralistic tone. Blaming "toxic" individuals is not an effective strategy of social critique, aimed at social transformation. Second, if the metaphor is to be taken seriously, it suggests insurmountable difficulties in breaking or changing the problematic bond. I prefer the adjective "damaged" to speak of unfree love, which is indebted to Theodor W. Adorno's criticism of "damaged life." Theodor W. Adorno, *Minima Moralia: Reflections on a Damaged Life* (New York: Verso, [1951] 2005). The term is better apt, I believe, to convey the social, structural, objective dimension of the problems affecting love relationships; what is more, it suggests that reparations, (re)constructive amends, are possible.

3. Harry G. Frankfurt, *The Reasons of Love* (Princeton, N.J.: Princeton University Press, 2004), 46.

4. Immanuel Kant, *The Metaphysics of Morals* (Cambridge: Cambridge University Press, [1797–1803] 1991), 203.

5. Frankfurt, *Reasons of Love*, 48.

6. Matthew S. Liao, "The Idea of a Duty to Love," *Journal of Value Inquiry*, 40 (2006): 1–22, 16; my italics.

7. The sexual connotations of this metaphor are not unproblematic, but I do not think it is particularly helpful to discuss them here.

8. Niklas Luhmann, *Love as Passion: The Codification of Intimacy* (Stanford, Calif.: Stanford University Press, [1982] 1986), 14.

9. See, for example, Luhmann, *Love as Passion*, 16.

10. Luhmann, *Love as Passion*, 32.

11. Luhmann, *Love as Passion*, 129.

12. According to Hegel, stability and continuity in time can be guaranteed only by legal marriage. G. W. F. Hegel, *Outlines of the Philosophy of Right* (Oxford: Oxford University Press 2008), § 161, addition.

13. Luhmann, *Love as Passion*, 138.

14. Anthony Giddens, *Transformations of Intimacy: Sexuality, Love, and Eroticism in Modern Societies* (Stanford, Calif.: Stanford University Press 1993), 182. The democratization of personal life also extends, according to Giddens, to friendship and to parent-child relations.

15. Giddens, *Transformations of Intimacy*, 62.

16. Giddens, 27.

17. Giddens, 63, 190. The notion of intimate relationships based on recognition and freedom, which Honneth has discussed in his *Freedom's Right*, and that we have already seen in chapter 2, is evidently very much under Giddens's influence.

18. This thesis has been famously defended by Karl Polanyi, *Great Transformation: The Political and Economic Origins of Our Time* (Boston: Beacon, 2001). As Nancy Fraser has argued, capitalism has from the very beginning needed to rely on background conditions that are not necessarily capitalist, like reproductive or care activities, "nature," and some form of political deliberation and action. Without such conditions, capitalism would not survive. In other words, paradoxically, in order to become autonomous, the economic system needs an anchoring in non-economic practices. Nancy Fraser and Rahel Jaeggi, *Capitalism: A Conversation in Critical Theory* (Cambridge: Polity, 2018).

19. Luhmann, *Love as Passion*, 30.

20. Karl Marx, *Economic and Philosophic Manuscripts*. In *Collected Works, Vol. 3, 1843–1844*, by Karl Marx and Friedrich Engels (New York: New York International Publishers, 2005), 324.

21. Marx, *Economic and Philosophic Manuscripts*, 326.

22. Eva Illouz, *Consuming the Romantic Utopia: Love and the Cultural Contradictions of Capitalism*. (Berkeley: University of California Press 1997), chapter 1.

23. Eva Illouz, *The End of Love: A Sociology of Negative Relations* (Oxford: Oxford University Press, 2019), 99.

24. Illouz, *Consuming the Romantic Utopia*, 87.

25. Illouz, 87.

26. Illouz, 111.

27. To tell the truth, Luhmann does make a similar point: he conceives of the function of the sphere of love as a response to the development of a distant world of cold and brutal work relations, aimed at accumulating capital or at survival. Illouz stresses however way more decidedly how the cold world has never been really abandoned, and now return with a vengeance within the erotic domain.

28. Adorno, *Minima Moralia*, 172.

29. As if paraphrasing Adorno, Illouz writes: "Numerous ads present romance as a realm of *pure feeling, sensuality,* and *instantaneous pleasure,* free of the frictions and power struggles of real relationships" (*Consuming the Romantic Utopia*, 87).

30. Eva Illouz, *Cold Intimacies: The Making of Emotional Capitalism* (Cambridge: Polity, 2007), 91.

31. Illouz, *Consuming the Romantic Utopia*, 193.

32. On this, see Jay Bernstein's illuminating discussion of Adorno's reflections on love, in *Adorno: Disenchantment and Ethics* (Cambridge: Cambridge University Press, 2001), 50.
33. When discussing, in a page quoted before, jealousy and possession, Adorno acknowledges this point as well (*Minima Moralia*, 79). In this aphorism, "Morality and Temporal Sequence," Adorno does problematize the "exclusive character of what comes first," both in erotic and in political relations: those who are already in a relationship, or in a country or a land, do not have the right to exclude those who might come next.
34. Adorno, 167.
35. On Adorno and coldness, see Estelle Ferrarese, "Acceleration and Reification: Revisiting Adorno's Idea of Coldness," *Iride* 30, no. 81 (2017): 442–48.
36. Adorno, *Minima Moralia*, 168.
37. Frantz Fanon, *Black Skin, White Masks* (Sidmouth: Pluto, 2008), 29.
38. Fanon, *Black Skin, White Masks*, 50.
39. Examples illustrating racial damaging factors in erotic bonds do predominantly refer to African Americans, since the literature targeting love and racial oppression in the U.S. context is large. In other social and geographical contexts, racial and ethnical relations might be characterized by different traits.
40. Averil Y. Clarke, *Inequalities of Love* (Durham, N.C.: Duke University Press 2011), chapter 3; Patricia H. Collins, *Black Sexual Politics: African Americans, Gender, and the New Racism* (New York: Routledge, 2004), chapter 8.
41. Patricia H. Collins, "Black Women's Love Relationships," in *Black Feminist Thought* (New York: Routledge 2000), 149–72.
42. Collins, *Black Sexual Politics*, 256. See also Audre Lorde, "Scratching the Surface: Some Notes on Barriers to Women and Loving," in *Sister Outsider: Essays and Speeches* (Berkeley, Calif.: Crossing, 2007), 45–52, 47–48.
43. Collins, *Black Sexual Politics*, 262. My few sketches are of course not enough in giving a proper sense of damaging racialized structures and norms in the realm of love. Much more descriptive work is needed. See, for example, how Celeste Vaughan Curington, Jennifer H. Lundquist, and Ken-Hou Lin draw upon Collins's work, among others, to analyze intimate relations across sexual orientation among Blacks, Asian, Latinos, whites, and multiracial persons in the United States. Helpfully, the authors illustrate in great detail the historical and social construction of damaging racial preferences, especially in the context of online dating and dating technologies. They argue "that the contemporary context of neoliberalism, consumerism, and the rise of new digital technologies give rise to a unique form of digital-sexual racism"; Celeste Vaughan Curington, Jennifer H. Lundquist, and Ken-Hou Lin, *The Dating Divide. Dating and Desire in the Era of Online Romance* (Oakland: University of California Press, 2021), 4.
44. Raven Leilani, *Luster* (Basingstoke: Picador, 2022).
45. For a reflection on the particular difficulties experienced by African American women in navigating polyerotic bonds, see Justin L. Clardy, "Towards a Progressive Black Sexual Politics: Reading African American Polyamorous Women in Patricia Collins' Black Feminist Thought," in *The Routledge Companion to Romantic Love*, ed. A. Brooks (New York: Routledge, 2022), 153–61. Clardy does not discuss *Luster*, though.

46. Collins, "Black Women's Love Relationships," 161–62.
47. James Baldwin, *Another Country* (New York: Vintage International, [1962] 1993). Collins speaks of a "Black gender ideology" that dictates that women be sexual, "wild," and yet complaisant, as well as that men be in control and strong: calling into question the norm of heterosexuality, within Black communities, seems even more difficult than in other communities. Baldwin's *Another Country* illustrates this difficulty very well and with dramatic tones.
48. Heikki Ikäheimo and Arto Laitinen, "Analyzing Recognition: Identification, Acknowledgement and Recognitive Attitudes Towards Persons," in *Recognition and Power: Axel Honneth and the Tradition of Critical Social Theory*, ed. B. van den Brink and D. Owen (Cambridge: Cambridge University Press 2007), 33–56.
49. Further critical inquiries into love could, moreover, lead to pinpointing other types of damages.
50. Jean-Jacques Rousseau, *Emile, or On Education* (New York: Basic Books, 1979), 322. With regard to Rousseau on love and recognition, see, especially, Barbara Carnevali, *Romantisme et reconnaissance. Figures de la conscience chez Rousseau* (Genève: Droz 2012).
51. Collins, "Black Women's Love Relationships," 156.
52. Fanon, *Black Skin, White Masks*, 41.
53. Axel Honneth, "Rejoinder," in *Reification: A New Look at an Old Idea* (Oxford: Oxford University Press, 2008), 147–59, 153.
54. Axel Honneth, "Recognition as Ideology," in *Recognition and Power: Axel Honneth and the Tradition of Critical Social Theory*, ed. B. van den Brink and D. Owen (Cambridge: Cambridge University Press, 2007), 323–47, 339.
55. I suggest here that social norms, roles, habits and identities are unjust and problematic insofar as they impede the formation of erotic bonds, or because they impair freedom. There might be other reasons, of course, for criticizing a social order.
56. My view in this part of the section relies upon mainly Jessica Benjamin's theory: see, in particular, Jessica Benjamin, *The Bonds of Love: Psychoanalysis, Feminism, and the Problem of Domination* (New York: Pantheon, 1988); and Benjamin, *Like Subjects, Love Objects*, 185.
57. As I have argued elsewhere, subjugation that is violently maintained might become unsustainable, leading to what I call "romantic femicide"; Federica Gregoratto, "Why Love Kills: Power, Gender Dichotomy, and Romantic Femicide," *Hypatia* 32, no. 1 (2017): 135–51.
58. See, for example, Kimberlé Crenshaw, "Mapping the Margins: Intersectionality, Identity Politics, and Violence against Women of Color," *Stanford Law Review* 43, no. 6 (1991): 1241–99.
59. See, for example, Baldwin, *Another Country*, 68–69. There operates here as well a form of complicit love, reproducing not only racial hierarchies but also the fantasy of Black sexual potency.
60. Baldwin, 46.
61. Beauvoir, *Second Sex*, 708.
62. Anna G Jónasdóttir, *Why Women Are Oppressed* (Philadelphia: Temple University Press, 1994); Anna G. Jónasdóttir, "What Kind of Power is Love Power?," in

Sexuality, Gender, and Power: Intersectional and Transnational Perspectives, ed. A. G. Jónasdóttir, V. Bryson, and K. B. Jones (New York: Routledge 2011), 45–59.

63. Jónasdóttir, *Why Women Are Oppressed*, 24.

64. My example of Zelda and Scott can be useful to better understand Jónasdóttir's theory: since the Fitzgeraldses' lifestyle is largely a stranger to capitalist and bourgeois values, the exploitative dynamic in their love relationship can be explained mainly by referring to gender norms and not to economic ones. It is important to clarify, however, that Jónasdóttir does not intend to deny economic exploitation of women, both in and outside the household, or that economic exploitation intersects with exploitative love. However, she believes that the sexual and romantic type of exploitation and oppression must be critically analyzed in its own right, as if it were a separate phenomenon.

65. Jónasdóttir, 97.

66. Jónasdóttir, 100.

67. Loving care should be further conceptualized as including "hermeneutic labor," which Ellie Anderson has brilliantly identified as the labor of understanding and coherently expressing one's own feelings, desires, intentions, and motivations, as well as discerning those of others and inventing solutions arising from interpersonal tensions; Ellie Anderson, "Hermeneutic Labor: The Gendered Burden of Interpretation in Intimate Relationships Between Women and Men," *Hypatia* 38, no. 1 (2023): 177–97.

68. Stanley Cavell, *Contesting Tears: The Hollywood Melodrama of the Unknown Woman* (Chicago: University of Chicago Press 1996), 30.

69. Cavell, *Cities of Words*, 111.

70. Beauvoir, *Second Sex*, 710.

71. Clardy, "Towards a Progressive Black Sexual Politics."

72. Angela Davis, "The Legacy of Slavery: Standards for a New Womanhood," in *Women, Race, and Class* (New York: Vintage, 1981), 3–29.

73. Beauvoir's first novel, *She Came to Stay* (New York: W. W. Norton, 1999), offers a painful illustration of such a dynamic in the damaged nonmonogamous relationship between the three main characters, Pierre, Françoise, and Xavier.

74. Clardy, *Why It Is Ok to Not Be Monogamous*, 90–91.

75. Brian C. J. Singer, "Thinking Friendship with and Against Hannah Arendt," *Critical Horizons* 18, no. 2 (2017): 93–118, 93–94.

76. Hanya Yanagihara, *A Little Life* (Basingstoke: Palgrave Macmillan, 2015), 225; my italics.

77. Sophie K. Rosa, *Radical Intimacy* (London: Pluto, 2023), 59.

4. AVALANCHE: EROTIC EMOTIONS AND AFFECTS

1. Theodor W. Adorno, *Minima Moralia: Reflections on a Damaged Life* (New York: Verso, [1951] 2005), 172.

2. Some classic studies on the rationality of emotions are: Amélie O. Rorty, ed., *Explaining Emotions* (Berkeley: University of California Press, 1980); and Ronald de Sousa, *The Rationality of Emotions* (Cambridge: MIT Press, 1987).

3. Martha Nussbaum, *Upheavals of Thought. The Intelligence of Emotions* (Cambridge: Cambridge University Press 2001), 22.
4. Nussbaum, *Upheavals of Thought*, 300.
5. Nussbaum, 462.
6. Nussbaum, 713.
7. Martha Nussbaum, "Constructing Love, Desire, and Care," in *Sex and Social Justice* (Oxford: Oxford University Press 1999), 253–75, 259–61.
8. Arlie Russel Hochschild, *The Managed Heart: Commercialization of Human Feeling* (Berkeley: University of California Press, [1983] 2012), 68.
9. Hochschild, *The Managed Heart*, 74.
10. Nussbaum, *Upheavals of Thought*, 173.
11. Nussbaum, 172–73.
12. Nussbaum, 62.
13. Andrea Scarantino, "Insights and Blindspots of the Cognitivist Theory of Emotions," *British Journal for the Philosophy of Science* 61, no. 4 (2010): 729–68, 735.
14. Scarantino, "Insights and Blindspots," 741.
15. Giovanna Colombetti and Evan Thompson, "The Feeling Body: Towards an Enactive Approach to Emotion," in *Developmental Perspectives on Embodiment and Consciousness*, ed. W. F. Overton, U. Müller, and J. Newman (New York: Erlbaum, 2008), 45–68, 57.
16. Christian von Scheve and Jan Slaby, "Emotion, Emotion Concept," in *Affective Societies*, ed. J. Slaby and C. von Scheve (New York: Routledge 2019), 43–51, 42. Note, in italics, the implicit reference to Nussbaum's view.
17. Von Scheve and Slaby, "Emotion, Emotion Concept," 43.
18. Von Scheve and Slaby, 38.
19. Deborah Gould, "On Affect and Protest," in *Political Emotions: New Agendas in Communication*, ed. J. Staiger, A. Cvetkovich, and A. Reynolds (New York: Routledge, 2010), 18–44, 32.
20. Jonathan Lear, *Love and Its Place in Nature: A Philosophical Interpretation of Freudian Psychoanalysis* (New York: Farrar, Straus, and Giroux, 1990), 68.
21. Lear, *Love and Its Place in Nature*, 177; my italics.
22. Lear, 216.
23. Simone de Beauvoir, *Memoirs of a Dutiful Daughter* (New York: HarperCollins, [1958] 2005),160; my italics.
24. William Wordsworth, "Prefaces of 1800 and 1802," in W. Wordsworth and S. Coleridge, *Lyrical Ballads* (London: Routledge, 1991), 233–58, 236.
25. Friedrich Schlegel, "Lucinde. A Novel." In *Lucinde and the Fragments* (Minneapolis: University of Minnesota Press, 1971), 51.
26. John Keats, *Selected Letters of John Keats* (Cambridge, Mass.: Harvard University Press, 2002), 60.
27. On this, see Allen's helpful discussion of psychoanalytical contributions to social criticisms: Amy Allen, *Critique on the Couch: Why Critical Theory Needs Psychoanalysis* (New York: Columbia University Press 2021), 23.
28. Ellie Anderson, "Hermeneutic Labor: The Gendered Burden of Interpretation in Intimate Relationships between Women and Men," *Hypatia*, 38, no. 1 (2023): 177–97.
29. Keats, *Selected Letters*, 93.

30. Herbert Marcuse, "Nature and Revolution," in *Counterrevolution and Revolt* (Boston: Beacon, 1972), 59–78, 74.

31. In his comment on Theodor W. Adorno's thoughts on private life, love, marriage and dwelling, Bernstein helpfully captures the meaning of passivity in love as follows: "For us the involuntariness of love models ethical passivity, the sense that our responses to others can be awakened by them, and that their unique, nonsubstitutable being is sufficient to engender a fully particular response from us. . . . In its immediacy and feeling love presents ethical objectivity—our concern for the welfare, interests, and flourishing of the beloved—as heightened subjectivity, our deepest concern as flowing from the sheer thisness of the loved one. For Adorno this is the moment of ethical truth in the bourgeois idea of love, a component of the value of loving and of what in loving is valuable." Bernstein, *Adorno*, 49.v

32. Theodor W. Adorno, *Negative Dialectics* (New York: Routledge, [1966] 2004), 232.

33. Adorno, *Negative Dialectics*, 299.

34. Adorno, 299.

35. Adorno, 299.

36. Adorno, 299.

37. We can also intervene in these aspects of our bodies, try to control and steer our chemical, neuronal, physiological reactions, today more than yesterday, thanks, for instance, to so-called neuroenhancing technologies. Some argue that such intervention does increase our freedom; see Brian D. Earp and Julian Savulescu, *Love Drugs: The Chemical Future of Relationships* (Stanford, Calif.: Stanford University Press, 2020). I am not entirely against this line of argument, yet in this chapter I am outlining an understanding of freedom not as power over our affectivity, but as the process through which we dive into noncontrollable affective dynamics and try to learn from them.

38. Hochschild, *Managed Heart*, 192–93.

39. Hochschild, 194; my italics.

40. Adorno, *Minima Moralia*, 172. The command Adorno is referring to in this aphorism is the individualistic, hedonistic one that urges to follow every passionate whim, collecting lovers and sexual escapades; resistance lies, in these circumstances, in practicing fidelity.

41. On critical naturalism, the version of naturalism that serves the interests of a critical theory of contemporary societies, see Federica Gregoratto, Heikki Ikäheimo, Emmanuel Renault, Arvi Särkelä, and Italo Testa, "Critical Naturalism: A Manifesto," *Krisis* 42, no. 1 (2022): 108–24.

42. Nussbaum, "Constructing Love, Desire, and Care," 255.

43. A defender of strong constructionism with regard to sexuality is, most notably, Catharine MacKinnon, *Towards a Feminist Theory of the State* (Cambridge, Mass.: Harvard University Press, 1989), who claims that sexual desire, sexuality, and sexual difference are the result of men's domination of women. One cannot engage in sexual relationships, in her view then, without upholding and reproducing such (violent) domination.

44. Nussbaum, "Constructing Love, Desire, and Care," 256.

45. In this respect, it is interesting that Eric Fromm rejects both the conception, promoted by "authoritarian thinkers," of human nature as "fixed and unchangeable," and the idea of a human nature as infinitely malleable; Erich Fromm, *Man for*

Himself: An Enquiry into the Psychology of Ethics (London: Routledge, 1949), 21. If human beings' brains, bodies, impulses, affects, and emotions were completely shapable by social arrangements, "norms and institutions unfavourable to human welfare would have a chance to mold man forever into their patterns." In his view, "intrinsic forces in man's nature" could be instead mobilized "to change these patterns." Such forces would contribute to make human beings into agents of change, lead them to judge and criticize society (21–22).

46. Sigmund Freud, *Three Essays on the Theory of Sexuality*, in *The Standard Edition of the Complete Psychological Works of Sigmund Freud, Vol. 7, 1901–1905* (London: Vintage, [1905] 2001), 168; my italics.

47. Teresa de Lauretis, *Freud's Drive: Psychoanalysis, Literature and Film* (New York: Palgrave Macmillan, 2008), 13.

48. Herbert Marcuse, *Eros and Civilization: A Philosophical Inquiry into Freud* (London: Routledge, [1956] 1998), 39.

49. Marcuse, "Nature and Revolution," 75.

50. Marcuse, *Eros and Civilization*, 41.

51. Marcuse, 77.

52. Marcuse, 103.

53. Marcuse, 156.

54. Marcuse, "Nature and Revolution," 67. In this essay, Marcuse explicitly depicts nature as both the result of a social and political transformation and the "motor" behind the transformation.

55. Marcuse, *Eros and Civilization*, 153.

56. There is a strong Romantic inspiration in Marcuse's theory, and, in general, the idea of naturalism about love is a Romantic one. On the Romantics' critical naturalism, see Federica Gregoratto, "Romances of Nature: Hegelian and Romantic Impulses for Critical Theory," *Verifiche*, 21, no.1 (2023): 39–62.

57. Nussbaum, *Political Emotions*.

58. Nussbaum, *Upheavals of Thought*, 661; my italics.

59. Angelika Krebs, *Zwischen Ich und Du. Eine dialogische Philosophie der Liebe* (Berlin: Suhrkamp, 2015), 207f.

60. Margaret Gilbert, "How We Feel: Understanding Everyday Collective Emotion Ascription," in *Collective Emotions: Perspectives from Psychology, Philosophy, and Sociology*, ed. C. von Scheve and M. Salmela (Oxford: Oxford University Press, 2014), 17–31.

61. Hans Bernhard Schmid, *Plural Action* (London: Springer, 2009); Mikko Salmela, "Shared Emotions," *Philosophical Explorations* 15, no. 1 (2012): 22–46; Mikko Salmela, "Collective Emotions and Normativity," *ProtoSociology* 35 (2018): 135–51.

62. Mikko Salmela and Michiru Nagatsu, "Collective Emotions and Joint Action: Beyond Received and Minimalist Approaches," *Journal of Social Ontology* 2, no. 1 (2016): 33–57, 36.

63. See Salmela, "Collective Emotions and Normativity."

64. Émile Durkheim, *The Elementary Forms of Religious Life* (London: Free Press, 1995), 218.

65. Durkheim, *Elementary Forms of Religious Life*, 217–18; my italics.

66. Durkheim, 424.

67. Randall Collins, "Social Movements and the Focus of Emotional Attention," in *Passionate Politics: Emotions and Social Movement*, ed. J. Goodwin, J. M. James, and F. Polletta (Chicago: University of Chicago Press 2001), 27–44, 31.

68. Randall Collins, "Interaction Ritual Chains and Collective Effervescence," in *Collective Emotions*, ed. C. von Scheve and M. Salmela (Oxford: Oxford University Press, 2014), 299–311, 299.

69. Collins, "Interaction Ritual Chains and Collective Effervescence," 299–300.

70. Randall Collins, *Interaction Ritual Chains* (Princeton, N.J.: Princeton University Press, 2004), chapter 6.

71. Salmela, "Collective Emotions and Normativity."

72. Percy Bhysse Shelley, "On Love," in *Selected Poems and Prose* (London: Penguin Classics, Kindle edition, 2017); my italics.

73. In "Epipsychidon," the erotic *we* is rendered with a music metaphor: "We—are we not formed, as notes of music are, / For one another, though dissimilar; / Such differences without discord, as can make / Those sweetest sounds, in which all spirits shake / As trembling leaves in a continuous air?" (Shelley, "Epipsychidon," in *Selected Poems and Prose,* lines 142–46).

74. The literature on this is prevalently of sociological nature, linked to concrete social movements; see, for example, Deborah Gould, *Moving Politics: Emotion and ACT UP's Fight Against AIDS* (Chicago: Chicago University Press, 2009); Wendy Pearlman, "Emotions and the Microfoundations of the Arab Uprisings," *Perspectives on Politics* 1, no. 2 (2013): 387–409; and Efser Rana Coşkun, "The Role of Emotions During the Arab Spring in Tunisia and Egypt in Light of Repertoires," *Globalizations* 16, no. 7 (2019): 1198–214.

75. Krebs, *Zwischen Ich und Du,* 206, 229.

5. JOY AS AN ACT OF RESISTANCE: EROTIC EDUCATION

1. Michel Foucault, "Friendship as a Way of Life," In *The Essential Works of Foucault, Vol. 1, Ethics: Subjectivity and Truth*, edited by P. Rabinow (New York: New Work, [1981] 1997), 136–37.

2. In an interview with James O'Higgins, Foucault states: "It is the prospect that gays will create as yet unforeseen kinds of relationships that many people can not tolerate." O'Higgins then presses him to explain what these new kinds of relationship would look like—maybe, he suggests, these would be relationships "that don't involve possessiveness or fidelity." Foucault answers evasively: "If the relationships to be created are as yet unforeseeable, then we can't really say that this feature or that feature will be denied." James O'Higgins and Michel Foucault, "Sexual Choice, Sexual Act: An Interview with Michel Foucault," *Salmagundi* 58–59 (1982–1983): 10–24.

3. Foucault, "Friendship as a Way of Life," 135.

4. It is maybe no coincidence, in this respect, that Beauvoir wrote an entire novel, *The Inseparables*, dedicated to her relationship with Zaza/Andrée/Élisabeth Lacoin that she has not, however, made public.

5. Foucault, "Friendship as a Way of Life," 136.

6. Foucault, 138.

7. John Dewey, *Lectures in China. 1919-1920* (Honolulu: University of Hawai'i Press, 1973), 76; 80; John Dewey, *Lectures in Social and Political Philosophy (China). European Journal of Pragmatism and American Philosophy* 7, no. 2 (2015): 1-39, 22-23; 25. For extended discussions around Dewey's critical idea of recognition and social struggles in his *Lectures in China*, see Arvi Särkelä, "Ein Drama in drei Akten. Der Kampf um öffentliche Anerkennung nach Dewey und Hegel," *Deutsche Zeitschrift für Philosophie* 61, nos. 5-6 (2013): 681-96; Federica Gregoratto, "Agonistic Recognition, Intersections, and the Ambivalence of Family Bonds: John Dewey's Critical Theory Manifesto in China," *Transactions of the Charles S. Peirce Society* 53, no. 1 (2017): 127-45; Italo Testa, "Dominant Patterns in Associated Living: Hegemony, Domination, and Ideological Recognition in Dewey's *Lectures in China,*" *Transactions of the Charles S. Peirce Society* 53, no. 1 (2017): 29-52; and Justo Serrano Zamora, "Articulating a Sense of Powers: An Expressivist Reading of John Dewey's Theory of Social Movements," *Transactions of the Charles S. Peirce Society* 53, no. 1 (2017): 53-70.

8. Dewey, *Lectures in China*, 77.

9. Dewey, 78.

10. Consider, very schematically, the example of social struggles around gender issues. One positive outcome of the first women's movement, the suffragette movement, consisted in the recognition of women *as equal to men* concerning participation rights (this was actually one of Dewey's favorite example with regard to struggle for public recognition; see Dewey, *Lectures in Social and Political Philosophy [China]*, 22). This kind of recognition brought forth, however, at least two further orders of misrecognition: first, by politically recognizing women *as men*, the specificity of the woman condition—the recognition of women as women, one might say—is overlooked or excluded from the political realm, thus generating further kinds of inequalities and injustices. Second, by recognizing the totality of women as a homogenous group, differences, imbalances and power differentials based on social factors like race, class, and sexual orientation are not taken into account, thus, again, generating further kinds of inequalities and injustices. Social conflicts can be then conceived of only as ongoing transformations; the resulting habits, laws, rules, and institutions have always to be regarded as fallible, and changeable.

11. Meggie Nelson, *The Argonauts* (New York: Graywolf, 2016), 7. I am grateful to Italo Testa who, after having read a first draft of the project for this book, told me it reminded him of some central motives in *The Argonauts*.

12. Nelson, *Argonauts*, 9.

13. Nelson, 13.

14. Similar arguments can be developed with reference to other social factors as well. One can, for instance, argue that interracial marriages, or marriages between people from different ethnicities or religions, have contributed and still contribute to an overall change both of the perceptions and of the practices damaging people of color and racial relations in general. With reference to the U.S. context, see, for example, Maria P. P. Root, *Love's Revolution: Interracial Marriage* (Philadelphia: Temple University Press, 2001).

15. Stanley Cavell, *The Pursuit of Happiness: The Hollywood Comedy of Remarriage* (Cambridge, Mass.: Harvard University Press, 1981), 103.

16. See, for example, Nicola Barker, *Not the Marrying Kind: A Feminist Critique of Same-Sex Marriage* (New York: Palgrave Macmillan, 2012), chapter 5; and Jaye C.

Whitehead, *The Nuptial Deal: Same-Sex Marriage and Neo-liberal Governance* (Chicago: University of Chicago Press, 2012).

17. Christian Klesse, "Marriage, Law, and Polyamory: Rebutting Mononormativity with Sexual Orientation Discourse?," *Oñati Socio-legal Series* 6, no. 6 (2016): 1348–76, 1365.

18. Klesse, "Marriage, Law, and Polyamory," 1365.

19. Klesse, 1367.

20. See also Eleanor Wilkinson, "What's Queer about Non-Monogamy Now?," in *Understanding Non-Monogamies*, ed. M. Barker and D. Langdridge (London: Routledge, 2010), 243–54, 245–46.

21. This is, in fact, explicitly admitted by Clardy in his defense of a marriage reform that would include polyerotic bonds; Justin L. Clardy, *Why It's Ok Not to Be Monogamous* (New York: Routledge, 2023), chapter 4.

22. See Federica Gregoratto and Arvi Särkelä, "Social Reproduction Feminism and Deweyan Habit Ontology," in *Habit: Pragmatist Approaches from Cognitive Neurosciences to Social Sciences*, ed. F. Caruana and I. Testa (Cambridge: Cambridge University Press, 2021), 438–58.

23. Impulses are an integral part of Deweyan social life. The concept of impulse is closely related to what I have called in this work "affectivity," and it is at the same time "natural" and "social."

24. O'Higgins and Foucault, "Sexual Choice, Sexual Act," 13.

25. Cavell, *Pursuits of Happiness*, 199.

26. Alison Jaggar's notion of "outlaw emotions" can be helpful for my argumentation here. See Alison Jaggar, "Love and Knowledge: Emotion in Feminist Epistemology," *Inquiry*, 32, no. 2 (1989): 151–76.

27. María Lugones, *Pilgrimages/Peregrinajes: Theorizing Coalition Against Multiple Oppressions* (London: Rowman and Littlefield, 2003), 110.

28. Lugones, *Pilgrimages/Peregrinajes*, 107.

29. See, for example, Janet Hardy and Dossie Easton, *The Ethical Slut: Polyamory, Open Relationships, and Other Adventures* (Berkeley, Calif.: Ten Speed, [1997] 2017), chapter 15; and Ronald de Sousa, "Love, Jealousy and Compersion," in *The Oxford Handbook of Philosophy of Love*, ed. C. Grau and A. Smuts (Oxford: Oxford University Press, 2017), 491–510.

30. See, especially, Christian Klesse, "Poly Economics: Capitalism, Class, and Polyamory," *International Journal of Politics, Culture, and Society*, 27 (2014): 203–20.

31. Christian Klesse, *The Spectre of Promiscuity: Gay Male and Bisexual Non-Monogamies and Polyamories* (Aldershot: Ashgate, 2007), chapter 6.

32. Plato, *The Symposium* (Cambridge: Cambridge University Press, 2008), 206b9-10.

33. Martha Nussbaum, "The Speech of Alcibiades: A Reading of Plato's *Symposium*," *Philosophy and Literature* 3, no. 2 (1979): 166.

34. Nussbaum, "Speech of Alcibiades," 166; my italics.

35. Plato, *Symposium*, 215e7-9, 216a.

36. Plato, 218d1.

37. Plato, 213c, 214d4.

38. Audre Lorde, "The Uses of the Erotic: The Erotic as Power," in *Sister Outsider: Essays and Speeches* (Berkeley, Calif.: Crossing, 2007), 53–59, 54.

39. Lorde, "Uses of the Erotic," 54.

40. Lorde, 56.

41. See, for instance, the depiction of her intense and troubled (and nonmonogamous) love story with Muriel in her autobiography, *Zami: A New Spelling of My Name* (Berkeley, Calif.: Crossing, 1982), in particular chapter 26.

42. Lorde, "Uses of the Erotic," 57.

43. Cavell, *Pursuits of Happiness*, 129.

44. Lorde, "Uses of the Erotic," 57; my italics.

45. Lorde, 58.

46. Lorde, 59. More extensively on this, see again her autobiography, which is at the same time an insightful compendium of love troubles.

47. Audre Lorde, "The Master's Tools Will Never Dismantle the Master's House," in *Sister Outsider: Essays and Speeches* (Berkeley, Calif.: Crossing, 2007), 110–13.

48. Alexandra Kollontai, "Make Way for Winged Eros: A Letter to Working Youth," in *Selected Writings of Alexandra Kollontai*, ed. A. Holt (Westport, Conn.: Lawrence Hill, 1977), 276–92, 289–29; my italics.

49. Kollontai, "Make Way for Winged Eros," 290.

50. Audre Lorde, "The Uses of Anger," in *Sister Outsider: Essays and Speeches* (Berkeley, Calif.: Crossing, 2007), 124–33, 132.

51. Lorde, "Uses of Anger," 132; my italics. On the epistemic import of Lorde's idea of feelings, both positive (joy) and negative ones, see Caleb Ward, "Feeling, Knowledge, Self-Preservation: Audre Lorde's Oppositional Agency and Some Implications for Ethics," *Journal of the American Philosophical Association* 6, no. 4 (2020): 463–82.

52. Martin Hartmann, "A Comedy We Believe In: A Further Look at Sartre's Theory of Emotions," *European Journal of Philosophy* 25, no. 1 (2017): 144–72, 162.

53. On anger, or, better said, on certain types of anger as transformative emotion, there is growing literature at the moment; see, for example, Matthew Congdon, "Creative Resentments: The Role of Emotions in Moral Change," *Philosophical Quarterly* 68, no. 273 (2018), 739–57; Myisha Cherry, *The Case for Rage: Why Anger Is Essential to Anti-Racist Struggles* (Oxford: Oxford University Press, 2021); and Federica Gregoratto "Between Anger(s) and Radical Hope: Emotions in Progress," *European Journal of Philosophy*, 15, no. 2 (2023): 1–19.

54. Hence, I do not agree with certain post-Marxist accounts of "political love," such as Michael Hardt and Antonio Negri, *Commonwealth* (Cambridge, Mass.: Harvard University Press, 2009); and Michael Hardt, "For Love or Money," *Cultural Anthropology* 26, no. 4 (2011): 676–82. For a elaborated critique of those, see Eleanor Wilkinson, "On Love as an (Im)properly Political Concept," *D: Society and Space* 35, no. 1 (2016): 57–71.

55. James Baldwin, *Collected Essays* (New York: Library of America, 1998), 365.

56. Baldwin, *Collected Essays*, 366; my italics.

BIBLIOGRAPHY

Adorno, Theodor W. *Minima Moralia: Reflections on a Damaged Life.* New York: Verso, [1951] 2005.

———. *Negative Dialectics.* New York: Routledge, [1966] 2004.

Allen, Amy. *Critique on the Couch. Why Critical Theory Needs Psychoanalysis.* New York: Columbia University Press, 2021.

———. *The Power of Feminist Theory. Domination, Resistance, Solidarity.* Boulder, Colo.: Westview, 1999.

———. "Recognizing Domination: Recognition and Power in Honneth's Critical Theory." *Journal of Power* 3, no. 1 (2010): 21–32.

Anapol, Deborah. *Polyamory in the 21st Century: Love and Intimacy with Multiple Partners.* New York: Rowman and Littlefield, 2010.

Anderson, Ellie. "Hermeneutic Labor: The Gendered Burden of Interpretation in Intimate Relationships between Women and Men." *Hypatia,* 38, no. 1 (2023): 177–97.

Angel, Katherine. *Tomorrow Sex Will Be Good Again: Women and Desires in the Age of Consent.* Verso: London 2021, Kindle edition, 2021.

Arendt, Hannah. *The Human Condition.* Chicago: University of Chicago Press, 1998.

Aristotle. *The Nicomachean Ethics.* Oxford: Oxford University Press, 2009.

Badhwar, Neera K. "Friends as Ends in Themselves." *Philosophy and Phenomenological Research* 48 (1987): 1–23.

———. "Love." In *The Oxford Handbook of Practical Ethics,* edited by H. La Follette, 42–69. Oxford: Oxford University Press, 2003.

Badiou, Alain. *In Praise of Love.* London: Serpent's Tail, 2012.

Baldwin, James. *Another Country.* New York: Vintage International, [1962] 1993.

———. *Collected Essays.* New York: Library of America, 1998.

Bair, Deirdre. *Simone de Beauvoir: A Biography.* New York: Touchstone, 1991.

Barker, Nicola. *Not the Marrying Kind: A Feminist Critique of Same-Sex Marriage.* New York: Palgrave, 2012.

Barthes, Roland. *A Lover's Discourse. Fragments.* London: Vintage, [1977] 2018.

Beauvoir, Simone de. *The Ethics of Ambiguity.* New York: Philosophical Library Open Road, [1948] 2015.

——. *The Inseparables.* Dublin: Penguin Vintage, 2021.

——. "It's About Time Women Put a New Face on Love." In *Feminist Writings*, edited by M. A. Simons and M. Timmermann, 76–80. Chicago: University of Illinois Press, 2015.

——. *Memoirs of a Dutiful Daughter.* New York: HarperCollins, [1958]2005.

——. *The Second Sex.* London: Vintage Books, [1949] 2011.

——. *She Came to Stay.* New York: W. W. Norton, [1943] 1999.

——. *A Transatlantic Love Affair: Letters to Nelson Algren.* New York: New Press, 1997.

——. "What Love Is—and Isn't." In *Feminist Writings*, edited by M. A. Simons and M. Timmermann, 99–102. Chicago: University of Illinois Press2015.

Berlant, Lauren. *Cruel Optimism.* Durham, N.C.: Duke University Press, 2011.

Benjamin, Jessica. *The Bonds of Love. Psychoanalysis, Feminism, and the Problem of Domination.* New York: Pantheon, 1988.

——. *Like Subjects, Love Objects: Essays on Recognition and Sexual Difference.* New Haven, Conn.: Yale University Press, 1995.

Bernstein, Jay M. *Adorno: Disenchantment and Ethics.* Cambridge: Cambridge University Press, 2001.

Blackwell, Courtney, Jeremy Birnholz, and Charles Abbott. "Seeing and Being Seen: Co-Situation and Impression Formation Using Grindr, a Location-Aware Gay Dating App." *New Media & Society* 17, no. 7 (2015): 1117–36.

Bogaert, Anthony. "Toward a Conceptual Understanding of Asexuality." *Review of General Psychology* 10, no. 3 (2006): 241–250.

Brake, Elizabeth. *Minimizing Marriage: Marriage, Morality, and the Law.* Oxford: Oxford University Press, 2012.

Brogaard, Berit. *On Romantic Love: Simple Truths About a Complex Emotion.* Oxford: Oxford University Press, 2015.

Brunning, Luke. "The Distinctiveness of Polyamory." *Journal of Applied Philosophy* 35, no. 3 (2018): 513–31.

——. *Romantic Agency: Loving Well in Modern Life.* Cambridge: Polity, 2024.

Brunning, Luke, and Natasha McKeever. "Asexuality." *Journal of Applied Philosophy* 38, no. 1 (2021): 497–517.

Butler, Judith. "Taking Another's View: Ambivalent Implications." In A. Honneth, *Reification and Recognition: A Look at an Old Idea*, edited by M. Jay, 97–119. Oxford: Oxford University Press, 2008.

Capra, Frank, dir. *It Happened One Night.* Columbia Pictures, 1934.

Carnevali, Barbara. *Romantisme et reconnaissance. Figures de la conscience chez Rousseau.* Genève: Droz, 2012.

Carson, Anne. *Eros the Bittersweet.* Dublin: Dalkey Archive, 1986.

Cavell, Stanley. *Cities of Words: Pedagogical Letters on a Register of the Moral Life.* Cambridge, Mass.: Harvard University Press, 2004.

——. *Contesting Tears: The Hollywood Melodrama of the Unknown Woman*. Chicago: University of Chicago Press, 1996.

——. *The Pursuit of Happiness: The Hollywood Comedy of Remarriage*. Cambridge, Mass.: Harvard University Press, 1981.

Chalmers, Harry. "Is Monogamy Morally Permissible?" *Journal of Value Inquiry* 53 (2019): 225–41.

Chambers, Clare. *Against Marriage: An Egalitarian Defence of the Marriage-Free State*. Oxford: Oxford University Press, 2017.

Cherry, Myisha. *The Case for Rage: Why Anger Is Essential to Anti-Racist Struggles*. Oxford: Oxford University Press, 2021.

Chodorow, Nancy. *The Reproduction of Motherhood*. Berkeley: University of California Press, 1978.

Clardy, Justin L. "Towards a Progressive Black Sexual Politics: Reading African American Polyamorous Women in Patricia Collins' Black Feminist Thought." In *The Routledge Companion to Romantic Love*, edited by A. Brooks, 153–61. New York: Routledge, 2022.

——. *Why It Is Ok to Not Be Monogamous*. New York: Routledge, 2023.

Clarke, Averil Y. *Inequalities of Love*. Durham, N.C.: Duke University Press, 2011.

Collins, Patricia H. *Black Sexual Politics: African Americans, Gender, and the New Racism*. New York: Routledge, 2004.

——. "Black Women's Love Relationships." In *Black Feminist Thought*, 149–72. New York: Routledge, 2000.

Collins, Randall. *Interaction Ritual Chains*. Princeton, N.J.: Princeton University Press, 2004.

——. "Interaction Ritual Chains and Collective Effervescence." In *Collective Emotions*, edited by C. von Scheve and M. Salmela, 299–311. Oxford: Oxford University Press, 2014.

——. "Social Movements and the Focus of Emotional Attention." In *Passionate Politics: Emotions and Social Movement*, edited by J. Goodwin, J. M. James, and F. Polletta, 27–44. Chicago: University of Chicago Press, 2001.

Colombetti, Giovanna, and Thompson, Evan. "The Feeling Body: Towards an Enactive Approach to Emotion." In *Developmental Perspectives on Embodiment and Consciousness*, edited by W. F. Overton, U. Müller, and J. Newman, 45–68. New York: Erlbaum, 2008.

Congdon, Matthew. "Creative Resentments: The Role of Emotions in Moral Change." *Philosophical Quarterly* 68, no. 273 (2018): 739–57.

Coşkun, Efser Rana. "The Role of Emotions During the Arab Spring in Tunisia and Egypt in Light of Repertoires." *Globalizations* 16, no. 7 (2019): 1198–214.

Crenshaw, Kimberlé. "Mapping the Margins: Intersectionality, Identity Politics, and Violence Against Women of Color." *Stanford Law Review* 43, no. 6 (1991): 1241–99.

Cukor, George, dir. *Adam's Rib*. Loew's, 1949.

——. *Gaslight*. Loew's, 1944.

——. *The Philadelphia Story*. Loew's, 1940.

Curington, Celeste Vaughan, Jennifer H. Lundquist, and Ken-Hou Lin. *The Dating Divide: Dating and Desire in the Era of Online Romance*. Oakland: University of California Press, 2021.

Cusk, Rachel. *A Life's Work*. London: Faber and Faber, 2008.

Davis, Angela. "The Legacy of Slavery: Standards for a New Womanhood." In *Women, Race and Class*, 3–29. New York: Vintage, 1981.

Delaney, Neil. "Romantic Love and Loving Commitment: Articulating a Modern Ideal." *American Philosophical Quarterly* 33, no. 4 (1996): 339–56.

Deranty, Jean-Philippe. *Beyond Communication: A Critical Study of Axel Honneth's Social Philosophy*. Boston: Brill, 2009.

Deutscher, Penelope. *The Philosophy of Simone de Beauvoir: Ambiguity, Conversions, Resistance*. Cambridge: Cambridge University Press, 2008.

Dewey, John. *Art as Experience*. In *The Later Works of John Dewey, Vol. 10: 1934*, edited by J. A. Boydston, Carbondale: Southern Illinois University Press, 2008.

——. *Lectures in China, 1919–1920*. Honolulu: University of Hawai'i Press, 1973.

——. *Lectures in Social and Political Philosophy (China): European Journal of Pragmatism and American Philosophy* 7, no. 2 (2015): 1–39.

——. "Philosophies of Freedom." In *The Later Works of John Dewey, Vol. 3: 1927–1928*, edited by J. A. Boydston, 92–114. Carbondale: Southern Illinois University Press, 2008.

Durkheim, Émile. *The Elementary Forms of Religious Life*. London: Free Press, 1995.

Earp, Brian D., and Julian Savulescu. *Love Drugs: The Chemical Future of Relationships*. Stanford, Calif.: Stanford University Press, 2020.

Emens, Elizabeth F. "Monogamy's Law: Compulsory Monogamy and Polyamorous Existence." *NYU Review of Law and Social Change* 29 (2004): 277–376.

Emerson, Ralph Waldo. "Friendship." In *Essays and Lectures*, 339–54. New York: Penguin, 1983.

Fanon, Frantz. *Black Skin, White Masks*. Sidmouth: Pluto, [1952] 2008.

Ferguson, Ann. "Love Politics: Romance, Care, and Solidarity." In *Love: A Question for Feminism in the Twenty-First Century*, edited by A. Jónasdóttir and A. Ferguson, 150–64. New York: Routledge, 2014.

Ferrante, Elena. *My Brilliant Friend: Book 1*. New York: Europa Editions, 2012.

——. *The Story of a New Name: Book 2*. New York: Europa Editions, 2013.

——. *The Story of the Lost Child: Book 4*. New York: Europa Editions, 2015.

——. *Those Who Leave and Those Who Stay. Book Three*. New York: Europa Editions, 2014.

Ferrarese, Estelle. "Acceleration and Reification. Revisiting Adorno's Idea of Coldness." *Iride* 30, no. 81 (2017): 442–48.

——. "Precarity of Work, Precarity of Moral Dispositions: Concern for Others in the Era of 'Emotional' Capitalism." *Women's Studies Quarterly* 45, nos. 3–4 (2017): 176–92.

Fishman, Lillian. *Acts of Service: A Novel*. New York: Hogarth, 2022.

Foucault, Michel. "Friendship as a Way of Life." In *The Essential Works of Foucault, Vol. 1, Ethics: Subjectivity and Truth*, edited by P. Rabinow, 135–40. New York: New Work, [1981] 1997.

Frank, Manfred. *The Philosophical Foundations of Early German Romanticism*. New York: State University of New York Press, 2003.

Frankfurt, Harry G. "Autonomy, Necessity, and Love." In *Necessity, Volition, and Love*, 129–41. Cambridge: Cambridge University Press, 1999.

——. "On Caring." In *Necessity, Volition, and Love*, 155–80. Cambridge: Cambridge University Press, 1999.

——. *The Reasons of Love*. Princeton, N.J.: Princeton University Press, 2004.

——. "Reply to Jonathan Lear." In *Contours of Agency: Essays on Themes from Harry Frankfurt*, edited by S. Buss and L. Overton, 293–298. Cambridge, Mass.: MIT Press, 2002.

Fraser, Nancy, and Jaeggi, Rahel. *Capitalism: A Conversation in Critical Theory*. Cambridge: Polity, 2018.

Freud, Sigmund. *Three Essays on the Theory of Sexuality*. In *The Standard Edition of the Complete Psychological Works of Sigmund Freud, Vol. 7: 1901–1905*. London: Vintage, [1905] 2001.

Friedman, Marilyn. "Romantic Love and Personal Autonomy." *Midwest Studies in Philosophy* 22, no. 1 (1998): 162–81.

Fromm, Erich. *The Art of Loving*. New York: Harper Perennial, [1956] 2006.

——. *Man for Himself: An Enquiry into the Psychology of Ethics*. London: Routledge, 1949.

Garcia, Manon. *The Joy of Consent: A Philosophy of God Sex*. Cambridge, Mass.: Harvard University Press, 2023.

Giddens, Anthony. *Transformations of Intimacy: Sexuality, Love, and Eroticism in Modern Societies*. Stanford, Calif.: Stanford University Press, 1993.

Gilbert, Margaret. "How We Feel: Understanding Everyday Collective Emotion Ascription." In *Collective Emotions. Perspectives from Psychology, Philosophy and Sociology*, edited by C. von Scheve and M. Salmela, 17–31. Oxford: Oxford University Press, 2014.

——. *Joint Commitment: How We Make the Social World*. Oxford: Oxford University Press, 2014.

——. "Mutual Recognition and Some Related Phenomena." In *Recognition and Social Ontology*, edited by H. Ikäheimo and A. Laitinen, 271–86. Boston: Brill, 2011.

Gilligan, Carol, *In a Different Voice*. Cambridge, Mass.: Harvard University Press, 1982.

Gould, Deborah, *Moving Politics: Emotion and ACT UP's Fight Against AIDS*. Chicago: University of Chicago Press, 2009.

——. "On Affect and Protest." In *Political Emotions: New Agendas in Communication*, edited by J. Staiger, A. Cvetkovich and A. Reynolds, 18–44. New York: Routledge, 2010.

Gregoratto, Federica. "Agonistic Recognition, Intersections, and the Ambivalence of Family Bonds: John Dewey's Critical Theory Manifesto in China." *Transactions of the Charles S. Peirce Society* 53, no. 1 (2017): 127–45.

——. "Between Anger(s) and Radical Hope: Emotions in Progress." *European Journal of Philosophy* 15, no. 2 (2023): 1–19.

——. "Loving Vulnerability: Eleven Negative Theses on Polyamory." *Compàs d'Amalgama* 4 (2021): 56–60.

——. "Recognizing Care, Caring Recognition: Democratic Love and the Problems of Care Work." *Thesis Eleven* 134, no. 1 (2016): 56–72.

——. "A Romance of Recognition: Nature, Gender, and (Sex)ism in Friedrich Schlegel." In *The Philosophy of Recognition: Expanded Perspectives on a Fundamental Concept*, edited by M. Congdon and T. Khurana. New York: Routledge, forthcoming.

——. "Romances of Nature: Hegelian and Romantic Impulses for Critical Theory." *Verifiche* 21, no. 1 (2023): 39–62.

——. "Why Love Kills: Power, Gender Dichotomy, and Romantic Femicide." *Hypatia* 32, no. 1 (2017): 135–51.

Gregoratto, Federica, and Arvi Särkelä. "Social Reproduction Feminism and Deweyan Habit Ontology." In *Habit: Pragmatist Approaches from Cognitive Neurosciences to Social Sciences*, edited by F. Caruana and I. Testa, 438–58. Cambridge: Cambridge University Press, 2021.

Gregoratto, Federica, Heikki Ikäheimo, Emmanuel Renault, Arvi Särkelä, and Italo Testa. "Critical Naturalism: A Manifesto." *Krisis* 42, no. 1 (2022): 108–24.

Haag, Pamela. *Marriage Confidential: Love in the Post-Romantic Age.* New York: HarperCollins, 2011.

Haigh, Andrew, dir. *Weekend.* Peccadillo Pictures, 2011.

Hardy, Janet, and Dottie Easton. *The Ethical Slut: Polyamory, Open Relationships, and Other Adventures.* Berkeley, Calif.: Ten Speed, [1997] 2017.

Hardt, Michael. "For Love or Money." *Cultural Anthropology* 26, no. 4 (2011): 676–82.

Hardt, Michael, and Antonio Negri. *Commonwealth.* Cambridge, Mass.: Harvard University Press, 2009.

Hartmann, Martin. "A Comedy We Believe In: A Further Look at Sartre's Theory of Emotions." *European Journal of Philosophy* 25, no. 1 (2017): 144–72.

Hawks, Howard, dir. *Bringing Up Baby.* RKO Radio Pictures, 1938.

——. *His Girl Friday.* Columbia Pictures, 1940.

Hegel, G. W. F. "Entwürfe über Religion und Liebe." In *Frühe Schriften, Werke 1,* 239–54. Frankfurt am Main: Suhrkamp, 1986.

——. "Jena Lectures on the Philosophy of Spirit (1805/06)." In *Hegel and the Human Spirit,* edited by L. Rauch, 83–183. Detroit, Mich.: Wayne University Press, 1983.

——. *Lectures on the Philosophy of Religion.* Oxford: Oxford University Press, 2006.

——. *On Christianity: Early Theological Writings.* New York: Harper Torchbooks, 1961.

——. *Outlines of the Philosophy of Right.* Oxford: Oxford University Press, 2008.

Heller, Zoë. "How Everyone Got So Lonely." *New Yorker,* April 4, 2022. https://www.newyorker.com/magazine/2022/04/11/how-everyone-got-so-lonely-laura-kipnis-noreena-hertz?fbclid=IwAR32rJoarW1FbE8wCIhVwIYW2J16OkrG91KyOdqbUfWNCB_7zI6pyNLRC8E, 2022.

Helm, Bennet. *Love, Friendship, and the Self: Intimacy, Identification, and the Social Nature of Persons.* Oxford: Oxford University Press, 2009.

Hertz, Noreena. *The Lonely Century: How to Restore Human Connection in a World That's Pulling Apart.* New York: Currency, 2021.

Hobbs, Mitchell, Stephen Owen, and Livia Gerber. "Liquid Love? Dating Apps, Sex, Relationships, and the Digital Transformation of Intimacy." *Journal of Sociology* 53, no. 2 (2017): 271–84.

Hochschild, Arlie Russell. *The Managed Heart: Commercialization of Human Feeling.* Berkeley: University of California Press, [1983] 2012.

Honneth, Axel. *Freedom's Right: The Social Foundations of Democratic Life.* Cambridge: Cambridge University Press, 2014.

——. "Recognition as Ideology." In *Recognition and Power: Axel Honneth,* edited by B. van den Brink and D. Owen, 323–47. Leiden: Brill, 2007.

——. "Rejoinder." In *Reification: A New Look at an Old Idea,* edited by M. Jay. 147–59. Oxford: Oxford University Press, 2008.

——. *The Struggle for Recognition: The Moral Grammar of Social Conflict*. Cambridge: Polity, 1995.

——. "Three, Not Two, Concepts of Liberty: A Proposal to Enlarge Our Moral Self-Understanding." In *Hegel on Philosophy in History*, edited by R. Zuckert and J. Kreines, 177–92. Cambridge: Cambridge University Press, 2017.

hooks, bell, *All About Love: New Visions*. New York: HarperCollins, 2000.

Ikäheimo, Heikki, and Arto Laitinen. "Analyzing Recognition: Identification, Acknowledgement, and Recognitive Attitudes Towards Persons." In *Recognition and Power: Axel Honneth and the Tradition of Critical Social Theory*, edited by B. van den Brink and D. Owen, 33–56. Cambridge: Cambridge University Press, 2007.

Ikäheimo, Heikki, and Arto Laitinen, eds. *Recognition and Social Ontology*. London: Brill, 2011.

Illouz, Eva. *Cold Intimacies: The Making of Emotional Capitalism*. Cambridge: Polity, 2007.

——. *Consuming the Romantic Utopia: Love and the Cultural Contradictions of Capitalism*. Berkeley: University of California Press, 1997.

——. *The End of Love: A Sociology of Negative Relations*. Oxford: Oxford University Press, 2019.

——. *Why Love Hurts? A Sociological Explanation*. Cambridge: Polity, 2012.

Jaggar, Alison, "Love and Knowledge: Emotion in Feminist Epistemology." *Inquiry* 32, no. 2 (1989): 151–76.

Jenkins, S. I. Carrie. "Modal Monogamy." *Ergo* 2, no. 8 (2015): 175–94.

——. *Sad Love: Romance and the Search for Meaning*. Cambridge: Polity, 2022.

——. "What Is Love? An Incomplete Map of the Metaphysics." *Journal of the American Philosophical Association* 1, no. 2 (2015): 349–64.

——. *What Love Is and What It Could Be*. New York: Basic Books, 2017.

Johnson, Sophie Lucido. *Many Love: A Memoir of Polyamory and Finding Love(s)*. New York: Touchstone, Kindle edition, 2018.

Jónasdóttir, Anna G. "What Kind of Power Is Love Power?" In *Sexuality, Gender, and Power: Intersectional and Transnational Perspectives*, edited by A. G. Jónasdóttir, V. Bryson, and K. B. Jones, 45–59. New York: Routledge, 2011.

——. *Why Women Are Oppressed*. Philadelphia: Temple University Press, 1994.

Julian, Kate. "Why Are Young People Having So Little Sex?" *Atlantic*, December 2018, https://www.theatlantic.com/magazine/archive/2018/12/the-sex-recession/573949/ (accessed May 28, 2024).

Kant, Immanuel. *The Metaphysics of Morals*. Cambridge: Cambridge University Press, [1797–1803] 1991.

Keats, John. *Selected Letters of John Keats*. Cambridge, Mass.: Harvard University Press, 2002.

King, Martin Luther, Jr. *A Gift of Love: Sermons from Strength to Love*. London: Penguin Classics, 2017.

Kislev, Elyakim. *Relationships 5.0: How AI, VR, and Robots Will Reshape Our Emotional Lives*. Oxford: Oxford University Press, 2022.

Klesse, Christian. "Marriage, Law, and Polyamory: Rebutting Mononormativity with Sexual Orientation Discourse?" *Oñati Socio-legal Series* 6, no. 6 (2016): 1348–76.

——. "Poly Economics—Capitalism, Class, and Polyamory." *International Journal of Politics, Culture, and Society* 27 (2014): 203–20.

——. *The Spectre of Promiscuity: Gay Male and Bisexual Non-Monogamies and Poly-amories*. Aldershot: Ashgate, 2007.

Kolodny, Niko. "Love as Valuing a Relationship." *Philosophical Review* 112, no. 2 (2003): 135–89.

Kollontai, Alexandra. "Make Way for Winged Eros: A Letter to Working Youth." In *Selected Writings of Alexandra Kollontai*, edited by A. Holt, 276–92. Westport, Conn.: Lawrence Hill, 1977.

Kottman, Paul. *Love as Human Freedom*. Stanford, Calif.: Stanford University Press, 2017.

Krebs, Angelika. "Between I and Thou—On the Dialogical Nature of Love." In *Love and Its Objects: What We Can Care For?*, edited by C. Maurer, T. Milligan, and K. Pacovská, 7–24. London: Palgrave Macmillan, 2014.

——. *Zwischen Ich und Du. Eine dialogische Philosophie der Liebe*. Berlin: Suhrkamp, 2015.

LaFollette, Hugh. *Personal Relationships: Love, Identity, and Morality*. Oxford: Black-well, 1996.

Lauretis, Teresa de. *Freud's Drive: Psychoanalysis, Literature, and Film*. New York: Palgrave Macmillan, 2008.

Lear, Jonathan. "The Authority of Love." In *Contours of Agency. Essays on Themes from Harry Frankfurt*, edited by S. Buss and L. Overton, 279–92. Cambridge, Mass.: MIT Press, 2002.

——. *Love and Its Place in Nature: A Philosophical Interpretation of Freudian Psycho-analysis*. New York: Farrar, Straus, and Giroux, 1990.

Leilani, Raven. *Luster*. Basingstoke: Picador, 2022.

Liao, Matthew S. "The Idea of a Duty to Love." *Journal of Value Inquiry* 40 (2006): 1–22.

Loick, Daniel. "'. . . as if it were a thing': A Feminist Critique of Consent." *Constella-tions* 27, no. 3 (2020): 412–22.

Lorde, Audre. "The Master's Tools Will Never Dismantle the Master's House." In *Sis-ter Outsider: Essays and Speeches*, 110–13. Berkeley, Calif.: Crossing, 2007.

——. "Scratching the Surface: Some Notes on Barriers to Women and Loving." In *Sis-ter Outsider: Essays and Speeches*, 45–52. Berkeley, Calif.: Crossing, 2007.

——. "The Uses of Anger." In *Sister Outsider: Essays and Speeches*, 124–33. Berkeley, Calif.: Crossing, 2007.

——. "The Uses of the Erotic: The Erotic as Power." In *Sister Outsiders: Essays and Speeches*, 53–59. Berkeley, Calif.: Crossing, 2007.

——. *Zami: A New Spelling of My Name*. Berkeley, Calif.: Crossing, 1982.

Ludwig, Paul W. *Eros and Polis: Desire and Community in Greek Political Theory*. Cambridge: Cambridge University Press, 2002.

Lugones, María. *Pilgrimages/Peregrinajes: Theorizing Coalition Against Multiple Oppressions*. London: Rowman and Littlefield, 2003.

Luhmann, Niklas. *Love as Passion: The Codification of Intimacy*. Stanford, Calif.: Stanford University Press, [1982] 1986.

MacKinnon, Catharine. *Towards a Feminist Theory of the State*. Cambridge, Mass.: Harvard University Press, 1989.

Marcuse, Herbert. *Eros and Civilization: A Philosophical Inquiry into Freud*. London: Routledge, [1956] 1998.

——. "Nature and Revolution." In *Counterrevolution and Revolt*, 59–78. Boston: Beacon, 1972.

Marino, Patricia. *Philosophy of Sex and Love: An Opinionated Introduction*. New York: Routledge, 2019.

Marx, Karl. *Economic and Philosophic Manuscripts of 1844*. In *Collected Works, Vol. 3, 1843–1844*, by K. Marx and F. Engels, 229–346. New York: New York International Publishers, 2005.

May, Simon. *Love: A New Understanding*. Oxford: Oxford University Press, 2019.

McCarey, Leo, dir. *The Awful Truth*. Columbia Pictures, 1937.

McKeever, Natasha. "Is the Requirement of Sexual Exclusivity Consistent with Romantic Love?" *Journal of Applied Philosophy* 34, no. 3 (2017): 353–69.

Miller, Nancy K. *My Brilliant Friends: Our Lives in Feminism*. New York: Columbia University Press, 2019.

Montaigne, Michel de. "On Friendship." In *Essays*, 91–104. London: Penguin, 1993.

Nelson, Maggie. *The Argonauts*. New York: Graywolf, 2016.

——. *On Freedom: Four Songs of Care and Constraint*. London: Jonathan Cape, 2021.

Neuhouser, Frederick. *Foundations of Hegel's Social Theory: Actualizing Freedom*. Cambridge, Mass.: Harvard University Press, 2000.

Nietzsche, Friedrich. *Thus Spoke Zarathustra: A Book for All and None*. Cambridge: Cambridge University Press, 2006.

Novakovic, Andreja. *Hegel on the Family Form*. Cambridge: Cambridge University Press, forthcoming.

Nozick, Robert. "Love's Bond." In *Examined Life: Philosophical Meditations*, 68–86. New York: Simon and Schuster, 1989.

Nussbaum, Martha. "Constructing Love, Desire, and Care." In *Sex and Social Justice*, 253–75. Oxford: Oxford University Press, 1999.

——. *Political Emotions: Why Love Matters for Justice*. Cambridge, Mass.: Harvard University Press, 2013.

——. "The Speech of Alcibiades: A Reading of Plato's *Symposium*." *Philosophy and Literature* 3, no. 2 (1979): 131–72.

——. *Upheavals of Thought: The Intelligence of Emotions*. Cambridge: Cambridge University Press, 2001.

O'Higgins, James, and Michel Foucault. "Sexual Choice, Sexual Act: An Interview with Michel Foucault." *Salmagundi* 58–59 (1982–1983): 10–24.

Pearlman, Wendy. "Emotions and the Microfoundations of the Arab Uprisings." *Perspectives on Politics* 1, no. 2 (2013): 387–409.

Peck, Raoul, dir. *The Young Karl Marx* [*Le jeune Karl Marx*]. Diaphana Films/Neue Visionen Filmverleih/Cinéart, 2017.

Pettit, Philip. *The Robust Demands of the Good: Ethics with Attachments, Virtue, and Respect*. Oxford: Oxford University Press, 2015.

Plato. *The Symposium*. Cambridge: Cambridge University Press, 2008.

Polanyi, Karl. *Great Transformation: The Political and Economic Origins of Our Time*. Boston: Beacon, 2001.

Race, Kane, "Speculative Pragmatism and Intimate Arrangements: Online Hook-up Devices in Gay Life." *Culture Health & Sexuality* 17, no. 4 (2015): 1–16.

Rooney, Sally. *Beautiful World: Where Are You*. London: Faber and Faber, 2021.

——. *Conversations with Friends*. London: Faber and Faber, 2017.

——. *Normal People*. London: Faber and Faber, 2019.

Root, Maria P. P. *Love's Revolution: Interracial Marriage*. Philadelphia: Temple University Press, 2001.

Rorty, Amélie O. "The Historicity of Psychological Attitudes: Love Is Not Love Which Alters Not When It Alteration Finds." In *Friendship: A Philosophical Reader*, edited by N. K. Badhwar, 73–88. Ithaca, N.Y.: Cornell University Press, 1993.

Rorty, Amélie O., ed. *Explaining Emotions*. Berkeley: University of California Press, 1980.

Rosa, Sophie K. *Radical Intimacy*. London: Pluto, 2023.

Rousseau, Jean-Jacques. *Emile, or On Education*. New York: Basic Books, 1979.

Salmela, Mikko. "Collective Emotions and Normativity." *ProtoSociology* 35 (2018): 135–51.

——. "Shared Emotions." *Philosophical Explorations* 15, no. 1 (2012): 22–46.

Salmela, Mikko, and Michiru Nagatsu. "Collective Emotions and Joint Action: Beyond Received and Minimalist Approaches." *Journal of Social Ontology* 2, no. 1 (2016): 33–57.

Särkelä, Arvi. "Ein Drama in drei Akten. Der Kampf um öffentliche Anerkennung nach Dewey und Hegel." *Deutsche Zeitschrift für Philosophie* 61, nos. 5–6 (2013): 681–96.

Scarantino, Andrea. "Insights and Blindspots of the Cognitivist Theory of Emotions." *British Journal for the Philosophy of Science* 61, no. 4 (2010): 729–68.

Scheve, Christian von, and Jan Slaby. "Emotion, Emotion Concept." In *Affective Societies*, edited by J. Slaby and C. von Scheve, 43–51. New York: Routledge, 2019.

Schlegel, Friedrich. "Fragments." In *Lucinde and the Fragments*, 141–256. Minneapolis: University of Minnesota Press, 1971.

——. "Lucinde, a Novel." In *Lucinde and the Fragments*, 41–140. Minneapolis: University of Minnesota Press, 1971.

Schmid, Hans Bernhard. *Plural Action*. London: Springer, 2009.

Sheffield, Frisbee C.C. *Plato's* Symposium: *The Ethics of Desire*. Oxford: Oxford University Press, 2006.

Shelley, Percy Bhysse. "A Defence of Poetry." In *Selected Poems and Prose*. London: Penguin Classics, Kindle edition, 2017.

——. "On Love." In *Selected Poems and Prose*. London: Penguin Classics, Kindle edition, 2017.

——. *Selected Poems and Prose*. London: Penguin Classics, 2017.

Sedgwick, Eve Kosofsky. *A Dialogue on Love*. Boston: Beacon, 1999.

Seresin, Asa. "On Heteropessimism." New Inquiry, October 9, 2019. https://thenewinquiry.com/on-heteropessimism.

Silvestre, Adrian, dir. *Mi vacío y yo*. Testamento P.C.T., S.L., 2022.

Simpson, Leanne Betasamosake. *As We Have Always Done: Indigenous Freedom Through Radical Resistance*. Minneapolis: University of Minnesota Press, 2017.

Singer, Brian C. J. "Thinking Friendship with and Against Hannah Arendt." *Critical Horizons* 18, no. 2 (2017): 93–118.

Singer, Irving. *Meaning in Life, Vol. 2: The Pursuit of Love*. Cambridge, Mass.: MIT Press, [1994] 2010.

Soble, Alan. "Union, Autonomy, and Concern." In *Love Analyzed*, edited by R. E. Lamb, 65–92. Boulder, Colo.: Westview, 1997.

Solomon, Robert C. *About Love: Reinventing Romance for Our Times*. New York: Simon and Schuster, 1988.

Sousa, Ronald de. "Emergence and Empathy." In *Institutions, Emotions, and Group Agents: Contributions to Social Ontology*, edited by A. K. Ziv and H. B. Schmid, 141–58. New York: Springer,, 2013.

——. "Love, Jealousy, and Compersion." In *The Oxford Handbook of Philosophy of Love*, edited by C. Grau and A. Smuts, 491–510. Oxford: Oxford University Press, 2017.

——. *The Rationality of Emotions*. Cambridge, Mass.: MIT Press, 1987.

Sturges, Preston, dir. *The Lady Eve*. Paramount Pictures, 1941.

TallBear, Kim. "Making Love and Relations: Beyond Settler Sex and Family." In *Making Kin Not Population*, edited by A. E. Clarke and D. Haraway, 145–64. Chicago: Prickly Paradigm, 2018.

Testa, Italo. "Dominant Patterns in Associated Living: Hegemony, Domination, and Ideological Recognition in Dewey's Lectures in China." *Transactions of the Charles S. Peirce Society* 53, no. 1 (2017): 29–52.

——. "How Does Recognition Emerge from Nature? The Genesis of Consciousness in Hegel's Jena Writings." *Critical Horizons* 13, no. 2 (2012): 176–96.

——. "Recognition as Passive Power: Attractors of Recognition, Biopower, and Social Power." *Constellations* 24, no. 2 (2017): 192–205.

Velleman, David J. "Love as a Moral Emotion." *Ethics* 109, no. 2 (1999): 338–74.

Yanagihara, Hanya. *A Little Life*. Basingstoke: Pan Macmillan, 2015.

Yao, Vida. "Grace and Alienation." *Philosophers' Imprint* 20, no. 16 (2020): 1–18.

Ward, Caleb. "Feeling, Knowledge, Self-Preservation: Audre Lorde's Oppositional Agency and Some Implications for Ethics." *Journal of the American Philosophical Association* 6, no. 4 (2020): 463–82.

Ward, Caleb, and Ellie Anderson. "The Ethical Significance of Being an Erotic Object." In *The Palgrave Handbook of Sexual Ethics*, edited by D. Boonin, 55–71. Cham: Palgrave Macmillan, 2022.

Weisberg, Joe. *The Americans*, dir. FX, 2013–2018.

Whitehead, Jaye C. *The Nuptial Deal: Same-Sex Marriage & Neo-liberal Governance*. Chicago: University of Chicago Press, 2012.

Wilhelm, Dagmar. *Axel Honneth: Reconceiving Social Philosophy*. London: Rowman and Littlefield, 2019.

Wilkinson, Eleanor. "On Love as an (Im)properly Political Concept." *D: Society and Space* 35, no. 1 (2016): 57–71.

——. "What's Queer About Non-Monogamy Now?" In *Understanding Non-Monogamies*, edited by M. Barker and D. Langdridge, 243–54. London: Routledge, 2010.

Wordsworth, William. "Prefaces of 1800 and 1802." In *Lyrical Ballads*, by W. Wordsworth and S. Coleridge, 233–58. London: Routledge, 1991.

Zamora, Justo Serrano. "Articulating a Sense of Powers: An Expressivist Reading of John Dewey's Theory of Social Movements." *Transactions of the Charles S. Peirce Society* 53, no. 1 (2017): 53–70.

INDEX

racial oppression, love and, 231n39
racial preferences, damaging, 231n43
racial relations, interracial marriage
    impacting, 238n14
racism, love relationships impacted by, 123
Radical Intimacy (Rosa), 147
reason, Romantics and, 160–61
reasons of love, 88
La Recherche. See *In Search of Lost Time*
recognition, 69, 102, 125, 224nn33–34;
    Aristotle introducing, 58; of co-
    presence, 70; dependence on, 127;
    dichotomous gender structure
    reproduced through, 133; of erotic
    bonds, 59–60, 203; of erotic *we*, 192;
    of friendship, 146–47; Gilbert on, 72;
    Hegel introducing, 224n28; Hegel on,
    56–57; mis, 238n10; of multiple
    partnerships, 194; mutual, 170–71;
    normative order conceded to
    through, 194–95; passive power of,
    196; passivity and, 161–62; power
    dynamics and, 66; power plays
    animating, 68; reciprocal, 222n10;
    roles, norms, and identities
    encouraged by, 130; for same-sex
    marriage, 192–94; social conflict and,
    190; social structures and, 237n7;
    transformative effects of, 63–64; of
    women, 238n10. *See also* public
    recognition
recognition theory, 52, 61, 224n31; bodily
    dimensions emphasized in, 62; erotic
    bonds illuminated by, 189–90;
    Hegelian, 14, 225n42; Honneth
    elaborating, 129–30; marriage in, 195;
    social order reinforced by, 193
recognitive acts, 125–26
recognitive dynamics, erotic love framed
    by, 102–3
relationship anarchy, 101
relationships, interpersonal relationships
    as power, 176
remarriage, comedies of, 74–79, 140, 179,
    197, 226n56
resistance, act of, 28, 149, 178
risk, in erotic encounters, 9

rituals, collective, 172, 175
robust concern theory, 14, 31–32, 35–36,
    41–42
romance, commodification of, 116
romantic agency, nonmonogamous
    relationships framing, 226n69
romantic confusion, cherishing
    compared with, 209
romantic femicide, 232n57
romantic ideologies, 91, 93–94
romanticization of commodities, 116
romantic love: agonism within, 222n93;
    ethical significance of, 222n1;
    friendship distinguished from, 30–31,
    94, 145; modern idea of, 25–26;
    self-transformation through, 91
"Romantic Love and Personal
    Autonomy" (Friedman), 39
romantic market, 122–23
romantic relationships, Friedman
    criticizing, 47–48
romantic relationships, sexual affairs
    contrasted with, 5
Romantics: critical naturalism of,
    236n56; on love, 91–92; polyamorous
    discourse anticipated by, 101–2;
    reason and, 160–61; romantic
    ideologies contrasted with, 93–94;
    beyond union theory, 91–93
Rooney, Sally, 95–96, 98, 100, 121, 182,
    221n87
Rorty, Amélie, 73
Rosa, Sophie K., 147
Rousseau, Jean-Jacques, 128, 232n50
Russian Revolution, 208

Salmela, Mikko, 171–72, 175
same-sex marriage, recognition for,
    192–94
Sartre, Jean-Paul, 67, 225n37
Savulescu, Julian, 21, 217n4
Sayre, Zelda, 136–39, 141–42, 233n64
Scheve, Christian von, 156–57
Schlegel, Friedrich, 91, 160, 209; gender
    dualism presupposed by, 227n22; on
    love unions, 218n14; *Lucinde* by, 25,
    92, 94, 101–2